SEND THE BOY TO SEA

SEND THE BOY TO SEA

The Memoirs of a Sailor on the Goldfields

by

James Montagu Smith

Edited by PETER CUFFLEY

The Five Mile Press

The Five Mile Press

The Five Mile Press Pty Ltd
22 Summit Road
Noble Park
Victoria 3174 Australia
Phone: +61 3 9790 5000
Fax: +61 3 9790 6888
Email: publishing@fivemile.com.au

First published 2001.

In-house editor: Maggie Pinkney
Designer: Zoë Murphy
Cover design: Sonia Dixon

Printed in Australia by Griffin Press.

Cataloguing-in-Publication data
Smith, James Montagu
Send the boy to sea: the memoirs of a sailor on the goldfields
Bibliography.
Index.
ISBN 1 86503 566 1.

1. Smith, James Montagu. 2 Sailors - England - Biography.
3. Goldminers - Australia - Biography. 4. Immigrants - Australia - Biography. 5. Gold mines and mining - Australia - History. I. Cuffley, Peter. II. Title.

994.031092

Editor's Note
In the interests of the manuscript's integrity, the nineteenth-century spelling of some words has been retained. 'Sic' has not been added after such words, because it was felt this would interrupt the narrative flow. The original capitalisation of some words has also been retained, but paragraph breaks have been introduced for easier reading.

Cover image:

Henry Gritten, *Hobart Town*, 1856 (detail)
Oil on canvas, 94 x 153.2 cm
Tasmanian Museum and Art Gallery
Hobart, Tasmania

CONTENTS

The Story Behind this Book

At some time between 1858 and 1868, James Montagu Smith filled four notebooks with his neat handwriting, describing his adventures from the age of fourteen – when he first went to sea – to the age of twenty-one. These events took place between 1851 and 1857. At various times throughout these years he kept notes, diaries and journals on which these 'memorandums' are based.

The four volumes eventually passed on to his daughter Viola, who looked after them until her death in 1940. She in turn bequeathed them to the present owner, Jean Truebridge (née Smith), her niece and James's granddaughter. On her retirement, more than forty years later, Jean made a typed transcription of the journals. They have never before been published, and give a fresh new vision of Australia in the 1850s.

OPPOSITE PAGE:
S T Gill titled this picture, *Interesting statement – quality of washing stuff*. Collection: Peter Cuffley.

Still mark if vice or nature prompt the deed,
Still mark the strong temptation and the need,
On pressing want, on famine's powerful call,
At least more lenient let your justice fall,
For him who, lost to every hope in life,
Has long with fortune held unequal strife,
Known to no human love, no human care,
The homeless, houseless wanderer of despair.

John Langhorne (1835-1779)

INTRODUCTION

James Montagu Smith was an intelligent, if troublesome, boy of fourteen when he began his years of adventure. By his twenty-first birthday in August 1857, he had made three return journeys from England to Australia including two via Cape Horn and one via Hong Kong. He had learned a great deal about humanity and the wider world, holding on to optimism, although at times he saw himself as 'The homeless houseless wanderer of despair'.[1] Australia captured his heart in spite of desperate times and dangerous moments. He fell in love with its natural beauty, its bright skies and sunny days, the feeling of democracy and a promise of unlimited prospects.

While all kinds of diaries, journals and memoirs have been published, few can offer such an engaging first-hand account of convict voyages, imprisonment and the great goldrushes, as well as the contrasts between Britain and Australia. His observations of people cover a broad spectrum of mid-nineteenth century society including some notable figures in the antipodean hierarchy. He writes of mateship when it was an essential means of survival, of cronyism and cruelty, of love and human relations. There is even a memory of lovemaking so detailed as to be a rare gem from an era when most diarists or published authors only hinted at such things. When James died in 1888, the first centenary of European settlement in this ancient land, his obituary described him as a 'thorough Australian'. He was also said to be 'honest, intelligent, bright and blunt ... the much loved Monte Smith'.

We have these important writings because four precious notebooks survived and came into the possession of Jean Smith, granddaughter of James Montagu Smith. That was in 1940, and in the 1980s when she had retired from teaching she set to work to transcribe them. While the original handwriting is neat and generally readable there was a need to interpret obscure, scrawled or shortened words. Jean also added punctuation at various points and created necessary paragraph breaks. In time her handwritten transcription was typed up and circulated amongst family and friends. She checked many of the references and researched much of the life of James and his family. As the editor of the journals, I have also undertaken considerable research for the present publication in an effort to identify people, places, ships, events and reference points. Documentation has been found to support the details and broad experiences of the seven years recorded by James with rarely a discrepancy between his account and 'official' records.

As to his life before January 1851, he gives some important clues, but there is great significance in what he leaves unsaid. Of his father there is not one word.[2] James writes of his childhood at Herne Bay, of the friends he made at Richard Winch's Academy, of his mother's friends and of 'birdsnesting' with Mr Richmond. Their address, number 7 St Georges Terrace, places the family in comfortable circumstances, though by 1845 they had left this home.[3] His mother Mary Ann Smith moved to Montagu Villa, Queens Road, St Johns Wood, one of the newer 'suburbs' in London's west. James and his sister Fanny were placed in London schools and we know James was a boarder.

According to family records, James Montagu Smith was born in London on 28 August 1836. His seaman's record states that he was born in Marylebone, though no parish register entry for a baptism has turned up, even when the actual date is known (4 December 1836). His sister Fanny was forty-nine when she died in 1884, giving a birth date of circa 1835.

Mary Ann Smith died on 13 October 1846. In her will she appoints her old friend Charles Hay and her aunt Sarah Gregory as both her executors and guardians of James and Fanny. 'Charles Hay the elder' was a lighterman living at Rotherhithe in Surrey.[4] James became a friend of his sons Frank and Charles junior. A lighterman would transport goods on the Thames, being particularly involved in the loading and unloading of ships. James writes of his guardian's connections with ship-owners and sea captains.

In 1852-53 Fanny attended Queen's College, a school established in 1848 by Frederick Denison Maurice and funded by the Governesses' Benevolent Institution. Maurice, a Christian Socialist, was professor of Theology at King's College. He became the principal and main lecturer at Queen's College and was a powerful advocate for the education of women.

James writes of Fanny and the young women in their circle of friends with a mixture of insight, condescension and self-depreciation. In March 1855 he had landed in England after years in the company of sailors and gold-diggers. 'Ever since I went to boarding school I had seen little or nothing of women.' He felt he had known only half the world. 'I was now thrown in an entirely new sphere, and behaved very ridiculously I know.' On Sunday 1 April 1855 he writes: 'made an April Fool of myself by going into one of her precious high churches with Fanny. St. Stephen's I think she called it, in Lincoln's Inn Fields.' Fanny must have moved between the Hay family and other friends. James stayed at Hay's on a few occasions, but was made to find his own lodgings. He sometimes went sailing with Frank or Charles in Frank's small yacht, the *Razor Bill*. James called at Hay's fairly frequently when he was in London, sometimes to borrow money from the 'Governor'. He enjoyed the family life and the occasional meal. Fanny also lived with the Burge family and again James was invited for Sunday dinner.

George Burge was a civil engineer and contractor, and is recognised as the 'founding father' of Herne Bay, having proposed the building of the pier in 1830, the central element in a large-scale resort project. He built the Pier Hotel, St George's Terrace and an assembly room and bath.[5] These developments were funded from a considerable fortune he amassed as an engineering contractor, though by the 1850s, some of his property investments had lost him money. James describes him as 'a clever man' and notes that as a contractor he was an important figure in two of Britain's great engineering feats of the first half of the nineteenth century.[6]

Also of importance in James's London life were the Burgess family who lived in the Brixton-Lambeth area, at that time a part of Surrey but now swallowed up by the great city. James Burgess was James's uncle (his late mother's brother), a kind man, 'but not quite pushing enough'. Poverty forced the Burgess family to live in 'a wretched neighbourhood', a situation contrasted by the life of William Burgess, his brother, who, having been convicted for receiving stolen goods, was sent to New South Wales as a convict and had done very well.

Uncle William became the pivotal force in the life of James Montagu Smith and brings to mind the character Magwitch in *Great Expectations* by Charles Dickens, first published in 1860. James's third trip to Australia, this time on that record-breaking 'Yankee' clipper the *Red Jacket,* was basically in response to an offer by William Burgess to provide for his sister's children. James was hopeful that his uncle might set him up on one of his farms, and in the end he did inherit 50 acres (20.25 hectares) on the Hunter River in New South Wales, not far from the river port town of Morpeth.

If James was at times headstrong and short-tempered, he was also disarmingly honest and deeply philosophical. His writings are so much more than entries in a journal. He called them 'Memorandums', a mixture of straightforward narrative, thoughtful reflection and wise observation. We share in both the adventure and the dreariness of life as a sailor, gold miner, labourer or traveller. The same goes for his perambulations in England and Scotland, where he is a young gentleman with prospects, or returned gold digger complete with beard, blue shirt and moleskin trousers. He writes, in turn, as a hard-living labourer, an intelligent observer of the natural world and an informed theatregoer in sophisticated London. At various times throughout these years between the ages of fourteen and twenty-one, he was keeping notes, diaries, or journals. It is believed that the four surviving notebooks were created from this material at a later date, though some sections include dated journal entries, which were probably copied verbatim.

Volume I was definitely completed before 1868 and it seems likely that all four were compiled after 1858 and before James was married in 1866.[7] He comments that he lost his notes of the voyage on the convict transport *Sir Robert Seppings* when he and some others deserted the ship. We know that his recollections of this period are reliable in every detail in that the captain's report of his rebellious behaviour is recorded in the ship's log and exactly parallels his version.

He comments on writing at greater length while at sea, noting the popularity of diary-keeping on long voyages. He leaves Maryborough on the Victorian goldfields and sails out of Port Phillip Bay nine days before the battle at Eureka Stockade on 3 December 1854, so he would have needed to refer to a published account to write details of the event. He did hear of the burning of Bentley's Eureka Hotel through Jimmy Barr, a Scottish digger mate who knew Andrew McIntyre, one of the three men charged and convicted. There would have been talk of those times when he was back on the diggings with his old mates in 1855-56.

On the causes of goldfields unrest he could write at first hand, having been at the great meetings in Castlemaine. 'I was fool enough to write out a lot of bills which we stuck up on the trees along the highway – very seditious they were too.' Politics could bring him to an excitable state and at one stage he writes that folks called this his 'radical humbug'. Experience in Australia certainly made him critical of the conservative insularity he found in England. Taken out of the relatively comfortable world of the British middle class, James experienced at first hand the inconsistencies and inequities of the rules and the law when applied to those without money, power or social status. He felt that adversity made him a better man, '... and at all events, more lenient to the vices of the poor and unfortunate.' His school chums who finished their schooling and went on to pursue careers in England would have found some of his experiences quite fantastic, with the ring of a work of fiction. For James it was very real and we are indebted to his desire to write it all down. The word 'private' is there on the cover of each notebook, so we are trusting that he would have approved of publication long after his own and the following generation had passed away.

PETER CUFFLEY
Castlemaine, Victoria, 2001

I

ON THE BLUE BRINY

Memorandums on a voyage in the ship 'Lancastrian' – Langley, Commander. 567 tons registered. Commences January 1st 1851. [1]

After committing sundry rows and breaches of the peace, such as blowing up the seat of the privy and bringing rum in to school in cocoanuts – all of which little innocent amusements originated from reading trashy novels, which shows how careful parents and teachers ought to be in the selection of books for children – I got expelled and sent to my Guardian, Mr. Hay.

He never had me to live at his house, although he frequently had my sister there during her vacation. I used to board at the house of Mrs. Willans in Paradise Street, Rotherhithe. She was a pew-opener at the adjoining church, her husband having been killed by a fall of the scaffolding during the erection of the said church, and left her with four children.[2]

Shortly after this the Governor got me a billet in the above-named ship, as a sort of trial voyage to Melbourne, for which I was to pay twenty pounds; which by the bye is a great take-in. Foolish fathers are delighted at the idea of getting their sons to sea as gentlemen; but directly their sons get on the blue briny they are taken less notice of than the poorest boy in the ship, and usually get all the dirtiest and most disagreeable work. The tars say, "What business has anyone at sea who has money enough to stay ashore," and it has given rise to the coarse, but veritable maxim – "Go to sea for pleasure. Go to hell for pastime."

My time between going to sea and leaving school was not so much wasted either, for I learnt to swim off Kenworthy at the Holborn Baths in six lessons for one guinea. He taught me all kinds of ornamental swimming. It has not been thrown away, for had I never learnt to swim, I should not now be writing this.

I also learnt navigation at Leuthwaites. The ship was lying in St. Katharine's Docks and as it was six weeks before she would leave I went on board every day, nominally to learn seamanship, but in reality to do all kinds of little dirty jobs that boys are usually set on their first trip. The first mate was an excellent seaman and a very good master, and had been placed on board by the Captain's father (who was the owner of the ship) as a kind of wet nurse for the Skipper, for he was but two and twenty and had not been many voyages to sea.[3] This was his first trip as Commander. He was a gentlemanly man and seldom interfered with the foremast hands. The cabin passengers complained that he did not find the cabin table well enough, but from the things that I saw go in every day I disbelieved it. They were a mixed lot – two runaway matches and several runs for debt; a solicitor's family, name of Read, who have since made a large fortune in Melbourne.[4] Indeed, anyone going out at that time with a little capital and staying in Melbourne until the great rush to the diggings was sure of a rapid fortune.

We hauled out into the stream and were towed down to Gravesend where we lay for the night. Everything was in confusion – pigs, sheep, fowls, spars, boxes – it seemed as though we should never get them away. The first two days are, in my opinion, the worst part of a voyage. I got very little sleep the first night. By the bye, I forgot to say that the night before, I dined at the Governor's house and thought that I could not be a sailor unless I drank freely. Accordingly did, and got outrageously drunk and had to be carried home. This was my first bout and therefore worthy of remark.

The next morning set sail, with pilot on board and let go the anchor at the Nore. At daybreak all hands were piped up to get the ship under weigh. It was severely cold. The boys always have the worst work, viz. to haul the muddy wet chain cable back from the windlass to prevent the chain riding. 'The Song of Cheerlymen', sung by the tars on hoisting the topsails, sounds very well for the first. The Yankees are the boys for singing – they have a new song for each rope.

I was placed under the Bosun who had a berth in the half deck with the steerage passengers, together with another lad called Harry whose parents had also paid twenty pounds for his passage. We all slept in the same berth. I was mustered in the chief mate's watch and Harry was in the second mate's or starboard watch. He turned out when I turned in, and vice versa. The boatswain kept watch all day, and therefore slept all night, and many a row did he kick up for being waked by our calls. There were two other boys besides ourselves. They were apprentices and consequently lived in the topgallant forecastle with the men.

The Bosun was an arrant thief and soon taught us to be as bad as himself. Grub, grog and tobacco are considered by all sailors to be common property. Our night-watch was frequently employed in wringing the necks of sundry fowls, cutting them up and making a scouse for breakfast. We lived very well considering, and the more we stole the better the Bosun liked us. We made a great slaughter among the passengers' wine until one night we were watched and I was nearly caught, but fortunately bobbed under the table and was passed by. In the morning it was traced to the Bosun's berth and in order to clear himself he told of me, and I was consequently mast-headed with one of the apprentices.

We had not been up there an hour when the mate hailed us, but receiving no answer sent up an able seaman who found us, made fast with a gasket to the topgallant rigging, and fast asleep. We were called down and made to walk the forecastle with a couple of handspikes on our shoulders; but we were released by the intercession of the solicitor's daughter,[5] who was about twelve years old, and said she was quite sure "the pretty boy" (that's me) would not steal any more wine. Instead of being disliked for it I became quite a favourite among the passengers, and for my own part I looked upon the whole of the punishment as a jolly lark. However I was more cautious for the future and was never *caught* again.

The ladies were awfully sick for the first week and we boys had the agreeable job of swabbing up the contents of their bowels. It must have been a great saving to the Captain, for meals came away almost untasted, and there was some rare pickings in the galley – commonly called "gubkins". They made up for it, however, when they got well. Any persons who require an appetite should try the sea-sickness. I was not sick at all, but I believe boys who are worked hard seldom feel it so much as elderly people who have nothing to do.

We encountered a severe gale in the Bay of Biscay, in which we lost a whole suit of sails and completely swept the decks. The oldest salt on board said he'd never met with anything like it. The cabin was completely filled with water and it was a mercy we did not founder. The gentlemen and ladies were swimming about up to their waists in water, some of them quite *en déshabillé*. I had no time to pity them for I had enough to do to look after myself. The Skipper did not leave the deck for two days and nights, but the wind abated after the first night, and we unbent the sails and bent new ones.

In crossing the Line we had some rare fun. Neptune and his wife came on board the previous night and were drawn round the main deck in a triumphal car. He enquired of the Captain if he had any new sons. The Skipper answered in the affirmative. It was really so well got up that Harry and I believed that they had come from the briny and, as they disappeared over the head, the illusion was complete. The next day he came aboard in all of his glory together with his wife and all his dependants – barber, doctor and bather. A spare main topsail was tied upon the quarterdeck and filled with water – over which was erected a rough scaffold. Neptune made a long harangue to the Skipper – the most prominent of it was that he wanted nothing but his dues – grog and shaving, and that after he had prescribed for the diseases of the new hands he should depart once more into his native element. After this, grog was served out and I'm sorry to say Neptune's wife partook rather freely of the alcohol. He apologised for her by saying that she was in a rather peculiar way and only did it for the good of her stomach. His sons were placed before him from which he selected anyone that took his fancy and placed him on the end of a plank.

After being blindfolded, he was well-lathered with a composition of tar and other equally nasty fluids. Neptune enquired his character – if good, he was shaved with number one razor, a smooth iron hoop; if bad with number three, notched like a saw, which took off at the same time beard, lather and skin. The barber put some questions to him and as he opened his mouth the lather brush was dabbed in. The doctor now took him in hand and after feeling his pulse assured us that he was in a high fever, bled him in the arm with a marline spike, and gave him a little opening medicine consisting of a mixture of pig, sheep and cow dung washed down with half a pint of liquid manure. The end of the plank was tilted up and he was resigned to the tender mercies of the bather. After being nearly drowned he was allowed to escape, only to run the gauntlet of the Captain, passengers and crew armed with buckets of water which they dashed unceremoniously at him; and instead of pitying the poor wretch, they seemed to glory in his misfortune, which they were soon doomed to share. Even the ladies did not come off free, for they, having assembled on the poop to see the sport, were drenched by a stream of water from the mizzen tap. After being thoroughly wet, they seized on the buckets and entered into the game with spirit.

The new hands having now got an insight into the trials that awaited them; some made desperate resistances but they were in vain. One of the cabin passengers locked his door and made a desperate stand, refusing either to pay tribute or to undergo shaving; he threatened to stab anyone who should use force, with a bowie knife that he held in his hand. They parleyed, and one of Neptune's satellites treacherously threw the bight of a rope round his neck and brought him to the deck. In the scuffle the salt received a severe stab in the fleshy part of the back. The passenger was disarmed and examined by Neptune's doctor who pronounced him to be a lunatic of a very dangerous description, and proceeded to give the necessary remedies. The day concluded with music and dancing and a glorious drunk among the shellbacks.

March 15th [1851]. Doubled the Cape of Good Hope. Strong breezes. In Latitude 43°6′ South and Longitude 27°53′ West blew a gale – fore-main and mizzen topgallant masts carried away, mainsail blew clean out of the bolt ropes, tremendous heavy swell. Saw a large school of whales.

March 21st [1851] Spoke the barque *David Clark* from London to Bombay. Eighty-one days out. Carried away fore-main and mizzen top-masts and jib boom. Latitude 36° and Longitude 14°. So it appears that she was caught and dismasted in the same gale in which we lost ours. The weather was very bad all the passage. We passed Port Phillip heads on May 1st and took the pilot on board to the universal joy. It was a long tiresome passage. Hobson Bay, where the vessels of large tonnage lie, is about forty miles from the heads.

We dropped anchor there the next morning, off Williamstown, and the passengers went ashore.

I had a bad back tooth which caused me so much pain that I got the doctor to pull it out, and as the ship was moored he charged me ten shillings. He told me to go into the pantry and wash my mouth out with a little spirits and water. I did so, and whether it was the strength of the brandy, the pain of the tooth or the weakness of my head I know not – suffice it to say that I got so drunk that I went and slipped into the second mate, who was no favourite of mine at any time, and kicked up a most tremendous row. I woke up the next morning with an awful headache and remembered nothing from the time I went into the pantry.

We commenced discharging cargo directly the passengers left the ship, and from that time till the time we took in ballast I scarcely ever saw the Bosun sober. The cargo consisted principally of stores, beer, spirits and iron. About half the beer and spirits had burst their heads out with the working of the ship and we pumped it up continually during the bad weather. The breakage, waste and plundering was shameful. It had nearly caused the loss of the ship and imprisonment of the crew; for not content with spirits, they broke open a case of jewellery and purloined a quantity of silver spoons. They got some scent of it ashore and the ship was placed under the surveillance of the police.

The third mate and Bosun were at the head of this business, as indeed they were at every other kind of roguery; and the former's conscience pricking him, when the police boat came alongside he told one of the apprentices to go into his cabin and throw a canvas bag filled with plate out of the port. It unfortunately fell close to the boat and they consequently placed buoys round the ship and dragged for several days, but they failed in picking it up. The ship was next searched but no plate was discovered. A few boxes of pickles were found in the chests of two of the sailors, and they would have been transported had it not been for the exertions of the solicitor, Mr. Read.[6] The Bosun and Chips, as I afterwards heard, had their booty stowed away down the chain locker, and disposed of it for crepe shawls to the Chinese merchants.[7]

About six hands had liberty to go ashore every Sunday. I was not much pleased with the town of Melbourne, and thought there was plenty of room for improvement. There was only one street of any consequence, called Elizabeth Street, and this was nearly up to one's neck in mud. This street is the lowest part of the town, being in a kind of gully running north and south. All the streets are very wide and run at right angles. Meat was wonderfully cheap – beef one penny a pound and mutton two shillings and sixpence the live sheep. I was told that it was hardly worthwhile bringing them down from the bush; they paid better when boiled down and converted into tallow. Several of the hands, amongst whom was the second mate, ran away. It was a fortune to any of those that stopped there.

Opposite to Williamstown was another small village, a wretched-looking place called Sandridge.[8] The towns have a most unprepossessing appearance, but the surrounding country was very grand and thickly wooded. Mt. Macedon and the You Yangs stand out in bold relief. The water of the Yarra Yarra is sweet and good above the falls. Vessels that draw over nine feet of water cannot cross the bar. It takes a circuitous route from the town into the bay.

We took on board a number of large old guns as ballast and I believe the Captain did exceedingly well by them in China. Also a quantity of stone ballast, very nasty stuff to handle. We shipped some fresh hands and the ship was once more swimming in grog. In fact there had always been more or less knocking about – it was the cause of most of the rows on board. The night that the new hands came on board there was some very severe fighting; one man lost his eyesight forever. It was a general mêlée, mates and all. Two of the new ones were sent ashore in the morning. Two of our London crew were discharged. One of them pretended to have ruptured himself while discharging cargo, but it was generally known to be a sell. The other one had a bad disorder and would have forfeited his wages, but the Skipper generously paid him. We took in water by means of floating tanks, and a quantity of livestock.

The third mate was promoted to the second mate's billet. The boatswain and carpenter, Harry and I had two of the foremost cabin berths given to us. With several little extras besides what we could appropriate (which was not a little) we were therefore tolerably comfortable.

We caught very bad weather the whole passage – there were heavy squalls and thunderstorms. One gale in Torres Strait lasted three days and we were forced to scud under bare poles or close reefed topsails. It was about three o'clock of the second day, and the wind had abated a little, when one of the ordinary seamen and myself were sent up to shake out a reef from the fore topsail. We had just let go the points and were about to cast off the casings when the Captain saw a squall boiling away at our stern. The sea appeared to be carried aloft and he sang out to us to make fast and lay down. I was just below the top when the squall struck us and the hail pierced my clothes like needles. Before I could say "ho!" there were two loud reports; the topsails had split to ribands. The worst was to come – we heard a third report louder than ten thousand cannons. We were mostly thrown off our feet by the shock. Half-blind we staggered to our feet aghast. "Sound the pumps!" was the general and awful cry. The Captain, pale as death, still preserved that most valuable thing in emergency, his presence of mind. The pumps were sounded and pronounced in no danger. We breathed more freely; it was not yet fated that we should part from our frail support.

The men returned to the forecastle and there found two of their shipmates apparently dead, their faces covered with blood. They had not been missed in the confusion, and were now attended to by the Captain (we carried no doctor). In a few minutes to our great joy they were restored to consciousness. Their account confirmed our former impressions that we had been struck by a thunderbolt – and by the mercy of the Almighty it had been guided by the cable chain through the hawsepipe, in lieu of the ship's bottom. They had turned hastily from their bunks on hearing the topsails burst, and the forecastle was instantaneously filled with a vivid flame; after which they remembered no more.

There are times when the sailor cannot help feeling humbled before that invisible being who "rules the raging of the sea", and in the present case there were few that did not feel better for that awful lesson. But the impression with most of them lasted only until fine weather returned; but even that little bit of repentance is about as good as a deathbed repentance. (NOTE – Later. I have since heard that the ship was lost the next voyage by a typhoon in the China Seas).

We made fast the fragments of the topsails, set the fore top-mast studding sail and [were] piped to grog. The next morning there was a lull and we bent new topsails. The weather continued squally until we sighted New Guinea where it fell a dead calm for two days, and the vessel was surrounded by fish of all the colours of the rainbow. Towards evening of the first day we caught a shark eleven feet long; slipped a running bowline round his tail and bowsed him aboard with a watch tackle. If the Skipper had have guessed what antics he was going to play he would have left him in his own element; for with a single blow of his tail he sent the skylight flying and smashed the binnacle to atoms. He might have done more mischief had not the Skipper been near with the ship's broad axe and without more to do rendered him harmless by cutting off his tail. The salts now had their no-longer-dreaded enemy at their mercy and amused themselves for some time by cutting and hacking him to pieces. When dead he was thrown overboard to feed his companions; and all the benefit that we derived was from his liver, the oil of which is said to be a first-rate remedy for the rheumatism by outward application. It is almost useless to mention that we stank of fish for a week afterwards.

The next day we lowered a boat and caught thousands of the prettiest fish ever I saw, about as large as dace and very paltry eating; so like many other things – the outside was the best of them. At sunset we caught a nice breeze from the west that seemed to give a refreshing smell of cocoanuts.

Two days after this I had my first miraculous escape. I was on the fore topgallant stay with an able seaman for whom I was passing the ball; the stay went under a cleat on the martingale, our united weights pressed it from under the cleat and twisted us up in the air. The able seaman caught hold of the flying jib stay, but I, trying to save the ball of spun yarn (for I knew I should *catch it* if I *lost it*), lost my balance, spun yarn and all. The ship was going about seven knots and smooth water. "Man overboard!" thrilled through the ship. I saw the huge bulk glide past me, pale anxious faces up and down from the rails; ropes were thrown as I passed, and then she gradually receded and left me alone with the deep. But I knew very well that I should not be left and therefore felt quite easy in my mind. When I thought of the eleven foot shark my conscience gave me a slight prick and made me kick about a little, as I had heard that they were loath to touch anything living. But finding the kicking business tiresome I gave it up, lay on my side and watched my wooden house as she gradually came into the wind's eye – and then I saw confused figures running about the poop.

They were evidently lowering the boat. I felt quite jolly at the idea, when of a sudden I saw the boat swing. They had let go one of the tackles, and if the other one gave way I was lost. A cold sweat came over me; and I could hear my heart beat, said "Our Father"; and felt considerably better. I saw the boat rise again and felt like a new man. Some hands got into it, lowered away, unhooked the tackles and gave way. They pulled three points from me – they were being directed by someone in the mizzen rigging who evidently could not see me. I hallooed as loud as I could and fortunately the Bosun heard and pulled towards me. He made a drive at me with the boat hook in his excitement, but fortunately only caught me on the shoulder. The boat's crew gave a loud cheer when they hauled me into the boat. It was responded to by those on board. The poor fellows seemed overjoyed and I was the pet of the forecastle for some time afterwards.

A glass of hot grog was prepared which I drank to the Skipper with great gusto. In case however I should feel inclined to go over again to get the same reward, I was solemnly informed that I should not have it next time. They informed me that there was a great confusion on board, and astonishing as it may appear, they could see nothing of me after the first few minutes and had given me up for lost. It is nevertheless true that when there is the slightest swell one cannot see anything from the deck – I mean such a small thing as a man's head – for any distance. If the man that was with me had been fated to fall he would have fared differently as he could not swim.

Bent down all the staysails and main royal yard – flying jib boom in.

Thursday, August 14th [1851] Unstowed bower anchor and got up cables and bent them. Latitude 19°30′ North, Longitude 114° South. The Chinese Sea is famous, or rather infamous, for sudden squalls and as they are usually the only chance one has, it would be useless to take in sails, so the plan is to let go the halliards until the storm is past. Our Skipper was a first-rater to carry on canvas, but the mate was the most reckless, as they generally are, because the responsibility is off their shoulders. I have frequently seen the lee bulwarks buried in the sea during a squall in his watch. She was very light and consequently not at all stiff.

On the 16th [August 1851] we saw several Chinese junks. The pilot came on board at five and we dropped anchor off Green Island.

Sunday 17th [August 1851] Light breezes and calms with hot sultry weather. Hove up anchor, made sail up to Tai Tam Bay and let go port bower abreast of Hong Kong. Stowed sails.

I was much pleased with the appearance of the land. Hong Kong is altogether a very pretty island. It belongs to the English. In the bay is a floating church, the first of the kind I have seen. The sermon I heard was a good one. The crew of the *Reynard* were there, nominally to return thanks for their deliverance.[9] She was one of the two ships that went in search of a shoal in the China Sea and ran on it herself. All hands were saved.

The instant we let go our anchor the ship was surrounded by all sorts and sizes of boats filled with all sorts of eatables and merchandise. The number was astonishing. I am told that they live entirely on the water. These are considered by the real Chinese to be beneath them – called Tartars, they are arrant thieves. Bananas, guavas, pineapples were in abundance, My pen can but ill describe the delightful sensation I experienced in sucking down these delightful fruits. Eggs were threepence a dozen. They are a little larger than bantams, but very good. The crepe shawls were a great article of commerce. I saw some that would make many a London belle's eyes sparkle; they were truly magnificent. The people must excel in all kinds of fancy workmanship. I also saw some very curious ivory chessmen and fantastic pictures.

Among the people were large numbers of women, but I only saw two real China women during our stay, and those were veiled. The boats are large and sail well. They have a verandah which protects alike from the sun and rain – not unlike gondolas – their sails are made of a kind of rush matting.

The people were employed in getting the guns and ballast out of the hold. The ordinaries and boys beat the rust off them, which was about an inch thick, and afterwards rubbed them all over with grease to make them look better. The Captain then brought someone on board to make a bargain with. The former appeared to have a good insight into the Chinese customs and the pantomime between them was most amusing. At length they struck and appeared equally satisfied with their bargain. I was told by another Chinaman that the man who bought them was as great a rogue as there was in Hong Kong, which was saying a great deal. I know that the Skipper made a considerable sum by them, and the only use they were was for old iron; as guns they were done.

We stayed here until the 26th [August 1851], then hove up anchor and set sail with fair wind – brought up at 6 p.m. – next morning at daylight made sail. The country on both sides of the river was flat and marshy. The Captain promised to take me to Canton with him, but forgot it. I have only repented it once and that has been ever since.

At 9 a.m. moored with both bowers abreast of Bamboo Town, Wampoa.[10] There were a great many Americans in the river and several frigates. The place appeared to be swimming with people, but it was a dirty-looking hole enough. We unbent all sails and stowed our running gear, for if we had not the Chinese would have saved us the trouble. Several ships have been completely dismantled by this rapacious though clever race. So stealthily had they done it that the crew knew nothing about it until the morning. They swim on board and climb up the rudder case, cut all the running gear and return with it on their shoulders in the same way. They are all excellent swimmers. The tide runs with very considerable force in this river. It has the colour of strong tea.

On the 2nd of September [1851] we commenced taking in cargo. The stevedores do this with almost incredible speed and great neatness, there being scarcely space enough left to put one's hand in.

On Sunday all hands were employed clearing decks; boys filling tanks and water casks from the river. This day of rest was about the hardest day's work I did during the voyage, and satisfies me that, putting all religious opinions on one side, Sunday is a very wise institution and ought to be kept holy, or at least quiet.

On the 6th the hold was filled and the hatches battened down.

On Wednesday 10th [September 1851] unmoored and dropped down the river; brought up again at night.

Friday 12th [September 1851]. At one a.m. weighed anchor and set sail. At four pilot left the ship. Macao bearing NNE distance 6 miles from which we take our departure. From this time until we reached the Line the wind was principally from the southward and westward, at times light, with occasional squalls attended by rain.

The awful effects of inconstant attachments were commencing to make themselves felt among the officers and crew. The chief mate, from being the most powerful man on board, became a mere skeleton and so weak that the veriest child might have pushed him down. The third mate was like a spotted leopard. The Bosun's penis was choked and half the crew were maimed in some way or the other. Thus the Skipper was the only officer on board fit for duty and he had an awful hard time of it. If we had had any very bad weather we should have been obliged to let go the halliards and cut away, for we had not hands enough to reef. However as it was we managed pretty well. The Bosun was able to knock about after a few days and became quite a great man amongst the small ones. We now lived like fighting cocks. It's worthwhile being a servant to the devil.

October 4th [1851]. Sighted two islands and a strange sail standing to the South West.

October 5th [1851]. Crossed the Line in Longitude 107° 43′. Light airs and calms. Caught a large shark. The weather very warm – the skin off my face and arms.

October 8th [1851]. Saw several small islands – a heavy squall struck the ship. Let go all halliards and tacks – blew away the flying jib. The weather continued squally and the wind foul until the 16th October when we sighted Java and came to an anchor at Anjer Point[11] in Latitude 6°3′ South and Longitude 10°5′ East . We sent the chief mate ashore to get medical aid. He was treated very liberally by the Captain. I pitied him; to see such a fine man completely wrecked was shocking . The crew were sincerely sorry for him. He was an excellent officer. I never heard of him since.

Several boats came alongside filled with fruits, fowls, and monkeys of all descriptions – moosedeer, a beautiful little miniature deer about six inches high, without horns but in every other respect perfect, and very brilliant eyes – mongoose, celebrated for the destruction of rats and other vermin. Great numbers were bought by the crew. I had a very fine one up to all sorts of mischief. He would frequently enter and eat the Captain's sugar. He did not complain until one day Jacko[12] killed two of his splendid grey parrots and plucked them. He was then ordered to be killed, but his life was saved by the interception of the Bosun – and I promised to keep him tied up for the future.

We weighed anchor the same day and made sail – had some very heavy thunderstorms. Passed a barque on the same tack, the *Mary Sanders*. Humphreys, the second mate, now took the chief mate's place. He was very lucky, for it is an occurrence that very seldom takes place. He had risen from the ranks of third mate and he was a very poor seaman too. He swindled me out of a splendid box of instruments and the Bosun got my sextant by similar disgraceful means. It shows what a mean race they are who will thus impose upon the credulity and innocence of a boy.

The American ship *White Squall* passed us within half a cable's length. She appeared to sail three knots to our one. Although the English are very loath to allow it, there is very little doubt that the Americans build much faster sailing vessels than us.

November 25th [1851]. Signalised the *Plantagenet* from Madras – 58 days out.

November 30th [1851]. Sighted land – rounded the Cape of Good Hope. We'd had very variable weather since we left Anjer Point and mostly light winds. They cannot be depended on in these seas. Bent the cables intending to go into Table Bay – the mountains now bore due East (at distance 6 miles) but the wind suddenly shifted, so we fished the anchors and unbent the cables again.

December 6th [1851]. We spoke the *Sea Serpent*, another Yankee. She had left Wampoa 35 days after us – she passed us fluking.

December 14th [1851]. Saw St. Helena bearing S.E. Bent chain cables and unstowed the anchors and got all ready for port. Next day we came to anchor with best bower in 25 fathoms water abreast of the town. It's a wretched-looking place and is enough to give anyone cold to look at it. I pitied Napoleon. It is well-supplied with water. We filled by means of floating tanks. A great number of mackerel were bought by the crew dirt-cheap. Several of the hands were very ill from them – at certain seasons they are very hurtful.

December 16th [1851]. Hove short. Made sail at 8 p.m. Jamestown bore SSE distance 8 miles. Unbent the cables and stowed them away. We were very comfortable with the Bosun and Chips. They behaved very well to us, principally because they were always at loggerheads with each other. The Bosun nearly killed the steward because he would not let him have any grog. The Captain interfered and got covered with the former's blood. He was threatened with the law when we got home, but he got off free, as indeed most of these cases do.

December 19th [1851]. We sighted the Island of Ascension.

December 28th [1851]. Were boarded by the Captain of the brig *Parramatta* sixty-five days from the Mauritius. They had a bottle of wine together in the cabin.

January 5th, 1852. Spoke the American ship *Garrick.* We crossed the Line on Christmas Day. It was very different from the last time. The Skipper only stood two bottles of grog, but the Bosun stole two gallons, so that made up for it. We had a tolerable pudding and enjoyed ourselves very well, but we were all very tired of our voyage and of each other. I don't think Russell[13] can ever have been on a long voyage or he would never write such humbug as his "Life on the Ocean Wave". The same dreary monotonous blue, day after day, is enough to weary the patience of a saint; the best of men will fall out on a long voyage. Our crew did not quarrel much because they knew that if they fought there were no officers to stop them before they hurt each other; but the Bosun got a hammering from a tall Irishman before the mast, the night after we were hauled into the docks. I was about as sorry for him as anyone, for although he was a great rogue I had got used to him and begun to feel a kind of sneaking regard for him.

January 9th [1852]. We have had very fine weather since our departure from St. Helena but we now began to feel it a little cold and many signs betokened the coming stormy weather. We therefore unbent our old sails and bent new ones. The Captain had got a new suit in China. Every ship has what they call a fine weather suit and a stormy suit.

For eight days we had a very severe gale. It was fortunately fair and on the 21st [January 1852] we sighted Scilly. The wind had increased and we were scudding under close-reefed fore and main topsail and foresail. The night was pitch dark; not a star was to be seen. I had turned in, but was awakened from a horrible dream in a very summary manner by being thrown violently from my bunk – four feet high – on to the deck. Hearing a tremendous row I rushed out but could see nothing, but the mainsail and topsail in ribands. I was soon enlightened and found that we had been run into by a brig which had probably gone down. She must have been outward bound, and at the rate we were going we must have done her considerable damage. She had evidently struck us with her starboard bow and glided off, carrying away our mainyard, quarter galleries and boat. The pumps were sounded and found all right. The most dangerous part of a voyage round the world is the English Channel.

The next night, to the satisfaction of everyone, we were anchored in the downs. The last of the moosedeers died today to the universal regret. He belonged to the carpenter. There were a good many bought at Java but none of them outlived the cold weather although every care was taken of them. None of these beautiful, unique animals has ever been reared in England. The monkeys thrived well with the exception of the tips of their fingers which they used to bite off when they were frost-bitten.

As we were being towed up the river, Frank Hay[14] came on board and did not seem to admire my rig at all. He got another suit and waited until I had cleaned myself; which by the bye is no easy matter after a long voyage. It generally happens that those boys that are brought up with the greatest care and attention become the most dirty and careless when they are cast adrift to shift for themselves. To speak for myself, I was an awful dirty young scoundrel, and although I had a splendid and expensive outfit on leaving, yet on my return I had scarcely a rag, and those of a very common description.

As soon as ever the ship touched the heads of St. Katharine's Docks I sprang ashore and had the doubtful honour of being the first ashore – and very glad I was to get there. After many years a man may get a liking for the sea – "Use is second nature" – others cannot get an opportunity of leaving and some are ashamed of leaving when they have once begun it – but there is not one out of five hundred that really like it. It's entirely against human nature that they should prefer salt junk, as hard as mahogany, to fresh meat and vegetables; or being turned out on a dreary wet night every four hours, and sometimes oftener, to getting all night in. I would not believe any man who should say that he liked seeing a dreary, restless expanse of water, with nothing for the eye to rest upon, better than green fields, trees and comfortable houses. I should never have gone after this voyage had it not been that I was so confident in saying that I should like it and never leave it, that I was ashamed to draw back now, and have it said that I was afraid, or laughed at. So I stopped at Mrs. Willans's until the Governor should get me another ship – like a soldier waiting for a hard day's work and praying that it will never come.

I could not get much money out of the Governor so I used to go to Nicol my tailor, who had been acquainted with my uncle, and got him to lend me money occasionally, and to stick it down in the bill for clothes. I gave my Jacko to Frank Hay, and crepe shawl to Fanny. But people don't seem to value the things that are brought them from abroad. If only they know half the trouble and rows boys have to bring them I am sure they would look on them as worth three times as much as they could buy the same things at home for. Poor Jacko got kicked from one to another until at last he was kicked back to me because he used to play nasty tricks before the ladies. I had no place to keep him so reluctantly I sold him to a wretch of a Jew in Ratcliffe Highway for four shillings, although I had given three times as much for him in his native wilds.[15]

I went to Chips's house. He was actively engaged in negotiating for the sale of his China crepe shawls and for that purpose we went into Graham's on Ludgate Hill to price some. They asked us five and ten pounds for some about the same quality as his. They were very polite until he pulled out his own and offered them for half the price they had asked. We were instantly shown to the door; and to tell the truth I was very glad to get out safe and sound, for I can't say that I altogether liked the look of those large shops. I never went with him any more, but believe he sold them for about an eighth part of their value to some plundering pawnbroker. The Bosun I heard of no more, and with him went my sextant, a couple of pounds and other small sundries.

The Governor was acquainted with Allen, shipowner, and he promised to get me into some ship and also to give me one pound a month as ordinary seaman. The ship proved to be a transport ship, the *Sir Robert Seppings*, chartered by the Government to carry female convicts to Hobart Town. She was lying in the East India docks and I went down to see her, but did not much fancy her from the first. I then went to the shipping office to get shipped and there found a number of hands waiting. Having a letter of recommendation from the owner, I had a seat given me near the mate. This piece of respect to me proved very much against me in the long run. The agent was much surprised on hearing that I had not a register ticket and I was sent to get one, which was obtained without much trouble. In consequence of not having it the first voyage I should lose one year of my time when I got to be mate – but as things have turned out it's just as well as it is.

II

SAILORS AND CONVICTS

A voyage in the transport ship 'Sir Robert Seppings' – Stewart, Commander (Richard Smith Stuart[1]), 628 tons registered. (From London bound to Hobart Town – commences 18th March 1852.)

She was lying down at Woolwich when I came on board – had my best clothes on and a watch in my pocket. The mate[2] was standing at the gangway and asked who I was. When told he seemed surprised and wished to know why I was not on board – did not know what business boys had making so much of themselves. He would soon take the nap off those fine clothes and let me know when he got me on the blue water.

Of course I saw through things in a minute and if I could have got into a boat I would have left everything and chanced all the rest. Indeed I had serious thoughts of swimming for it when he came ordering the boy Smith. That's the thing that cut me up, although it was quite just; yet I was getting a pound a month and therefore considered myself equal with the ordinaries so long as I could do my work as well. But it is mostly the way in the English Merchant Service. It is next to impossible for a boy to distinguish himself and to rise quickly. *They* have had to serve their time before *they* got to be able seamen, and they think it is but just that everyone else should do the same. They will not allow that anyone can be competent unless they are bound apprentices. Therefore time is everything; abilities and perseverance nothing. The question is not,

"What can you do?" but "How *long* have you been to sea?"

This was the cause of the mate's dislike to me. As he expressed himself, "He is too knowing and cheeky for me, that young shaver is!" At all events, whatever the cause might be, I experienced the effect just the same, and it is a very bad job to make an enemy of the chief mate; he has more opportunities of annoying anyone he dislikes than all the ship's company put together.

I've heard a good deal about the courage and generosity of British seamen, but it is in truth only to be found in Dibdin's songs and novels.[3] Certainly when they get ashore they are so unacquainted with the ways of the world and have so many sharks at their heels that they invariably get taken in and lose their money. They revenge themselves however on many of the unfortunate landsmen that venture on their element, and make not the slightest excuse for the poor wretches' blunders – I mean those supernumeraries who are either working their passage, or are commonly called "Jenny Ducks".

When a boy leaves the home of a fond mother with his chest (donkey) crammed with every little luxury that maternal love can think of, the generous tars steal or frighten him out of almost everything he has – to swear and bully him for his smallest blunders without giving him the least instruction. If he is a high spirited boy his life is made a burden and his young ideas are crushed, unless by some bold stroke he frees himself from them. I have heard that sailors are like spaniels – the worse you treat them the better they like you. The old saw, "Give them an inch and they'll take an ell" is very applicable to matelots; certain it is that they will growl, so it is perhaps as well to give them cause. The few man-o-war sailors that I have seen were a superior class to the merchantmen – more clean and mannerly although not such good seamen. Jack always says that the *last* ship was the best – "used to get every luxury in that ship;

never had an afternoon watch on deck, and the mate such a nice fellow; but in this bl—y hooker everything is directly opposite."

It may be remarked that the cook is usually the worst billet on board a small ship. Even if he is a good one he is always getting growled at. He suits Jack best if he is a good fighting man. I was eye-witness to a specimen of it when in the Hobart Town coasters. There was a disagreeable little fellow always growling and bullying until he had risen to be a complete cock of the ship, either because the hands were afraid, or did not wish to be bothered with bringing him down a peg or two. Besides he was a very good seaman, and they are allowed the privilege of a little extra growling. The cook was a quiet inoffensive fellow, tall and thin as a spare topgallant mast – looked as if his food did not do him much good, and it had such as long way to go down that I hardly wonder at it. He went by the cognomen of "Lamppost".

One day Growling Jim had been having a civil growl with the mate and, not being able to vent his spleen upon him, he began on the doctor about the duff. He was answered civilly enough that the duff was a good one, which was the truth, but it had got broken in turning it out of the bag. Jim took the cause of dispute in his two hands and politely observed, "Call that a good 'un, you long b——r; then put it where you put the rest of your good things," at the same time heaving it with all his strength in the Lamppost's skylights. There was an angry growl and before anyone could interfere Lamppost had seized Jim by the collar, and placing his right hand on his crutch he hove him over the bulwarks into the sea. A loud splash announced that Jim had landed safe in the briny. There was instantly a cry of "Man overboard!" An awful cry it is – seems to thrill through every limb and paralyse it.

In a moment the helm was put hard down by the Captain's orders – he was, luckily, on deck at the time and threw over the lifebuoy.

The vessel was soon aback, and after a much longer time than it would have taken on an ordinary occasion the boat was cleared of lumber and lowered. Lamppost and the Skipper were the only ones that had preserved their usual presence of mind. The lifebuoy had fortunately fallen close to Jim. When he was got on board he was very repentant and acknowledged that it was his own fault. Although I believe he liked Jim after this "as the devil does holy water", yet he was always very respectful to him, and drew in his horns forthwith.

We were all much pleased that he was on board safe and sound. The loss of a man at sea causes a greater gloom over a ship than anything I know. It is supposed to be the forerunner of greater misfortunes.

But, to return to the *Seppings* – the women were sent on board three days after I came on board, two hundred and fifty of them, besides children.[4] Their appearance was anything but promising; that greatest ornament of women, hair, had been cut pretty close, and there was a great deal of crying and yelling together with a considerable sea-sickness. When one reads of thieves and other bad characters one thinks of them with disgust and abhorrence. But if you see them every day, this feeling gradually wears off and you find that there is not so much difference between them and the rest of the world after all; and come to look at things a little closer and one finds that the fault does not so much lie in the act but in the way it is done. The sailors soon became intimately acquainted with them, and I was frequently employed to write love letters for the old salts.

The Captain was a good commander and an able seaman, but very proud – never condescended to speak to a sailor himself. Therefore everything was done through his chief officer, which generally answers very well. A captain cannot keep himself too distant. The two mates were bad men and much addicted to drink. About the seamen I will make no remark for they are mostly all alike, with a few exceptions.

If anyone doubts let them read the papers and see the daily accounts of the brutality of officers to those they dislike and the insensitivity of the crew to the suffering of their shipmate. It is only the worst cases that are brought before the public; viz. those that have a tragical end, whilst nine out of ten escape notice.

As I said before, the mate disliked me much and always set me at the most dirty and disagreeable work, besides keeping me up on my watch below to get up water every afternoon. I am the worst person possible to conciliate one who has offered me an injustice, and my answers were put down for impertinence. Things went on this way until after we had doubled the Cape, when they came to a head. (I lost all my notes on leaving this ship, and therefore am obliged to write from memory. I think nothing momentous occurred until this time.) The weather had been moderate; there was no shaving on the Line; and as it was the government orders not to risk anything the Skipper reefed topsails on the smallest change of weather. We scarcely carried away a rope yarn.

After we had doubled the Cape we caught a gale of wind from the Westward which lasted about two days. The ship rolled very heavily, she being built of teak and being considerably lightened of her provisions. Two seamen and myself were hauling taut the weather main topsail brace. The nearest to the pin of course belayed the brace. The mate d——d me and asked why I did not belay it and when I answered called me a young liar.

"Well," I said, "If that's one, there is little harm in telling another. You're a gentleman!" With that he up his fist and let me have it in the mouth. I turned to and gave it him again, and together with the roll of the ship, for I was to windward, he fell down the half deck hatch, but did not hurt himself much. Whereupon the second and third mates came to his assistance, for all hands were on deck having been reefing topsails. I was collared and with some difficulty got in the poop.[5]

The Captain came up and the mate related the affair after his own fashion. He would not allow me to speak. Suffice it to say that I was put in irons, viz. handcuffs, which they put on so tight as to tear the skin from the back of my wrist, and made fast to the mizzen mast. The weather was miserably cold, and having nothing on but a blue shirt, I was nearly frozen. One of the boys brought me an oilskin, for it was hailing, but the Skipper told him to take it away again. Being kept up there until night it was a wonder I did not lose the use of my limbs. Fortunately one of the hands brought me a pannikin of hot tea with some rum in it which kept me up.

At eight o'clock I had everything taken off and rigged with some dry things, and then locked up in the Black Box. This was a box made like a coffin standing on its end – one can neither sit or lie, nor indeed stand comfortably – with little holes at the top to breathe through. It is anything but a pleasant place. It was placed on board for the use of the women – there were some placed in there every day. I was kept there till 12 o'clock the next day, so I had been fourteen hours without food.

The women were a curious lot enough, nearly all short sentences, seven or fourteen years. Every sailor had one or more sweethearts with whom he carried on a correspondence by means of letters. They were allowed on deck during the day and in fine weather had their meals there; but were all sent below and locked up at sunset. The only way of communicating with the 'tween decks being by means of the hospital in the after part.

The system of government was founded on the old proverb "Set a thief to catch a thief". Several of them were promoted and promised rewards to watch over the rest – thus, one not being able to trust the other, they were all kept under. These constables were far more tyrannical to their fellow prisoners than free ones would have been. They had several fights among themselves, and once there was a general mêlée caused by the tyranny of the constables. This made more noise than all the fiends of hell and Bedlam let loose, but did very little damage. The hatches were put on and some of them were informed that the sailors would leave in boats and scuttle the ship if they were not quiet. On this lie getting wind, they raised such awful yells that it was truly horrible to hear them. Fancy the lungs of two hundred and fifty well-conditioned women, and pretty good lungs some of them had too. They were soon quieted and the officers were sent down to apprehend the most violent.

They were taken on the poop and put in irons. The mate was very violent to several of them. One of them gave him such a tongue-whacking that he was trying to gag her, but he was served out for she caught his fingers between her teeth and bit them to the bone. He struck her violently in the face with his disengaged hand. At this unmanly act there was a great shout among the women and enquiry was made into the cause by the Skipper, and the mate was severely reprimanded.

They were all exceedingly good when they imagined that they were nearing their destination. The doctor[6] had sole charge of the women. He was, I believe, a good doctor, but at the same time an infernal old scoundrel. He had two very pretty girls to make his bed and clean his berth. To see him stalking down the 'tween decks he put one in mind of a lecherous old Turk in the midst of his harem. *On dit* – that one of these women got in the family way and threatened to ruin his reputation by swearing the child to him and that he kept her quiet with a sleeping potion which caused her to be delirious until the day of her death. This happened shortly after her landing. How far this may be true I know not.

They all went ashore at Hobart Town and were instantly taken to a factory called the Brickfields[7] where they were detained until they were hired out, which is never very long. It is too handy to get a servant for a mere nominal charge. But on the event of a complaint of bad conduct being made by the master or mistress they are sent to the Cascades[8] and placed at the wash tub for a time; and what they bewail far more, their hair is cut short. I believe that this punishment is feared next to death by the young ones, but they get used to it after a little colonial experience. The dread of transportation is far worse than the reality. It is the best thing that ever happened to many of them. Directly they arrive at the Colony they are comparatively free, and in a short time completely so. Some of them get a year or two's probation at Millbank or some other prison in England which I have heard is worse than all the rest. If they behave well their time is considerably shortened. Any free man or ticket-of-leave can, by applying to the Governor, marry any of the newly-arrived convicts. Some of the richest men in the Colony are old convicts, commonly called lags.

The city of Hobart is a fine place built at the foot of a large mountain called Mount Wellington, the top of which is continually covered with snow. The scenery from the mouth of the Derwent is exceedingly pretty, very mountainous and thickly-wooded. The trees grow to an enormous height, but I shall have occasion to speak of this presently.

One woman and three children died on the passage.[9] This one was transported for life in consequence of a murder committed by herself and husband at their house in Liverpool. The husband was hanged but the evidence not being very clear against her, the sentence was mitigated. But her conscience was a far worse punishment than death, than which a more useless and barbarous law was never made. She refused to eat and literally died of starvation. A burial at sea is a peculiarly mournful affair and when the body goes it seems as if a great weight is off one's chest.

Everyone has somebody to chum with on board a ship. My chum was a young man about two and twenty, well educated and had been several years in a man-o-war. He was in my watch, and often have we sat on the pump well and talked away the dreary night watch, about the past, present and future; the disagreeable sounds that usually roused us from our pleasing reveries were, "Smith, loose the main royal! Smith, what time is it? Smith, what are you doing there? Come up and walk the poop. Not a word, you impudent scoundrel, you're always at your games. Ah, sir, do you dare to answer me!"

I expect Wilson[10] has been a rackety chap. At all events he did not stick to me as he ought to have done. He had scarcely any clothes, and I used to share mine with him. I had a first rate fit-out, more useful but not as expensive as on my former voyage. Sailors hate to see that anyone is above them in education, or stick together at all, and Wilson and I were not liked in consequence. Although some of them said that they would sooner have me with them up aloft than any of the able seamen; which proves that the mate's aversion was as groundless as it was despicable.

We landed the prisoners [8 July 1852] and the very night after came the tug-o-war. Anchor watch was to be kept, viz. a man and a boy every two hours. I had already kept from six to eight. The Bosun ordered me to keep from ten to twelve, the mate having directed him to do so. I refused to be imposed upon and would not go. I knew what the consequence would be perfectly well, but as we were now in port I wished to be taken before a magistrate, and lay a complaint against the mate. But I had yet to learn that there was law without justice for the poor man, and that the boasted justice of English law was the fabric of a vision.

The mate, hearing that I had refused, came forward accompanied by the second and third mates and Bosun and attempted to haul me out of the lower forecastle, but could not succeed.[11] He wanted the carpenter to come and lend him a hand, but Chips declined, adding that if he went in it would be the worse for him. He was logged for disobedience.

I agreed to go quietly before the Captain, and if he said that I was to keep the watch well and good. But no sooner had I got before the windlass than the treacherous villain struck me, and with the second mate kicked me about the head and face till they were a complete mass of bruises. They were afraid to do it in the forecastle because of provoking the wrath of the men. I was then taken before the Captain and put in irons. The mate complained that I had behaved in a very shocking manner; but in spite of his efforts to prevent me I told the Captain it was a lie and moreover swore that until I was taken before a magistrate I would not do a hand's turn on board.

He said that he was determined to support his officers in the execution of their duty, and ordered me to be ironed and placed in the Black Box. The mate taunted me and said that he had a hundred pounds in his pocket and it should all go to put me in jail. Both the mates were in liquor at the time. The doctor's assistant took my part and said that the mate was less than a man to strike a boy in the manner he had. "The time may come," said he "that he will stand before you as a man and then what excuse will you make to him!"

But enough of this! It is anything but a pleasing story to think of. Suffice it to say that I was locked in the box until next morning, and then taken ashore by the police boat. The cook had refused duty and went with me.[12] Both were glad to leave her and hoped never to see her again.

We were taken to the Lock-up. This was the first time that I had been to any of these respectable houses, and I do not regret it. It has given me a little insight into the mysteries of justice that before I had only read of in novels. Newspapers talk about English justice – pshaw! Let anyone try them – without a shilling, or friend and a rich adversary. They'll find their mistake out, I'll be bound. I believe that it would be quite possible to get a dozen honest poor men transported if one only had money enough. Everyone has his price and is to be bought, from the magistrate to the constable. There are exceptions to every rule.

Then again the cleanliness of the prisons, so much vaunted. When the public go to examine them they are well enough; but it's when "the cat's away that the mice will play". To find out abuses in anything one must commence as an inferior. Everything is so varnished over before the Upper Class see them, so that, albeit they are good benevolent people and really wish to assist their poorer brethren, yet they are unable to find out the way or even to see that they require it. Why should not lesser offenders, and those that are awaiting sentence (often innocent men) be treated as well as convicted felons? But no; they are all poked into a little stinking room without a blanket, the floor covered with the dung and urine of drunken men, who, being shoved in there during the night, lie and wallow in their filth until morning, swearing, fighting, singing or crying as the fit takes them. This is the beautiful place that any poor man is taken to who is given in charge by the gentry, although perhaps proved innocent when tried, and discharged.

At daylight the policeman on guard, in order to save himself the trouble, calls out one of the prisoners who gets a mop and bucket and smears the floor over – which is considered sufficient. He gets rewarded by a crust of bread; the other prisoners get nothing unless they have the money to buy it.

We were kept in this pigsty until eleven o'clock the next day. Then we were taken before the magistrate. There was no-one in court but the Captain and the mate. The first question was, "What are these men charged with?"

"Insubordination and refusal of duty," replied the Skipper.

"Guilty or not guilty," said the magistrate to us. I began to explain to him the treatment of the mate.

"There, that will do," he said, "I suppose you want to go to the diggings, but you'll get sixty days' hard labour instead. Clear the court!"

"But, sir," said I, "Will you hear what I have to say in my defence?"

"Remove that man," said he to the attendant constables, and in the twinkling of an eye I was pushed outside the court. Few people would believe this to be true, but I solemnly declare that it is word for word exactly as it happened. I shall not easily forget that diabolical wretch's look of triumph as I was shoved out.

We were taken back to the lock-up, and in the afternoon to the Penitentiary, commonly called "Tench".[13] They searched us at the door and passed us on to the wardrobe man. All the officers are prisoners. This gentleman was waiting dressed in a gaudy suit of yellow with a bracelet on his leg. He kindly assisted us with our toilette, and, probably having a tender regard for our health, he removed our hair completely. A superfluity of clothing being unnecessary, we were told to strip and put on a suit of dirty grey and a leathern cap with a number on. We were conducted to a large stone building where the free men are kept, viz. those who are there on short sentences for a misdemeanour. There were about one hundred and fifty men there all dressed alike, and any person unaccustomed to them would have difficulty in distinguishing the one from the other. Ninety of these men were sailors who had either been caught attempting to run, or who were like myself.

A great many of them were walking up a large wheel, apparently very uselessly, for they never got up any higher.[14] We were told to get up; it was very difficult at first, for we were frequently missing the steps and hurting our shins, but we soon got used to it and walked up as well as any of them. The place was well enough in the short winter days, if we had a little more food, for we worked from daylight until dark. The allowance consisted of one pint of skilly, or flour and water boiled, and half a pound of bread for breakfast; one pint of very wretched broth and a tiny bit of meat and potato for dinner, and supper the same as breakfast. These may seem pretty good for anyone who has nothing to do, but it is only enough to keep life in a working man.

Three days later ten more sailors were brought in from our ship, having refused duty in the hopes of getting off clear after having served their time. For the diggings were all the rage about this time and even the coasters were offering fabulous prices for sailors. But they were disappointed, for unfortunately the *Seppings* was again chartered by the Government to fetch prisoners from Norfolk Island. And therefore the Captain, on applying to the Governor, obtained permission to take us all out by representing that otherwise he would be shorthanded. Half of them went willingly, but the others, amongst whom was myself, refused to go and they were not authorised to force us.

The Skipper soon after came with another order to take us on board whether we went willingly or not, and that if we did not work we should be kept in irons. "Needs must when the devil drives", so we went. But I have been since told that if we still refused to work that, it being against the law, they would not have forced us to sea. It is like the man said when they put him in the stocks, "You can't put me there!" – and at the same time he *was* there.

The business the ship was on was to bring three hundred of the Norfolk Islanders to Port Arthur, the Legislature having taken a freak into their heads that all the prisoners should leave Norfolk

Island.[15] They have since had reason to repent it. Several of them have escaped from Port Arthur and committed the most fearful murders in the adjoining country. They were all men who had been twice convicted of the most heinous crimes, and rendered desperate by the most horrible cruelty and ill usage. It has been not inaptly called the Ocean Hell; and it has frequently happened that two of them would toss up together whilst working in the quarries to ascertain which of them would knock the other's brains out, thus causing the less fortunate one to be hung after he had committed the murder, almost immediately.

Dalton and Kelly were passengers by our ship. They escaped shortly after being landed at Port Arthur. They stole a whaleboat and arrived safely in Port Phillip. They inhumanly murdered every soul they met on the road to the diggings. They were captured after a desperate resistance and hanged in Melbourne.[16]

We were three weeks on our passage – took a detachment of soldiers for the relief of those there. The mate dared not be abusive now because of the soldiers, and on the passage back we were obliged to unite against the common enemy, the prisoners. We brought up at the Cascades.[17] There is no port or shelter of any kind and had the wind increased much we should have been forced to cut away. As it was we lost the pee of one of our anchors.

The island is a beautiful place, a perfect little paradise inhabited by demons. It was originally covered with fruits of all kinds but they have been destroyed by the Governor's orders in consequence of the prisoners escaping and living on them. The lemons they have been unable to eradicate, and they were brought on board by the thousands for the use of the ship's company together with a large quantity of sweet potatoes which are very nice baked, very much like chestnuts.

The prisoners were brought on board, the soldiers standing over them with loaded pistols. A more villainous looking herd of wretches I never saw. They were all in irons, one leg being fastened to the other by a chain just long enough to allow them to walk. A conspiracy was formed to take the ship before we had been many days out. They removed the fore-scuttle although it was well fastened down by some iron bars; and by that means they got into the hold. In another hour the ship would have been theirs and probably all hands murdered, for the boarding pikes and some muskets were in the after hold. But fortunately one of the apprentices had been sent down for water and placed his hand on one of the prisoner's heads. With the most praiseworthy presence of mind he refrained from giving any alarm; and pretending that he had not noticed him he went on deck to get the pump. He went quietly to the Captain and informed that there were prisoners in the hold.[18] A detachment of soldiers was marched down with fixed bayonets, and as the former were unarmed they were easily secured, taken on deck and chained to the anchors and cables.

The soldiers and sailors were all aft, the former on the port side, separated by a bulkhead fore and aft and from the prisoners by a strong one athwart-ships pierced with musket holes which commanded the whole of the main deck. Thus, although our force was inferior, we had them like rats in a corner. A fearful mêlée broke out between those that had been in office and the others. The berths were torn down to form weapons of offence and dreadful blows were given indiscriminately. They were not quieted until a volley of blank cartridges had been fired along the 'tween decks. When they were quiet the soldiers entered and removed nine insensible men awfully smashed about the head and face.[19] None of the wounds was mortal as they had no edged tools.

We arrived at Port Arthur after a very favourable passage, to the satisfaction of all hands. Had we been much longer there is very little doubt that we should have lost a number of our men. Port

Arthur is pretty, very thickly wooded and mountainous. The second class in the scale of crime is confined here. We left this and brought up once more in the Derwent from which place we were intended to go to Madras; but I had resolved never to go in that ship and only waited an opportunity to make my escape.

All the ship's company were very anxious to run away just as much as I was, but from a very different motive. I wanted to get away from a man that I abhorred, and they merely wished to get to the diggings. At all events, I have the satisfaction of knowing that it was through me that the mate lost his hands this time.

The boat was hoisted up every evening and when the word was given we all came aft. One evening we came aft as usual but the boat was not up – four hands, able seamen, had pulled ashore in her. The guns were fired for the Police Boat but without effect. Three of them were afterwards caught and brought aboard. The Skipper was in a towering rage at this, for it was his boast that no man dared run from him; and I heard that he had a bet on the subject with the Captain of another vessel in the Harbour. The anchor watch was now doubled and a soldier was ordered to pace the deck with a loaded musket. In fact the ship was so well guarded that I began to despair of escaping.

Then one night the long-wished-for opportunity arrived. From twelve till two was my watch, and as I was on the poop I had an opportunity of making friends with the sentry. I plied him well with the brandy bottle, and then told him it was not the slightest use for two to be on the poop, so I would keep watch whilst he had his smoke. He went into the galley and as I had expected fell fast asleep. I lost no time in getting the carpenter and five others I could trust, told them the plan and then went on the poop to lower the boat. Having filled the blocks with slush so that they should not creak, we hauled her under the bows and got Chips's chest into her, together with a few other things. Wilson was on the forecastle and I gave him my watch and about three pounds worth of dollars, thinking that if I was taken I should lose them. Afterwards I repented, for he was but a poor chum if he would not bolt for friendship's sake.

I was just going to step into the boat when I heard the mate's voice calling for the boy of the watch. My heart came into my mouth. It was an anxious moment, but I ran aft and answered him. "Oh," said he "It's you, is it (hiccup)? Mind and keep a good look out!" He went to the side board and took a neat swig of a black bottle until I really thought that it had grown to his cursed lips, and then with a deep sigh staggered to his berth. I fervently thanked the pigs and returned to the forecastle. By the loudness of the sentry's snores I saw that it was all right, and the alcohol had done its work; jumped into the boat, pushed off and hoisted the sail. As we passed rapidly by the infernal tub I felt for a moment as pure and delightful a sensation as ever it fell to the lot of poor mortals in this wilderness of woe. My happiness was indescribable. I was free![20]

We set sail for the mouth of the Derwent. In the morning we ran into a bay called Peppermint Bay,[21] and, seeing some smoke ashore, landed in hopes of getting some grub, for in our hurry we had forgotten that very necessary commodity. We came to a bark hut and before it an old man was standing with a remarkably long gun pointed very disagreeably at our persons.

"Now then," he growled, "If you don't wish for this ball in your carcase move off – sharp is the word!"

Asked him several questions but all we could get from the old curmudgeon was, "None of your blarney, all serene," and sundry other short pithy sentences; and ended by fetching out a remarkably savage dog. Thereupon we made a precipitate retreat. In all probability he took us for runaway convicts. It is that which makes it so difficult to escape from a ship in this port. You can scarcely move along the high road without being questioned. However, we put to sea again and landed lower down where we found some splitters and sawyers. They advised us to sink the boat and take to the bush for it.

This advice was none of the best as we afterwards found – and they did it to get the boat up again when we were gone, and dispose of her. Not knowing any better at the time, we did as they advised and sank her filled with stones. One of us stripped and pulled her out. The plug was removed but it was not filling very fast. He left and she drifted too far inshore so that you could see her plainly at low water, it being very clear. I wished to take her out further but was overruled by the majority. It would have been as well had they taken my advice.

We then went several miles into the bush, which is very thick. If one gets off the track it is almost impossible to walk at all. The trees are of enormous magnitude. They principally consist of stringy bark growing on the high ground and several kinds of gums on the plains. The latter is much used for shipbuilding and the former for palings or slabs. It is very easily split and one often sees trees that have been half cut through, split up forty or fifty feet. Therefore, in cutting a tree it is necessary to knotch it on both sides with the axe. The American axe is in most use in these colonies and I have always found it the handiest.

We found two splitters on Port Cygnet Hill;[22] ticket-of-leave men. They instantly slung the billy for us and served out cold mutton and damper which they use at every meal. The damper they bake in the white wood ashes, plenty of which are indispensable. It is merely flour and water mixed into a pretty hard dough, about two inches thick and as large round as one thinks proper. A hole is then made in the hot ashes away from the flame and the dough is placed in it and covered up carefully, the ashes being renewed until it is done. It is very nice indeed, and if well-baked not so heavy as one would imagine.

They drink tea at every meal, usually green tea and very weak. The extravagant use of this luxury would quite alarm any old lady in England. The mutton was corned. This was the first time ever I had tasted it salted and I very much enjoyed it. I cannot understand the reason for never having it in England. The men were very kind and showed us a place where there was a nice hut built of palings surrounded by an almost impenetrable bush, so that as long as we stopped, there was no danger of discovery. We passed our time very comfortably here for about six weeks.[23]

The surrounding scenery was wild and beautiful in the extreme; stupendous mountains covered with enormous trees interspersed in all directions by clear running streams which dashed over the rocks and rushed into the valleys beneath. Nor were living things wanting to fill up the measure of bliss; birds of all the colours of the rainbow. In no other country is there such a variety of the feathered tribe with magnificent plumage. Kangaroos are occasionally seen but they are very shy. The hindquarters of these remarkable animals are excellent eating. I was told that they grow seven, and rarely, nine, feet high when standing on their hind legs, and that when brought to bay will make a desperate stand, frequently killing both men and dogs with the formidable claws on their hind feet. They leap a tremendous distance. That is their only way of travelling, the fore legs being considerably shorter than the hind ones.

In Adelaide the hounding of these sagacious and beautiful animals forms a very favourite amusement and exciting sport. The squatters complain that one kangaroo eats as much grass as a whole flock of sheep. They carry their young in a pouch beneath their belly. Opossums do the same and are very plentiful. Every gum tree contains one, but as they are night animals it is very tedious work shooting them. Their skins make splendid rugs. Their food consists of the leaves of the gum tree. When taken young both these animals are easily tamed. Mosquitoes abound much. They frequently bunged one's eyes up and covered the face with lumps. They are a dreadful plague.

I was the only person among us that had any money and it had to be used with great caution in more ways than one as there were very few houses about and it was questionable if some of those inside would not inform the police of our whereabouts to get the reward. Chips was the caterer, or rather cadger. He sometimes got a damper, by spinning a pitiable yarn, for nothing. The money gradually dwindled away, and when it was gone we often had to go to bed with empty stomachs; but even this was better than having to leave the land of gold, with very little chance of any wage – and we were uncertain if the ship had sailed.

However, the fewer mouths to be fed the better – and I determined to chance it and dare the dangers of the road rather than an empty belly. One of the hands, an apprentice, and myself set off for Melbourne. We camped out the first night and, being without food or covering, we were very cold, and in the morning not in a very fit state for a long walk. However we pegged along until we came to a township called Brown's River;[24] and then came the tug-of-war. Our apprehension proved our destruction.

I bound my head round with a handkerchief and turned up my sleeves to appear like a sawyer, and we then separated and walked through the town. I was the first to meet anyone, and he unfortunately happened to be a constable. Seeing my strange appearance he questioned me. Some of them I answered, but finding that I was only getting further in the mud, pushed by him and went on. He instantly pulled out a pistol and levelled it at my head, telling me that if I stirred another step he would blow my brains out. I asked him what right he had to stop me; that I would do anything reasonable.

"Well," said he, "Come with me and answer a few questions, and then you can go on again."

Thinking discretion the better part of valour I went with him, affecting to treat it as a joke – when who should we meet but my chum. Directly he saw me he foolishly remarked, "Hallo Jim, where are you going?".

Thus we were sold directly, for I had represented myself as a sawyer going to town by myself to order some rations. He took us both off to the Watchhouse, although had it not been for the pistol I should have tried conclusions with him. We were then examined by the inspector, told lies and contradicted them again; suffice it to say we were not old enough in deception to be a match for them, and were accordingly locked up until we should be identified unless we would tell who we were, and then they would allow us to have the run of the kitchen.

It was not much use, we thought, holding out any longer because they must find us out before long, and the sooner it was over the better. So we told them that we were run-away seamen belonging to the *Seppings*. We were then let out and some dinner was given us. Our friend the constable looked upon us with pride, and well he might, for he was sure of a handsome reward.

Word was sent to the ship for someone to come and identify us, and in three days the two mates came. This was the worst cut to me. I would have given one of my limbs rather than he (the mate) should have the satisfaction of saying he had caught me. His object was to find the boat, but on this point I was determined to be dumb, and he could not prove that we took the boat at all. He threatened us with transportation for taking the boat. I retorted upon him that he had stolen some of the government firearms, and that instantly quieted him.

I was taken before the district magistrate, and am happy that he was quite a different man from the other. He heard my story and regretted that I had not seen him on the former occasion; but, as it was, he should be obliged to punish me for desertion unless I chose to return to the ship. This I promptly refused. He then sentenced me to one month's imprisonment with hard labour, adding that it was the shortest term allowed by law for the offence. The mate was vexed and asked if he was not going to punish me for the boat.

"Silence," said the magistrate, "I command here. How dare you dictate to me!"

I never saw a man look more sheepish in my life. He put his tail between his legs and walked off. It was the last I saw of him; but I may see him some time under different circumstances and then a day of reckoning will come.

The 'prentice was taken on board where they could refine their cruelty – no one to prevent them. I afterwards heard that he was locked up in a cabin-berth and kept on bread and water until he told the Skipper where the boat was sunk. He was taken to the spot by the Police Boat, the stones thrown out and the boat raised. If they had taken her where I advised the deuce a bit more they would have seen of her. I do not think he told of the others, which, considering the hardships he must have had to put up with, proved him a brick. He made another desperate attempt and succeeded in getting on board one of the coasters where he stowed away in an empty water cask; but he was unfortunately discovered by the police and taken on board to bc subjcct once more to their infernal tyranny.

Anyone that has been to sea must know that what I say is not exaggerated. There is no place where a man has greater opportunities of displaying a tyrannical disposition than at sea, where the captain is an absolute monarch. He has the opportunity of making either a hell or a heaven of the ship. I will maintain that no man, no, not even the best, is fit for absolute power; poor human nature cannot endure so much – he is sure to abuse it in some way or other.

Accompanied by an officer, I was taken to the Hobart Town Penitentiary where I underwent the same disagreeable operations as before, of cutting of the hair and changing clothes. This place is like a small city. It is surrounded by a lofty wall and contains eating rooms, kitchen, chapel, hospital, washing rooms and wardrobe. The treadwheel grinds all the flour for the prison consumption and the bread is made by the prisoners of whom there are three kinds; the free men, the probationers and the second sentences. They do not mix together, therefore I know nothing about the two latter classes – but will describe our treatment.

We all sleep in separate cells, about nine feet by four; in each cell is placed two blankets and a counterpane, a jug of drinking water, a Bible and prayer book and a tub with a lid to it. After prayers which are read in the wheel room everyone toes a line and at the word "Right about face!" turn half-face to the right and march in single line. Everyone being numbered, they have only to march straight forward, and on arriving at the door of each apartment halt, and, at a given word, open the door and walk in, closing it after you. It is then locked by the jailer. In the morning you are awakened by a bell and before the next bell rings, which is five minutes afterwards, you have to be dressed and your blankets rolled up in the manner directed. At the sound of the second bell you must open the door, come out and stand before it tub in hand. At the word of command "Right about face!" march to the wash houses, put down your tubs in rows, take off your jackets and wash. Then at the word, form a line and march to the wheel room.

There is room on the wheel for just thirty hands who accordingly mount, the remainder sitting down forbidden to speak on pain of three days' solitary confinement. A bell rings every three minutes, the right-hand man getting down and one of the idlers gets on the left-hand side; and so on – thus each hand is on one hour and a half, and the duration of the rest depends on the number of hands. At light all go to breakfast to which half-an-hour is allowed; one o'clock to dinner – three-quarters of an hour allowed; and supper at seven. After that prayers and proceed as before.

Anyone who misbehaves is taken before the Superintendent and usually sentenced to three days' solitary confinement in a stone cell, perfectly dark, the same size as the sleeping cell, but very cold – only one blanket allowed at night which is taken away in the day time; and last not least, only half a pound of bread per day which is barely sufficient for the necessities of nature.

The security of this prison cannot be impeached. The prisoner must first escape from his cell, after which he must avoid the numerous constables, who being all thieves, are up to everything. Then he has to scale a formidable obstacle, and after all this he is no further forward than if he were still in bed, for he has on the prison clothes which condemn him in an instant; and moreover he is in a convict city where he can trust no one. Very few escapes have taken place from this penitentiary. As for transportation being an object to dread or a means of reformation, why it's all stuff and nonsense. In a worldly sense they are better off than before. Solitary confinement is the punishment most dreaded, and I had an opportunity of proving that it was not without reason. No man could endure it for any length of time without either leaving his senses or the world, even if he had sufficient to eat – here it is solitary and starvation combined.

On Sunday there is a grand review – the different companies being formed in the prison yard. Superintendent Boyd[25] passes round and carefully examines them, sometimes accompanied by Governor Denison.[26] In fact it is carried on exactly as an army is reviewed in England, the companies going through their evolutions in the same manner. On these occasions every man is present and attends divine service which is always perfectly orderly and apparently attended to well. At least it would seem so to a casual observer; but for a deep reasoner it is easy to perceive that the ministers are not in earnest and only consider it as a disagreeable duty that they wish to hurry through with the greatest possible dispatch. To the prisoners it is a change from their usual dull routine and they like it. Whether they are actuated by any deep religious feeling or not it is for one only to determine, but it is my private opinion that they cannot look on the discourse in that light that appears to me to embody this, "I am your master and therefore you ought to obey me. I behave very well to you and put you in jail for your own good, therefore you ought to pray for me. In fact while you are here you must make me your God, and worship your governors and those that are put in authority over you, as the giver of all good things."

But to return to myself. I found two other hands belonging to the *Seppings* and I must say that I was pleased with finding company that I knew. But the days were getting very long, the number of wheelmates was few, and therefore the work was much harder than when we were there the first time. We therefore determined to knock off and refuse to work any longer. They had not power to prolong our sentence and the worst they could do was to give us solitary. We did so, and were taken before the Superintendent and sentenced to seven days' solitary which he assured us would be quite enough to make us wish to come back to the wheel.[27]

It is true that an awful punishment is in these words. To have no acquaintances, no friends, to be separated from all the social and intellectual pleasures – from the softer sex – without which things the little man's life's worth would be entirely destroyed. Truly, I pity the poor unfortunates who have to endure it for years. Let the fools who talk of death being the greatest punishment try the slow starvation and solitary system. Let the epicure who turns up his nose at the greatest delicacies see with what relish the poor wretch devours a mouldy crust. And worst of all, never to see the light of the glorious sun and feel its genial heat without which the brightest and most beautiful landscape is tame and insipid. The feeble heart shrinks from it, and the firm mind doubts and hesitates.

I think it probable enough that had I had sufficient food I should have felt even more lonely and depressed. Thus it is that one evil nullifies another, and the pain of the stomach drove away the anxiety of the mind. No man can undergo more than a certain amount of suffering. How thankfully would I have received the crumbs which fall from the rich man's table. Little do we think, whilst we sit round our luxurious tables, of the poor wretches who dwell, perhaps in the same street, and who would give years of their miserable lives to obtain the scraps that are thrown out to our dogs. Oh, how much indeed have those men to answer for, who, living in useless magnificence, close their ears to the cries of the sick and hungry. Nor are those who are without money to exempt themselves from such duties. More good is often done by a kind and judicious word than with much gold.

These reflections passed rapidly through my thoughts as I sat in my miserable dark cell, and looking back I would not that I had never been there – for as Shakespeare says, "Sweet are the uses of adversity."[28] I feel that it has made me a better man, and at all events, more lenient to the vices of the poor and unfortunate.

As I had refused to work with the intention of remaining in solitary until my sentence was up I determined not to be beaten and stuck to it after the seven days were up. Thus I was three weeks in this horrible cell. Every Sunday we attended divine service and I fainted, for the first time in my life, on the reviewing ground. Want of food, at just the time of life when a lad most requires it, had so weakened my frame that the sudden transition from darkness to light had this effect upon me. I was carried off and had some water thrown in my face – soon recovered. It is a common occurrence and caused no confusion. I have read that the prisoners confined alone in the Bastille when brought to the light went mad. I doubt it not. The other men went and worked on the wheel after the seven days had expired.

After the thirty days I had my clothes returned and left the prison rejoicing. In a foreign land without a friend or a home; but a sailor never need want a home long at that time; and as I walked down the quay I was saluted by the Captain of one of the coasters who instantly perceived by my appearance that I was a tar just from "The Tench", no uncommon thing at this time – more shame to the Government. He offered me ten pounds a month, and almost prayed me to come. But I did not want much pressing, so I instantly went on board and the Skipper sent me to the galley to have a feed. And like a fool I ate very heartily of meat, soup and potatoes – and in about an hour afterwards I was in agonies. Talk about the choler-oh! I went ashore and found one of the soldiers who had come from Norfolk Island with us. He took me up to the Barracks and treated me very kindly. All the next day I was laid up.

In the meantime the schooner had gone, but I was not long in shipping on board the *Harriet Nathan*, a barque, (Captain Lindsay) bound to Melbourne with general cargo.[29] Ten pounds per month. I went there and back in her. What a difference in the treatment of those colonial traders in the time of the diggings, and the limejuicers. In the former you have good grub, good treatment and good pay; but in the latter just the opposite.

When I returned to Hobart Town I found the carpenter and the rest of the boat's crew come from the bush. After we left them they had found a friend in one of the huts who had supplied them with food in lieu of Chips's tools; and one of them had found one half sovereign in the lining of my boots which I had placed there on my first incarceration and forgotten all about it. Chips had taken a small house and they used to live there pretty cheap.

I had now an opportunity of seeing more of the town. There is only one theatre there and that is but a poor one. Johanna's and Gipsy Poll's, two large singing houses, are very popular. The number of prostitutes are unequalled in any town in the world of the same population.

I shipped again almost directly aboard the *Allert*, a Brigantine.[30] The Captain was a very nice old man, but the mate was a great bully called Mitchell. The cook was a good one; but unfortunately all three of them were lushingtons.[31] The doctor used to get drunk for a week at a stretch and then I had to take his place, although it was a billet I was not at all partial to. We went in her to Launceston. The town is about forty miles up a river called the Tamar, the banks of which are covered with splendid farms and orchards. The soil is so rich that it requires very little cultivation and no manure. The river is exceedingly tortuous, and from the height of the banks very difficult to navigate. There is a small town at the mouth called George Town. Launceston is a small and dull place, but the surrounding scenery is remarkably fine. The river is not navigable higher on account of the falls and rocks.

We stripped the schooner to a gantline and sent up new riggings, and then ran round to the Leven in ballast (it is a small river to the Westward) for a cargo of palings. The scenery is grand in the extreme. There is no inhabitant within twenty miles except a few splitters who came there on account of the fineness of the timber. The river is overhung by rocks and trees of great height and bulk. There is only ten feet of water on the bar at high water. We struck on it going out, and in spite of anchors and all kinds of exertion we remained there nine days. There are plenty of fine fish in the river and we amused ourselves with catching them in the evening, or bathing. The latter nearly cost one hand his life for a shark had just turned on his back to give the fatal grip when he was perceived and frightened off by the cook who threw the oar at him. We never bathed after this, and the next Sunday we caught the rapacious monster which proved to be a ground shark, which accounted for our not seeing any of them before.

As we had to load her ourselves we were not very quick about it, and consequently we had two months' pay to draw on reaching the Derwent (sixteen pounds). With this I determined to try the far-famed gold diggings – shipped on the *Swordfish*[32] and when I arrived in Melbourne my savings amounted to about twenty pounds. Albeit a man obtains good wages in these coasters, yet they are none of the pleasantest, for one encounters very bad weather in Bass's Straits at times and wrecks are not infrequent. Bad enough anywhere but worse on this coast which is iron bound and there is small chance of saving the hapless crew. It was nearly a case with us in the *Harriet Nathan* on the St. George's rocks.[33] We nearly drifted on in a calm and had the catspaw[34] been five minutes later we should have had a lodging in Davy Jones' Locker.

III

IN PURSUIT OF GOLD

(Memorandums of adventures on the Victorian goldfields – July 1853 to November 1854)

I set off to Mt. Alexander Diggings with three of the hands and two old lags who had come as passengers with us from Hobarton; not without misgivings, for the accounts were so exaggerated that it appeared that nothing short of a miracle could keep one's throat safe from the knife of the bushrangers. It just shows what folly it is to be guided by those lying tattlers, newspapers. I am sure I have been in Melbourne at all hours of the night and was never molested, at the very time when if one looked at a newspaper for a description of the town it would make one tremble to see the fearful array of robberies and murders. The Bible says, "Put not faith in Princes"; an addition would be an improvement, i.e. or Newspapers or Rumour – in fact, to believe nothing you hear, nor one half that you see, is the colonial saying.

We got an old Irish carter to take our swags on his dray and accomplished what we considered great work – twenty miles the first day – and quite knocked ourselves up. Sailors are the worst hands in the world for walking; they are so unaccustomed to it. The first twenty miles is very flat and insipid scenery, and at that time of year the roads were awful bad. I said "roads", for in reality they were only tracks without a bit of metal on them. The wheels frequently sank up to the axle and then all hands would have to push and prise it out with levers, up to our waists in mud. It was no uncommon thing for drays to be stuck for several days. They offered no impediment to the traffic for the road was ten miles wide on Keilor Plains and therefore plenty of room to choose.

Keilor is a small town situated on the Salt Water River which empties itself into the Yarra below Melbourne. It is ten miles from the latter. At this place you lose every vestige of tree, and in summer, of water, until you get to the Gap – exactly ten miles. It may be called a landslip – it has probably been formed by heavy floods. We got there the first night and camped the plain side; a bad plan, for horses are not nearly so ready for a heavy pull in the morning as when warm. There was so little wood about here that we had difficulty in getting the fire alight to boil the billy. The horses are hobbled, viz. the forelegs made fast together by means of two straps joined by a short chain. They are then allowed to go where they please, and although they are hobbled sometimes manage to stray so far that the drivers have great difficulty in finding them.

After supper we spread the tarpaulin over the dray and all slept underneath. We were so stiff that we could hardly move the next morning, and a prodigious hard job we had to get up the other side of the Gap. Indeed we never should have managed it had not the driver borrowed a leader from another dray. Now we began to enter the bush and it had the appearance of a gentleman's park. The trees are not nearly so large or so close as in Van Diemen's Land. In fact, there was nothing particular to see on this road except the Black Forest at Mount Macedon which is very grand.[1] As most of the newcomers go to these diggings without seeing other parts they generally go away dissatisfied; whereas if they went to the right places there is as fine scenery in Australia as in any part of the globe.

We only made sixteen miles today. Our feet were so sore, and one of the men took off his boots to ease his feet, but he had reason to regret it; for after walking a short distance he could not get them on again in consequence of his feet swelling so, and had to cut them down the back. There is nothing like good woollen socks for walking in; a clean pair twice a day, easy boots with soles an inch thick, and the feet placed in cold water, the cooler the better, at night and one can walk thirty miles per diem with greater ease than persons who are not so provided can twenty. If a blister forms instantly prick it with a needle; if it fills prick again. This is my own experience and if it is not right I'll eat my head.

We camped tonight at Collier's station.[2] We had to pay one shilling per pound for flour, but got a hindquarter of mutton for three shillings. The ants are very numerous and very useful. They will pick the carcase of a bullock in an incredibly short time and far cleaner than the most skilled anatomist. By the bye, the bones would be worth a trifle if in the Old Country. One could get a shipload with very little trouble. There are a great many different ant tribes; it is most amusing to watch their movements. I have sat for hours as intent as if reading a book, and I have remarked that all the tribes, although some of them are very large and have the most formidable stings, yet they are all afraid of the smallest tribe, little black ones called pissants. I have frequently taken one of the large ones and pushed him into the tribe. They instantly seized him and if he did not very quickly make his lucky escape he was torn limb from limb. When the pissants walk abroad on their several business they form a kind of road or line of themselves like a regiment of soldiers an inch wide, and I have followed them up for thirty-three yards where they were feeding on the body of an opossum, one side going to it without anything and the other coming back to the nest heavily laden. I did not see any come back empty handed. I calculate they do it in this manner for fear of getting lost, for if you take one out of the line any distance they are so small that they cannot find their way back. They sting very unpleasantly.

I don't know anything about the classified names, but in the colonists' phraseology, there are green wood ants who make their nests in rotten trees; they are quite harmless. There are the yellow pincered ants, a size larger than the wood ant, and bite and sting second only to the bulldog ants, which are the largest and most ferocious, some of them being three inches long. They are very courageous; if you shake a stick at them they will run after you like a dog. He'll bite and sting the stick for a moment, and then if he finds he makes no impression, make for your legs; and woe be unto you if he gets at them. Thick moleskin trousers are no protection from their sting and pincers. Their sting is worse than the hornet's and in fact, than anything I know.

When we lit the fire, and having found plenty of dead wood we made a rouser, I went to fill my billy with some pretty fair water – at least for the bush. I have seen an English housewife go into fits at the bare mention of making tea with better water. As I was setting it on the fire – no easy matter with a wood fire – I was so startled by the cries of one of my mates that I let go the billy into the fire; and turning round saw him writhing, jumping, kicking and shouting in such a ludicrous manner that my alarm was quickly turned into laughter. The carter instantly saw how the matter stood. He had incautiously lain on a bed of bulldogs. The former told him to pull off his trousers, but he paid no attention and rushed furiously into the waterhole. This cooled his own courage considerably but had little effect on the furious insects, and the carter having prevailed him to listen, he came out and pulled off his trousers. And there they were, sure enough. For want of oil he rubbed the stings with some clean beef suet which allayed the pain a little, but poor fellow, he was awfully bitten.

Misfortunes never come single they say. It came on to rain heavily that night, and the rain formed a perfect little creek under the dray, wetting us through, and our blankets, flour, sugar and everything. Live and learn! We ought to have made a trench round it. We got up very miserable and bad-humoured, and wrapping a blanket over our shoulders stood by the fire all night in the pouring rain. Lucky we had made such a good one. This was a rare opportunity for the carter to dispose of a keg of very bad brandy which he now offered. In consideration that we were new hands and had not much money, he let us have it at one shilling a wine glass, the regular price being one and sixpence. Three of my mates eagerly swallowed the bait with a view to get wet inside as well as out; but Dick and myself, although we willingly took one, were proof against a second and were accordingly set down as humbugs, which on the whole is preferable to being fools. In a very short time the conversation became highly edifying; the first half-hour they were great friends, quite loving; in the next they were stripped to fight, and before the third was out they were lying here and there in puddles or any other nice comfortable place they could pick out. This kind of game did not suit Dick or me, but we did not mind it for once, and as it was a wet night let it pass.

Next morning before they were able to move they must have a nobbler or, as the saying is, "a hair of the dog that bit them", and another one now and then during the day to keep the cold out, so they were seedy all day and all ill-tempered. Dick and I walked ahead. Our prospects looked gloomy and it was a mizzling rain. We said little, but thought much. We passed the Bush Inn[3] and entered the Black Forest. This is a very thickly wooded place – very mountainous – both of which things cause it to rain more than in other places. The consequence is that the ground is soft and marshy and we had the sight of numbers of bullock drays completely stuck in the mud.

One man told us he had lost his bullocks and had been seeking them for ten days. We were frequently accosted with, "Good day, mate! Have you seen two strawberry bullocks with hobbles on?" or "a black horse branded so-and-so?" In fact, horses being in great demand were continually stolen. The carter told us that he had a friend on the roads who had lost seven horses in three months – which itself proves what a first-rate thing must be made of carting. A hundred pounds per ton was thought cheap.

The bullock drays seem curious enough to a new hand – some of them take as much as three tons, and, as there are but two wheels, the weight upon those makes it sink up to the axle if the ground is not very firm. But the united strength of a dozen well-driven bullocks is immense. It greatly depends upon the driving, so that every bullock has an equal strain upon the yoke chain. Some men can drive them without a blow, but others use them very brutally. It is a common occurrence to punch their eyes out and cover them with cuts. They frequently drop down dead from fatigue. The society for the prevention of cruelty to animals is much wanted here. The drays are very strong with a pole in the middle. The bullocks are yoked two and two in a very simple way – a piece of wood is placed on their necks with four holes in it; through these is passed a piece of bent rod iron rivetted at the top to prevent its falling out, and the yoke is complete. They take much longer on this journey than horse drays.

We camped near the Black Forest Inn[4] and as everything was wet we had much difficulty in lighting. The process of lighting a bush fire is more difficult than one would imagine – it took us nearly two hours, and even then we should not have managed it had not the driver cut up a small case which he had in the dray. New chums should always mate with an old hand if possible, and the latter is very unwise if he mates with them if he can help it.

The night passed very uncomfortably. Our three mates still remained in a state of half-fourpenny. Dick and I had a little private conversation on the subject, and we decided upon dissolving partnership if they did not discontinue their bad habits. They had their drams as usual and a civil growl when we hinted at what we had been speaking. They instantly told us to mind our own business, and we agreed to part on our arrival at the diggings. The driver, of course, sided with them as there was more to be got from that quarter; in fact most of their hard earnings was gradually transferred from their pockets to his own, thus realising the truth of the old saw, "Sailors earn their money like horses, and spend it like asses."

An accident occurred showing us that there were snakes in the country. A little dog that we had picked up in Hobarton and brought with us, and which we had all grown very fond of, was bitten by a deaf-adder.[5] It had incautiously played with it. It appeared to suffer great agony and died in about half-an-hour, the body much swollen. We all regretted it much, but it probably spared us a growl as we should not have been able to settle who it belonged to, satisfactorily. The snake is not very numerous in this country. The deaf-adder is the most poisonous; the black snake the largest.

The driver told us that a woman was bitten by the former in the ankle in a house that he had sojourned at. In a few hours she was delirious. A doctor was sent for but before he could arrive she was dead. Three hours after death the body became much swollen and emitted an unpleasant smell, showing that putrefaction would soon ensue. She was buried the next day. Her husband was a stockrider and came home a few hours after her death. The shock was so sudden to him that he took to drinking and ended by cutting his throat from ear to ear. A subscription was raised among the drovers who frequented the house and amounted to forty-six pounds which was given to the unfortunate orphans. It would have taken all the carters in the Old Country to have raised a like sum.

We managed to get through with considerable difficulty, this being about the worst portion of the road; leaving Mount Macedon on our left. Rain is very prevalent here. It is the opinion of old diggers that gold is likely to found in large quantities in this part.

In the evening of this day we sighted the promised land, Forest Creek.[6] It certainly looked anything but promising. We had expected to see hundreds of ferocious-looking men armed with revolvers picking up nuggets as fast as they could stoop; at the former we were agreeably disappointed, but the latter we saw neither sign nor colour of.

I had often heard of men coming to the diggings and returning without trying a single hole, and had laughed at their faintness, but I was less inclined to do so now; for I was half inclined to turn back myself, everything looked so dreary and miserable. There was a man here and there standing in what looked to us a ploughed field knocking a spade about in a tub, or hauling buckets out of the holes. We were told that the reason there were so few people was because there was a large rush a little further up the creek; but being too tired to go any further that night we camped near the old Post Office.[7] Our three companions, the lushingtons, gave way to their wounded feelings in the brandy keg and were soon in a happy state of forgetfulness.

The next morning Dick and I bade them goodbye, which rather astonished them as they had been thinking that we should forget it. But it was no use, and we went to the new rush which happened to be a place called Growler's Hill, Campbell's Creek. This appeared very lively. Tents were going up in all directions; the sinking was not over ten feet and quite soft. Unobserved, I watched a man wash a dish of stuff and saw a quantity of yellow metal in the bottom of his dish. This was satisfactory and we pitched our swags down at once and determined upon camping where we were.

We had a bed tick, and with that and a blanket we made a tolerable "mi mi", although, as we were afterwards told, it cut such a wretched figure in the eyes of the old hands that they took us for bushrangers and kept a very sharp look-out on us. The "mi mi" was made thus – a stick placed upon two forks about two feet high; over that the bed tick, and covered with leaves and branches.[8] At first we used to cook our meat by throwing it on the ashes, or holding it over the fire with a stick; but latterly we rented a frying pan.

The people appear very ill-natured and will not show a new hand anything. He has to find it all out himself. If they catch one looking at their dish or wash-dirt they are very wrath. We were much alarmed by seeing the Traps or Mounted Police come round after licences, and as we had none and could not afford to purchase, we made our lucky escape down a hole until they were gone. Every man on the gold diggings is supposed to take out a licence, thirty shillings a month. It is paid willingly by none except the very timid. If caught without one the luckless fellow is dragged off, handcuffed like a common felon and fined five pounds – in default three months on the road – and until he can be sent to Melbourne he is chained to a log. The troopers are mounted and well-armed with carbine, sword and pistols, which they are allowed to use if a man does not stop when called on. These diabolical proceedings irritate the diggers much and will some time or other cause them to repent it.

We bought some picks and shovels, but were altogether so green that we got cheated in the article and the price. We tried some old holes, not venturing to sink one. We worked as we saw others do, but the deuce a speck could we get; and for the first week we never saw the colour. Our living, for we did not live at all expensively, came to about twenty-five shillings a week each, so it would not do to go on long at this rate. Some Irishmen at length took compassion on us and showed us how to wash the stuff and where to get it from.

The shaft is sunk until one arrives at the bed-rock which consists of slate, sandstone or pipeclay. The gravel above this is taken for one inch to twelve, as the case may be, and tried in a flat dish. One sifts it about in the water until the gold, being the heaviest, sinks to the bottom; and gradually washes the dirt away sifting it the whole time. If there is a pennyweight in the dish it is considered payable (although we should have been very well satisfied if we could have got the colour); and he [the digger] drives out the bottom of the claim – i.e. undermines it about three feet high, taking care not to leave too great a portion of it without support or it is likely to bury him. As to saying that a man who is willing to work can always get good wages on the diggings – it's all humbug. There is a good deal of science required in it besides main strength and stupidness.

Gold digging is quite as much a trade as a carpenter or any other mechanic, and takes quite as long to learn in all its branches, besides being very amusing to the reflecting man. It is not nearly so much chance work as so generally imagined. When I became acquainted with it I found it a delightful and exciting study. There are some men, and I am sorry to say – the majority of the world – who never look at anything in any other light but a plain, matter-of-fact, pounds, shillings and pence one. To these, gold digging and the beauties of nature and art are plain and insipid enough. I have been frequently disgusted by hearing people who pretend to know everything and in reality know nothing about it, talk about countries they have never been to and men they have never seen.

The stay-at-home Englishman is the most prejudiced man living. He says, "Australia is not fit for the cultivated refined man; it is only the uneducated labourer that does well there". The first I allow – the nearer a man approaches the acme of refinement the more useless and senseless he becomes. I do not mean true politeness, than which nothing can be more delightful – but that artificial humbug which throws a wet blanket over one, and gives me the cold shivers. The second part I deny in toto – a man requires a solid common sense education to do well in this country. It is these men that have done and do well.

It is false to say that there are no pleasures for the refined man. Is there no delight in wandering through unexplored regions; in seeing the boundless forests as yet undefiled by the axe of white man? Is there no pleasure I say, to sit at the summit of a mountain, three or four thousand feet above the level of the sea, and see the glorious sun setting behind the ocean of foliage? – and to think that I am alone, with God; I am independent; I am free. It is in the freedom that one's joy lies. What man can say he is free in a large town? If he does how can he prove it? The richer he is, the more dependent he is. But here I can grow my own vegetables; I can breed my own sheep; I can make my own clothes – and I am dependent only on my God. The man who fails to enjoy, to find pleasure in such things as these, in the beauties of nature unadorned, is less than a man. In what is a man greater than a beast? Is it because he has reason? No – a beast reasons; a dog reasons quite as well as a man. He reasons on the food he eats. If a man only reasons how to get food, money and the necessaries of life he is not a bit better than the dog. It is by his sense of the beautiful in nature and art, and by expressing that sense that he shows his superiority as much as anything.

And what's the next thing they say? The educated man has not been brought up to bear hard work and hardships, and therefore he soon sinks under them. The latter part is false. I have seen men of excellent education and tenderly nurtured keep their health and spirits under circumstances which some of their companions, ignorant labourers, completely sank under and lamented like children. And as for work – I had a mate, a weak delicate young man, well-brought up and very intelligent, who drove round two Cornish miners who were taking spell and spell to cut him off; instead of which he not only cut them off but drove completely round them, quite astonishing my cousin Jacks when they knocked in.

What was it that bore these men up with their troubles and made a man unaccustomed to hard work so strong? It was the mind, the good solid common sense. And it's just the same with the living – neither the working ignorant labourer nor the educated mechanic had been accustomed to this mode of life. So the latter is naturally more fit for it than the former. The poorest man in England never washes or cooks for himself, or mends his clothes, or keeps his house tidy; yet he will have to do it here. Some of them roll in filth because they have not got the mind – they haven't got the moral faculties to do that which they have not been accustomed to.

But leaving this subject alone! We were a considerable time before we could realise anything to speak of. Having no cradle or tub we could not get on very fast. The tub is used for puddling or battering the dirt about until all the lumps of clay are broken and washed away, nothing remaining but small stones and gold. This is passed through the cradle, which is simple and ingenious. If well made and set, little or no gold is lost. We gradually got more into the method and were getting along comfortably having a frying pan, billies and plenty to eat; not yet having raised enough to buy a tent, they being very expensive about this time.

One morning an old digger came to us, who appeared to have been all night on the spree, and asked us if we wanted a mate – that he had fallen out with his former one. He had a good tent and tools, and moreover a payable hole. We were strongly advised to accept this offer by the Irishmen who said that, albeit he was a lushington, he was a very lucky digger. It was altogether too good an offer to be laughed at, and we joined. His hole averaged five ounces to the load, and, as we soon learned the art, we began to amass money. But soon found that our prosperity was to be disturbed by our new mate who made a practice of getting drunk the instant the stuff was washed up. In his fits he would leave off work and kick the things about the tent; playfully fire off his double-barrelled gun behind us – just, as he said, to let us know that Uncle Ned was at home. I did not like this, especially when he went on the spree and stayed away from work for two or three days; and in expostulating with him we had a few words and I left them, Dick preferring to put up with the lush as long as he could keep the hole.

I then joined a Dutchman by name Van Scrogin. He had been cook on an English ship and could speak the language well. He commenced to teach me Dutch but I was so inattentive a scholar that he discontinued it. We managed very nicely together and had a comfortable tent on Growler's Flat, two stretchers, a table, knives, forks, plates, candles and books. There was a rush on Lushington's Hill which turned out very rich.[9] We got a claim there and were fortunate enough to get about twelve pound weight of gold. It was nothing however to some of the holes.

It is a very exciting sight to see a large rush. If men take a fancy to a place they usually sink a shaft. If they strike gold, although they keep it as quiet as possible, it soon gets wind and the diggers will leave their old holes, albeit very good ones, and mark out claims at the new rush on what they suppose to be the lead; and it is here that an experienced man shows his superiority in finding out which is most likely to be the deep ground. Although it does not always lie in the deep, invariably in the richest leads it forms a gutter or channel. Large trees sometimes point out deep ground. The rock on the surface, the colour of the strata sunk through, large stones and many other things are signs not to be smiled at. Few men like to sell their claims until bottomed; they say it's selling their luck.

Van Scroggin was a very near man. He had placed some gold in the Private Escort and it had broken up, being unable to run as cheaply as the Government one; so Van sent the receipt down by a storekeeper who promised to bring him the gold. He did not come back at the time expected which put Van in great fear about his money, so he took an axe and rushed frantically up to the store and threatened to cut everything to pieces if his gold was not given up. The man in charge endeavoured to pacify him but it was no go – his gold he would have. I tried to get him away and got my hand nearly cut off for my pains. He commenced to cut down the porch when the man consented to give him half the sum and the other half when the master came. To this Van consented. If he had lost his gold I am sure he would never have survived it. He determined that he would no longer tempt the fickle goddess; but that he would return to his "faderland", where, as he told me "for von hundred pound me can buy von farm, von wife, von servant and drink von glass Genever[10] every morning." Not a bad country to live in! I had been with him about six months.

Dick had left the lushington very little richer than when I left him, He, the lushington, got a tremendous licking one day from a little fellow that he had insulted. By the bye fighting is not uncommon at the new rushes. A ring is formed by joining hands and fair play is shown impartially. The 'Tips', or South of Ireland men, are very quarrelsome, but their rows usually end in a general mêlée in which picks and shovels are used indiscriminately – but I shall have occasion to speak of this by and bye.

Washing stuff was frequently stolen at this rush – and some of great value. It is usual to have it carted to the tent. A great deal of gunpowder is wasted up here – almost every digger has pistols and a gun which they load and fire every night. But in spite of all the talk of robbing tents and murders in the diggings only one case came under my notice.[11] A young man was awakened by someone drawing his trousers from under his head. He put his hand out and laid hold of one of his pistols which were lying on the table and fired in the direction of the hand. There was a slight shuffle, and all was still. His mate on the other side of the table sang out "Halloa, what's that?" The young man replied and told him, adding that he supposed the wretch was gone, for he could hear nothing. He felt that the tent had been slit up on his side. They did not get up but went quietly to sleep again. In the morning what was his surprise and consternation – a man lying outside the slit weltering in his blood! He was quite dead. The ball had gone right through his heart and his death must have been instantaneous. The dead man was taken to the Commissioner, to whom the young man gave himself up. The verdict was justifiable homicide.[12]

I now joined Dick and another young man and we sewed both our tents together lengthways, thus making a fine roomy saloon; and besides that we erected a chimney which was, however, a very bad one at first. At last we got a tolerable one built of sods – turf cut with a spade, the size of bricks. It is amusing to see a new chum build a turf chimney. He usually has a good many tumbles before he succeeds. The only art of it consists simply of crossing every joint with a fresh sod and backing them.

We were not alone here. There were five tents besides ours, all erected in a line, thus forming a kind of street. They were mostly all Scotchmen, one Isle of Manxman – and more hospitable, better disposed men I never met with. I look upon this as about the happiest portion of my life. There were several rushes about this time.

The Scotchmen were working on the hill we were camped on – called "Jabba Hill", with several aliases. The sinking was from ten to thirty feet and the hardest ever opened in the country. It was solid white conglomerate mixed with quartz, from the surface to the bottom which was composed of sandstone and rotten slate. They drove in this stuff and knocked the wash-dirt down overhead, which is the usual way on all hard hills. The seven white hills of Old Bendigo were worked this way and much gold was thrown away in the drift which would pay well to wash again.

We were working on a hill close by called the "Devil's Hill". It had about two feet of crush and was about twelve feet deep. The gold lay in a gutter which ran right along the crown of the hill. It was pretty good, washing about eight ounces to the load; but we lost the best of our ground through foolishly telling another man that it was good. He sank right on the edge of our claim. We also laid a highland man on to the claim below us; and afterwards we took him into our party, the other young man leaving shortly after to go bullock-driving. He had fallen in love with the owner of the animals' daughter. He was an old lag and grog seller, and I remember one day, going to have a nobbler with one of the Scotchmen, we found the old man in great distress. On asking him what was the matter he replied in a very mournful Irish howl, "Ochone, och sure, and I've lost the thing that told the time!"

"What? Have you lost your watch?"

"Och no! I've lost the thing that told the time and sure I'm ruined intirely!"

"Well, tell us what it is and perhaps we can find it for you."

"Sure, and it was the thing that hung against the wall, and when the gentry came in they looked at it and then they wrote it down, and faith, it was the thing that told the time. Ochone, they'll never come any more!"

It proved to be an old almanack which, one of the Scotchmen, knowing his deep veneration for it (he could not read a syllable) had purloined. It was restored to its place the next day, much to the joy of the old hand, who determined to keep a stricter watch on it for the future.

The winter was now almost over and there was great talk about a large water hole in the creek under Growler's Hill[13] which was supposed to hold an almost fabulous amount of the precious metal. The first summer of the diggings had been a very dry one and the creek had become completely parched, all but this water hole and to it all the very rich stuff from the Red, White and Montgomeries Hills and Forest Creek was carted.

Time always adds greatly and the oft-told tale gathers much. So it is with the diggings. The first of the diggings is looked upon as being the richest, whereas, in proportion to the number of diggers, there were as many men hard up then and unfortunate as there are now. In fact the escort returns, allowing for numbers, proves that they are so. When I went first to Mt. Alexander I heard diggers who were leaving say that the diggings were done. The best and richest diggings that were ever opened, the Old Bendigo, was left and the men returned, saying that there was no gold on Bendigo. I am quite confident that there will be as rich goldfields in Australia fifty years hence as there are now. Observe what an immense tract of land lies as yet unexplored, and also in how many different parts goldfields have been discovered.

Gold was first discovered at Summer Hill Creek, which runs into the Macquarie, by Hargraves the geologist.[14] He had been at Sydney before and when the California diggings broke he ventured there. He was astonished to find the country assimilate much to New South Wales, and on his return he resolved to try it and discovered it in February 1851. The first large field was the Ophir on the Turon River which is said to have been rich.[15] But the diggings in this colony never came up to the Victorian fields in richness; the gold is more scattered. The great rush to Victoria almost deserted the Sydney diggings. Those who stayed there did well. The Ophir is about 144 miles from Sydney, and the gold is mostly found in the banks and in the beds of the creeks. The road over the Blue Mountains is very bad for drays – the Victoria pass and Mt. Lambie are 3400 feet above the level of the sea. The scenery is magnificent. Hargraves has since been well rewarded by the colonists, as indeed he deserved to be. Gold is said to have been frequently found before, but no notice was taken of it.

But to return to the Great Water Hole.[16] The old diggers said that at the commencement of the diggings very little was known about washing the stuff, and therefore much gold had been lost in the cradling and had gone into this hole. Three distinct runs had also been traced to the hole, but they were unable to follow it further in consequence of the water rushing so fast that they were unable to keep it down with bailing; but it was supposed to be impossible to contend with such an immense body of water without machinery, which would have been too expensive. The Scotchmen were anxious to try their luck at it, and we accordingly made up a party. Twelve strong able-bodied men with a tolerable capital can overcome much. We applied to the Commissioner for a grant which he willingly allowed us, commencing at it very early in the season in order to keep possession, for many eyes were turned towards the hole which contained such a mass of the precious.

We set to work in Diamond Gully[17] (so-called from containing many bastard precious stones) to cut piles and bark for the dam. The stringy bark is the strongest and is to be obtained in large quantities here. It is very useful for many things, making fine warm huts for the winter and very cool ones in summer. The tree is notched all round as high as one can reach, and being cut in the same manner at the bottom, is opened and gently forced from the trunk with the axe; when off, [it is] placed on the ground and flattened by heavy logs. You then have a fine sheet, sometimes eight feet square and about an inch in thickness. No rain will penetrate this, and it is the coolest covering one can have in hot weather.

Having cut about twenty loads, we carted them to the creek and commenced upon the drain or race. We cut it about a quarter of a mile long to give a good fall to the water – twelve feet wide and ten deep. We drove two rows of piles firmly across the present course of the creek, about three feet apart, placed the bark on the inside, filled the space with stiff yellow clay, beating it firmly in so that no water could penetrate, and concluded by covering the whole with bullock hides. The next thing was to bail out the hole – this was the most difficult part of it. To accomplish this we required pumps, and chain pumps, besides being very expensive, would cost more than their value to bring them from town. Even if we obtained them we were dubious they would not answer as they would no doubt get choked by sand in the sucker.

"Necessity is the mother of invention." After many pros and cons we determined to manufacture them ourselves on the Californian principle. We obtained four planks from the sawyer – thirty feet long, six inches wide and an inch and a half thick. We nailed these together and bound them with iron hoop, this making a tolerable box. We made a large drum and passed an iron spindle through it, made so as to ship two handles. This was fixed at the top of the box. At the other end there was a small roller and round these two was passed a canvas belt running through the box, and on the belt we nailed flat pieces of wood closely fitting the box; the lower end being put in the water, the pump forming an angle of 45°; the handle being turned by two hands, the buckets forced the water up the box thus throwing a continuous stream. We made four of these, and, considering there were no carpenters among us, they were masterpieces of genius.

With these formidable machines we made a rapid gain on the water and soon hoped to have it dry enough to work; but alas, man is altogether a poor insignificant creature. In one night our six months' labour was annihilated. We had returned to our tents and laid our heads trustfully on our trousers (for on the diggings we always turn them inside out and make a pillow of them) when, in the words of the poet, loud roared the dreadful thunder, and the rain – coming down from the mountains with irresistible force – swept away our dam, pumps, race; every mortal thing was carried down the stream for miles.[18] Even our race was carried away. These floods are common enough in the Colonies. The ground is parched and dry; when a thunderstorm comes the rain runs off it like a spit on a hot shovel and often causes great damage to the flocks and the farms on the banks of the rivers.

The next morning we wandered down the creek with dejected countenances in search of the pumps. Everyone knew how it would be – they had said so all along. They were very consoling, as people generally are in like cases. They knew there was an immense quantity of gold in the hole, but it was impossible to get it out. All this only made us the more determined to see the bottom of it.

This day I had an opportunity of seeing that very peculiar animal called by naturalists *Ornithorhynchus paradoxus* – by colonials, the platypus.[19] It had probably been washed there by the flood. We shot it and even then had considerable trouble in getting it. The body was of beautiful soft fur, the bill and feet like a duck; it is amphibious, rearing its young in a hole in the bank of a stream. They are not at all plentiful. I should have liked much to have obtained its skin, but the man who the gun belonged to claimed it.

The natural consequence of this flood was that we all went to Castlemaine, a pretty little township situated at the junction of Barker's and Forest Creeks, and got on the spree. I am almost ashamed to say I was among the number. This lasted for several days. Liquor here cost a pretty round sum – 1/6 a nobbler (wine glass) being paid for brandy and five shillings a bottle for ale and porter.

There were no licensed public houses at this time, and consequently it was all sold on the sly – notwithstanding the heavy penalty, sometimes imprisonment and confiscation of all goods found on the premises, awarded to all the sly grog shops discovered; the informer getting half the reward. But the immense profits and the opportunities to pass off villainous poison on the unwary digger were too great an inducement to desperate old lags to carry on this obnoxious trade.

A circumstance occurred which brought us all to our senses. One of our mates had, in the exuberance of his spirits, strayed into the company of strangers, who had induced him to go and have a wet, enticing him into one of these dens of iniquity. His grog was drugged, commonly called hocussed; he was robbed of everything valuable and left a short distance from the township. He was discovered a few hours afterwards insensible. It was a lucky thing for him that he was found so soon; two hours more and he would never more have spoken. As it was he remained in a very precarious state for six weeks, and but for the tender care of that "Ministering Angel", woman, it is doubtful if he would have ever recovered his health.[20]

He did not live with us, being camped beside a store kept by a very respectable widow, "fair, fat and forty". It appeared to me that there had been a slight intrigue going on between them. At all events she was very fond of him, although quite old enough to have been his mother and having a daughter seventeen years old. But however that's neither here nor there – suffice it to say, that when he got well he rewarded her for her tenderness by taking possession of her store and uniting in the indissoluble bonds of matrimony. By the bye though, they are not nearly so indissoluble here as they are in the Old Country. If a couple disagrees here they divorce themselves without the expense and bother of going through the Ecclesiastical Court. The wife says, "Well, Bill, you and I don't seem to hit it together. Now there's Jack yonder, he and I get along first chop and I know you have got a kind of striking regard for Jack's wife, so you better make change for change."

"Agreed," says Bill. And after that it's all settled without more bother.

This little incident checked us in our mad career and we again tried the hole minus two of our hands; and Dick amongst the number showed the white feather, leaving us with only nine good men and true. We repaired the race and set two aborigines at work to cut bark for us, they being so much more ready at it than Europeans. They are a curious race, and are said to be very low in the scale of humanity because they live without working and with very little fighting – which in my humble opinion shows their wisdom rather than their stupidity. The European makes a slave of himself for gold – and calls it industry – and then hops off the twig before he is able to enjoy it; he fights and murders his brethren, robs them of their wealth and devastates their country – and calls it honour and glory.

The aborigines wander about a fine country, view the beauties of nature as they come fresh from the hand of their Maker and in their hearts they rejoice and glorify Him; they carry with them neither scrip, nor staff; they take no thought for the morrow; they make hearty meals of their kangaroo, opossum or wild duck; when tired they lie down by the side of their gins (women) and sleep; they are happy and contented, or at least were so before the white man came and stole their country. They resist him not, but move farther into the bush and as the whites progress they retire. They have tasted his firewater and like it much, and also approve of his weed. They resist all his attempts to make them abandon their habitual ease and independence except when tempted by rum and tobacco, for which they will readily work. It is vain to try to fetter them to houses or towns. They have tasted freedom and prefer God's canopy to Man's.

And for this they are called barbarians; and for this they are despised. Pshaw! the European has much to learn, although he thinks himself so very wise.

Well, we got the dam up again on an improved style, making an oblique angle of it, that the body of water should glide off without meeting so much resistance; and after much labour we reduced the water in the hole, enabling us to get out a great deal of tailings which we passed through long toms, but found very little gold in them. Still we persevered in hopes that the bottom would turn out better.

It is necessary to mention that extensive meetings and riots occurred about this time, having in view the reduction of licences which was greatly needed being very exorbitant, and the expenditure of the public money was enormous, with nothing to show for it. The roads were a rotten system of jobbery and piecework. They have been made where they were not required, whilst the main road is still as it were untouched. The traffic on these roads is enormous, and the plan the drivers adopt is to use one tract as long as it is practicable and then cut out another. Thus on Keilor Plains alone you may see tracts as wide as the eye reaches; then they erect bridges which fall from their own weight. They pay fabulous prices for bullock drays, sometimes as much as ten pounds per diem and two shillings a foot for sawed stuff.

Then there are the government officers – they receive whatever they choose to ask for and some of their salaries are enormous. They talk of starting Governor La Trobe[21] off about his business – the sooner the quicker! The way those infernal scavengers the "Traps" behave is shameful. They drive free men about like a lot of pigs, and hunt them with guns, with orders to shoot them if they don't stop – just as if one was a wild beast. If found wanting a licence they chain the unfortunate wretch, whose only crime is being poor, to a log. He is kept there until tried and then if he cannot pay the fine he has to work ignominiously on the roads like a common felon – not, mind you, on the road to the diggings where it would do any good to the country, but in some out of the way hole that's no use to anyone. If one says anything about it, some timid fool, who calls himself a friend to order, says, "Ah, but you must have protection or we should all be murdered in our beds, and get up some morning and find ourselves dead!".

A fig for their order! The troopers are the scrapings of jails, the lowest of the low. Even if one does apprehend a bushranger and give him in charge they'll let him go if he can bribe them well. Again there is no criminal court nearer than Melbourne, and therefore it must be a very important case indeed or it would not be worth a man's while to prosecute. Horse-stealing, for instance, is wonderfully prevalent; if you turn a horse out to grass overnight it's ten to one in favour of his being stolen before morning, and it's the general belief that the troopers have a share in it – or how is it that the thief invariably escapes? One would think it was easy enough to find a man with such a large thing about him. Supposing him to catch the man in the act – the only way he can punish him is by shooting him, for to prosecute would absorb more than the value of the animal.

Grog tents were frequently seized because they (the troopers) got half the reward. But even in these seizures they showed no more humanity than the brute. The tent was burnt, everything confiscated, the proprietor imprisoned and his family turned adrift penniless. Being informed against for selling grog usually showed the man's innocence rather than his guilt – which I'll prove thus. If a man was a confirmed grog-seller, usually a lag, he would take precious good care to bribe the traps, and in that case he could not only sell grog, but live right alongside the camp; and he would be patronised largely by the very men who ought to suppress. On the other hand, many dodges were executed upon the unwary – such as coming to a likely tent habited as a distressed digger and demanding a glass of grog. If they obtained it they would press the acceptance of one and sixpence. This was quite sufficient to convict anyone. Many other like dodges were tried.

The meetings commenced at Old Bendigo, and were carried on there with much vigour. But at Castlemaine they were a complete hoax got up by Jackson,[22] a Methodist parson, and Itchcock[23], a storekeeper, who used first to harangue the diggers and afterwards to go and take a nobbler with the Commissioner and have a rare laugh over it. I was fool enough to write out a lot of bills which we stuck up on the trees along the highway – very seditious they were too. Very long petitions were ultimately sent to the Governor, and very formidable threats were issued in case of refusal, but La Trobe showed his wisdom by granting it and in the course of time the licence was reduced from thirty shillings per month to two pounds for three months[24]. The outrages were ameliorated. Public houses were licensed[25] in order to put down sly grog shops and petty courts established. But the greatest evil, the armed troopers, remained.

To return to the hole. We made rapid progress and at the lower end we sank a large paddock about twenty feet square, bottoming it all over. All we obtained was four ounces by tomming. This was the spot where it was to be so rich. But when folks saw this bottomed – "It wasn't there! Oh, no. The middle was the place. They said it all along." Well, we bottomed the middle, and the devil a grain there was there. Then it was the top that met with the same fate, and now all we had to trust to was the bank.

The work, by the bye, was anything but pleasant. For two months, I solemnly declare day after day, except Sundays, I never had a dry rag on me, and sometimes up to one's waist in slush. And the worst of it was that when one goes to one's tent in this state, instead of having dry clothes to put on and a nice dinner or supper, one has to light a fire – no easy job where there is a scarcity of dry wood – and cook one's grub, the best possible way. And yet during all these hardships, that would halt the strongest constitutioned men in England, who can't even get their feet wet, without going off the hooks, immediately sending the old lady into hysterics, I never had a cold, and with the exception of the man that was hocussed, not one of the party had a day's illness, which should prove to anyone of common sense the salutary and delightful effect of the climate. It is indeed a glorious climate. I am not exaggerating in the smallest when I say that it is the finest in the world, as proved by the convict returns twenty years ago in New South Wales.

Now, thoughtless people and the stay-at-home-with-us Englishmen (those who never knew what it was to have a meal's meat except on Sundays before they came here) the latter if sent to heaven would not be satisfied, and would growl and say, "Humph! this is a d——d hole. There is no comfort like there is in England." The comforts mean a foggy damp atmosphere and ice about six feet thick and seeing the sun once a week. They complain that it is unbearably hot in summer, but the atmosphere is so clear and dry that one does not feel it so oppressive as a hot day in London. One of these last-named bipeds who had often cursed the country for being too hot, got into an argument with me about it; when I asked him what more he wanted he said that the country was not so bad but there wasn't the comforts of Old England. "Now what is there in England that you can't get in this country?" said I. He hesitated a little. "Well, now" said he, "There is no comfortable coal fire to sit down at!" This was the man who complained so much of the heat, and yet the wretch wanted a nasty, smoky fire when he had glorious fire which sheds light and life on all. You seldom hear a sensible man speak against the country. At all events if they don't like it they have their alternative – the likes of those are not wanted here. The hot winds are disagreeable while they last, but it lasts no time and when the sea breeze comes you enjoy it. Why, a man wouldn't know the pleasure of filling his belly if he was never hungry.

Because a few people, from drinking and working in the drives, get inflammation in the eyes they must needs go to extremities and say that everybody is subject to bad eyes. There is a kind of blight certainly, but you see it principally among people who drink much. All the time I was at the diggings I never had a mate or any acquaintance that caught it – and only saw about half a dozen with it altogether; so it can't be very prevalent.

Men travel in this country without having wherewithal to cover themselves at night, and experience no ill-effects. The aged and consumptive folks get on very well here, the latter frequently getting cured. I don't think there has ever been a case of consumption in the country, excepting of course where it is hereditary. The climate is fruitful in another sense, and many a barren woman before now becomes a happy mother. The children of New South Wales are very tall and well-formed with, in most cases, pleasing features. They are called "Cornstalks". The girls arrive at the age of puberty much sooner here than in England; their passions are hot and they frequently get married when from fourteen to sixteen years old. The Van Diemonians are famed for their fine children – and potatoes. They are called Gum-suckers. I have not yet heard a name for the Victorians.[26]

Well, can you tell me where I left off? Oh, oh, I recollect! We began at the bank – when we got the hole so dry it drained the flat so that the holes they had been obliged to leave on account of the water were now workable and turned out very rich. The most extraordinary thing was that they got gold in large quantities right to our race, which of course we would not allow them to work. We sank all along the bank, and, not being able to find anything, opened the race and discovered a high reef running north and south right up and down our trench which had evidently stopped the gold – accounting for the last holes being so rich. I heard they took eighty pounds weight out of the one next to our drain.

It was very provoking, but there was no help for it. Two or three remained about the hole making a living out of the tailings, for we were all pretty hard up. The Scotchmen and Manxman still had some money which they generously shared with me and some others. I never met with better-hearted men than these. How the deuce Scotchmen got the name of stingy I can't conceive it – I have found more true generosity and hospitality among them than among the English – but, as the saying is – there is good and bad in all countries. But, I hope, I may die if there is a more prejudiced man under heaven than a stay-at-home-with-us Englishman.

We were lamenting on our hard fate when one day a Welshman who was living nearby showed us about sixteen ounces of gold in one dish he had just bottomed on the Garden Flat; so called, from a man having cultivated a bit of ground there. We all went down, took out four claims and began sinking all round him – there were six of us now. The Welshman was in a towering rage, though why he should be I don't know. At all events we all went down and be hanged if we did not all miss it. It was only a patch.

When he (the Welshman) was worked out he went and sank again on the same flat, and hit it again, heavier than the time before; I never saw such a lucky fellow. Well, we all set in around him again and all missed it. Very hard up we were too and running in debt to a store-keeper. We sank a hole on the Garden Flat, at least I and another did, and bottomed on a tremendous dip. We followed it down one side, and although we got a few pennyweights yet it being so awkward to work we left, and heard afterwards that some other men went into it and drove up the other rise, struck the run and took thirty pounds weight of the precious out of it. Holes are frequently left in this way, but it is impossible to guard against it.

At this time, luckily for us, a large rush broke out at the Tarrengower-Long Gully[27] in which they said that plenty of gold was found, but the water to wash the same was anything but plentiful and carting was very dear. It was about twelve miles off, and as of course we wanted to go and had no money – unity gives strength and therefore we joined five more men not unknown to us; thus making eleven altogether; six were to go to the new rush and the rest to fossick at the 'hospital' and keep them in grub. But I'll never do so any more, for if one does get a good hole it amounts to nothing among many. Two is the best party; three is bad; four is better than three; and any above that is no good at all.

The hospital was ground that we kept for these occasions. It would not pay wages, but it was what is commonly called a tucker-hole. We drove the old hole about seventy feet and, the stuff getting very inconvenient to throw out so far, we determined to sink another shaft. Now this ground had been all left once and a tent was pitched close to where we intended sinking. We however sank as near as we could to the tent, and the Cornish men to whom it belonged were very wrath to find a hole go down so near to their castle; so out of spite they commenced sinking a hole on our claim. We were not down more than five feet, and it was twenty feet sinking. We warned them that we should drive their bottom out if they continued sinking, but they only laughed at us, saying that was not the first pick and shovel work they had done, and that they would be down before we got many feet further. But the proof of the pudding, etc. We not only bottomed but drove theirs so completely out that they slipped through into our drive. They were very wrath, but they could do nothing.

We followed this bit up until the vein ran out and then up house and moved off to Tarrengower, but it was not so rich as had been reported.

We found however that our mates had got two pretty good claims on Growler's Point – got about ten pounds weight out of each, but it was nothing among so many. One of our mates styled himself Yankee Tom. He had been in a slaver for many years but was at last captured by a British man-o-war, and narrowly escaped hanging by pretending he was a Portuguese. The crew were put on shore somewhere on the coast of Africa, and after much hardship arrived at Sierra Leone.

I got a small bit of ground on the same point. Out of it I obtained four pounds of the precious which went to the general fund. When these claims were worked out we agreed to separate and go in smaller parties, being all sick of large ones. I joined two of the Scotchmen and the Manxman, all very nice chaps. Jimmy, the Glasgow man, went by the cognomen of "the Wee Hairy Man" from the quantity of beard he had.[28] We all had aliases – mine was Lissy, the Hawick man's was Dan, a very intelligent, well brought up young man.[29] As was usual on such occasions at the separation we had a great deal of spree and noise, spending our money like green, green gooses – very fast and repenting it at our leisure.

This was a very extensive goldfield, but not nearly so rich as Forest Creek. The quartz veins paid well, but they had not yet got machinery to crush them. There was a large rush at Porcupine Flat[30] and we shifted over there. We jumped two claims; for it was a practice to mark out a number of claims and by taking out a spit of each and leaving a pick or shovel to keep possession, although at the same time sinking another, that there's a chance if the one turns out a shicer of having two strings to one's bow. This is called shepherding. Jumping means to watch where the party is working and, having proved him to have more than one claim, to jump into the other and sink it yourself. This practice is the cause of many disturbances, which are settled sometimes by fighting, or bullying, or by the Commissioner.

In the new regulations each man was allowed twelve square feet, but much more was usually taken. Therefore when a man finds that the ground is good, it behoves him to drive it out as quickly as possible and to pile his washdirt, so that no one else can set in on the surplus ground.

We did not get much in these claims, but as the winter was coming on we built snug chimneys and made our tents very comfortable by lining them with green baize. We also fed very well, having meat at every meal very well cooked. We baked our own bread and, although I say it, it would not disgrace any London baker. We made our yeast as leaven, by mixing some flour into a paste in a small keg, keeping it covered in a warm place for a few days until it had a beery smell. It was now fit for use. Then take about eight pounds of flour and mix with the yeast and knead well into dough. Warm the camp oven and sprinkle it with a little flour; put your dough carefully in and keep turning the oven before a good fire. When you think it has risen sufficiently cover the oven with the hot ashes until done, which you can easily tell by sticking a clean knife into it. Take it out and stand it on its edge until cold. Box wood makes the best ashes when green. Stringy bark usually turns to charcoal which is not so good as the white ash.

A Cornishman living near us had some famous kangaroo dogs and we made several excursions with him to the other side of the Loddon River[31] that is to say, when we could borrow horses; and we had some glorious hunts. Men come here and say that there's no sport – no game. No, because they can't see an inch before their noses. Do they expect the game to come to them if they don't look for it? Why, there are lots of men come to Melbourne, stay there for two or three months perhaps, never going a hundred yards from the house they lodge in, take another ship and go home again. These are the men that are sure to have a long yarn about the horrors and hardships of Australia!

Talk about hunting – why, the deuce take it – there's none in the world equal to kangaroo hunting. Fancy a thick bush tangled with brushwood – here and there a fallen tree or huge block of granite, rotten branches strewing the ground, and you will have some idea of your hunting ground.

"Hark, what's that! Our dog Possum's off – and there goes Dick's Jabba. What are they after, Dan?"

"After? Why, look! Don't you see? Ah – ho – he'll away! There he goes, a huge man kangaroo – over brushwood, stumps, fallen trees – twenty-thirty, fifty feet at each bound! He looks like a bomb as he flies through the air. Oh, the dogs will never catch him – away – away!"

The horses catch the excitement, and rush madly on. This is a dangerous game. A projecting bough would put an end forever to your hunting and the ground is none of the evenest. But who thinks of such things as these in the glorious excitement of the moment. Ah! The first man, Jack, is down, and with such force too. His horse has tripped up on a rotten branch. He must be dead! But, who cares for that in such a moment? The dogs are gaining on the magnificent creature. They are far ahead of us, almost out of sight. On, on we go. The pace begins to tell. The horses will not stand it much longer. When suddenly he turns! There is an opening in the trees. It is a vast plain on the banks of the Loddon, covered with lumps of granite. "Now then! Now then, we shall have him!" But he knows a trick worth two of that. He does not follow the plain, but takes across to the river. The dogs follow at full speed, but with drooping tails and frothy tongues, as if they knew that their only chance was gone.

We had now got to the plain, and, there not being a single tree on it to offer any impediment to our view, we had a splendid sight of the magnificent race. By mutual consent we reined in our sweating steeds, with all eyes fixed upon the splendid animal whose strength appeared unabated. He reaches the river and with one bound he is over. The dogs hesitate – not to plunge into the rapid stream, but the opposite bank is steep and it takes them some time to find a place where they can get up. By this time the old man has gained the bush once more and all is lost. "But, stop! What makes him start, and swerve aside? Whence comes that loud hallo?"

"Ah, there are dogs! There are men on horseback." He turns and recrosses the stream. Both horses and dogs had got a breath of wind, and one and all we thundered over the plain. The diggers were soon left behind. The stockmen had found a crossing and with their dogs they turned his left flank. On, on they went; we were not a patch on them for riding. They went like the wind. One could hardly see their horses' feet touch the plain.

The dogs were close at his heels – the kangaroo could not hold out much longer. Ha, Possum has grasped him and he is at bay. He is determined to sell his life dearly. It seems a pity to kill such a noble creature. I almost wish he would escape again. He fights desperately and inflicts some frightful gashes on Possum. Jabba, more cautious, has pinned him behind. The stockmen are in – they belabour him with their whips, but take care to keep out of his reach. He gets bewildered, fights more desperately but less cautiously. He makes one desperate spring. By Heavens, he will get clear. He throws the dogs from him, rips a cattle dog belonging to the stockmen clean up and springs clear of them. Ah, ah! The genius of man overtakes you now – the diggers have come up and five shots are fired. Instantly he staggers, he shakes his head, the blood pours in streams from his neck. The dogs are on him once more. He casts a dying look of deep reproach upon them, as he should say, "There's too many of you," and with a spasmodic shiver he yields the life he has defended so nobly.

I think we all felt a melancholy steal over us and that we would much rather that he had got clear. But however that soon wore off, and driving away the dogs we commenced to skin him. This was performed very dextrously by the stockman who claimed the skin for his share of the booty. The dogs had so mangled the fur that it was good for nothing but leather, and therefore we gave it him readily. Having quartered him we slung the quarters to our saddles and slowly retraced our steps, when whom should we see making towards us but Jack followed by his limping horse. He looked very pale and his head was bound up with his handkerchief. It had been bleeding profusely. His shirt was torn off and his shoulder had been frightfully bruised. Luckily he had pitched on the grass. The horse appeared to have sprained his shoulder, but was not much hurt. Poor Jack! He did not seem to fancy the way we left him at all. Indeed, I don't know who would. The fact of it is, that until we saw him we had entirely forgotten that he had ever been born.

This threw a damper on the party and, as we were obliged to walk, we got no further than Catto's Station[32] where we camped for the night – obtained some Holloway's ointment and some pills for Jack, the only things we could get, and which indeed are thought a sovereign remedy for all diseases. They are very popular in this country. Every store, whether it has anything to eat or not, has some of these. I speak for myself that I believe the ointment to be a very excellent thing for cuts – or any place where the skin is broken. I have had a very bad foot cured by it when everything else failed.

We reached home the next day, and as it rained all day and being wet through we were heartily tired of kangaroo hunting for some time. But it did not always turn out such a race. Sometimes they were young and easily shot. Plenty of wallabies and kangaroo rats were also obtained in a like manner – they are beautiful eating. We all had a splendid spread of hindquarters of the kangaroo, which albeit was very tough roasted, but very nice stewed. It eats very much like venison. We celebrated it in bumpers and the consequence was, fourpenny, and we shan't go home until morning.

As we did not get another hole for some considerable time we, as usual, got hard up. In fact this is an awful starve-gutted place. We ran into debt to Tom Brice, partner of D.K. Campbell's, storekeeper, and a very nice fellow.[33] Some people get ruined by giving trust, but he made his fortune by it – for people who know nothing about them can say what they like about the diggers, but I'll maintain that, taking the average, there is not an honester body of men on the face of the earth, and they never forget a kindness. The consequence was that Campbell's store got all the custom. He sold his things moderately for the times; he was affable and obliging; and moreover when a man was unfortunate he would trust him to any amount, and I never heard that he lost a farthing by it. I am confident from the business he did that he must be worth his tens of thousands by this time – and began with a mere nothing. The more credit to him.

Well, as I was saying before, we got hard up, and as there was no fossicking ground here, no hospital, we felt it acutely; but it served us deuced well right. It was always a man's own fault if he got hard up in these times. But "experience teaches fools." There was some talk of a rush at the Avoca.[34] Two of our water hole mates went there and did extremely well – and after that they struck gold on the White Hills about twenty miles the other side of the Loddon. As there was nothing doing there we up tent and away. By the bye, knowing the evil attending large parties we divided and I went with Dan, the Hawick gallant. D.K. Campbell sent a branch store there so we were not hard up for the necessaries. For a long time his was the only store there – he being very [business-like] made considerable money, and, what was more in his favour, he did not stick on at the time of the rush as he might easily have done, being the only one.

We pitched our tent on the White Hills,[35] but found all the ground that was good taken up. An old Aberdonian had been there some time working on the sly and had heaped up about a thousand loads of surfacing which was said to be very rich. They had thrown up a dam and were lying in wait for the rainy season. Water was very scarce here and the population was not large enough to pay water carts. The way we managed was by putting a little alum into a bucket of muddy water and had to walk three miles with that. There is nothing to hold the water here, and the heat of the sun soon dries it up in sandy soil.

The majority of the diggers soon left this place as there were a great number of rushes about this time, and they gave credence to the most unlikely yarns. The story generally went that a man looking for his bullocks had come across some men in the bush working on the quiet, and getting fabulous sums of the precious. The diggers ever on the alert for such stories would instantly, without doubting the truth, up tools and away in search – sometimes travelling for days without success and often losing themselves and coming back half-starved. Nor did repeated failures show them their folly. The only thing I wonder at, that there weren't more people lost. Nor let anyone think that I was wiser than the majority. I was even worse, never being comfortable but when travelling in search of these never-had-been Eldoradoes.

Two others and myself set off one morning in search of one of the richest gullies ever heard of in the annals of gold diggings, at which place there was said to be only six persons who were carting hundredweights of the yellow to Melbourne. We took provisions with us for one day, hoping to reach it in the evening, but of course no such place was to be found, and we were two days without any grub – under the unpleasant necessity of eating wattle bark and gum. In the afternoon of the third eventful day we met a man in search of his horse, and found from him that we were within a mile of the White Hills which we were steering right away from; and very glad we were too, I can tell you, to get back to our mates who had given us up for gone men. Luckily there had been a shower the beginning of that week or we should have been in want of water as well as food. The wattle gum is by no means so bad, and is a fine thing for dysentery. I have no doubt that it will become ultimately an article of commerce. The bark is also very strengthening.

Soon after this gold was struck in a small gully in the Iron Bark Ranges, which much pleased the Bendigo digger who considered this as a sure sign of alluvial soil. The iron bark tree itself, by the bye, has a very noble appearance, the dark red bark projecting from the trunk, sometimes nine inches. It burns well and the wood makes tolerable pick handles. To this rush we went and put down without finding gold in sufficient quantities to pay. In one hole we obtained about two ounces which paid the butcher for a short time. They traced this little gully into a long flat and there they lost it. The reason appeared to be because they came to some white clay which they found a little gold on and thinking it the bottom left it.

Jack and the Wee Hairy Man had made their way up here and had joined Yankee Tom again and two young Welshmen. They were always fond of large parties. They were as hard up as ourselves. Then all at once gold was struck heavily on the flat, some enterprising man having gone through the white clay and proved it to be a false bottom, thus discovering as rich a lead of gold as has ever been opened in the Colony. It was almost incredible to see the stores go up, and tents, as if by magic as soon as the news got wind at Tarrengower and Bendigo, which did not take more than three days. The roads were lined with drays and diggers; and the ground, that a week before had scarcely been trodden by the feet of twenty white men, was now covered with myriads of white tents which seemed to have sprung up like mushrooms. In less than a fortnight there were forty thousand people on this place, which was now christened Maryborough.

In the meantime we had sunk and sunk again without success, and were at the last gasp when I jumped a narrow strip of ground between two others. It had been left as waste ground and was upwards of forty feet long but not more than six feet wide.

"Well," said Dan, "We will try once more at all events" and we commenced sinking. We bottomed at about thirty feet upon the side of the reef and saw fine gold in the stuff, but nothing to speak of. We had not however driven far into the dip when we came upon it and filled a large match box with the precious metal. This was good work and gave us fresh courage. At the last diggings we had been at the wash dirt was very thinly scattered over the bottom and the gold was so light and fine that, although we saw a great deal in the dirt it washed very little. Now these diggings were just the opposite – for every speck one saw there were twenty escaped notice in consequence of the dirt being like red ochre. As this was a gutter, for the holes on each side of us bottomed at about ten feet and we were thirty, the wash dirt was about four feet deep – all of which would have paid first rate, but, having no water to try it, we did not know this and consequently threw all this gold away among the drift. It was a remarkable thing too that only the gutter holes, and sometimes the two reefers on each side, had this white clay or false bottom, all the rest of the flat bottoming shallow. Thus all those holes that had been before left as duffers now turned out rich holes, much to the mortification of those who had left them.

It was a very lively sight to see the line of windlass all hard at work, some of them night and day, for about three miles down the flat. And the long street formed on the side, in which there were few less than thirty public houses, stores of all descriptions and sizes – bowling alleys were in great demand, even casinos. Theatres and rifle galleries abounded. The diggings never appeared so active before and the deposits of gold found in the gutter were in some cases immense; but it was not a general thing, the gutters being in some places no more than three feet wide and in no case more than thirty. Yet every claim on the gutter was sure of something. The farther we drove the more gold we got. It appeared very rich, but we had no idea of the true riches of it, or of the quantity of gold thrown away.

One evening, I being cook for that week – for we took week about to light the fire, fetch water and provisions and cook the grub – the cook having to rise early (before sunrise) and boil the billy, fry the chops and when ready call the other one. Cooking was a great bore when one came home tired after a hard day's work . Well, as I said – home I came to get supper ready and had just lighted the fire, when up comes Dan, his face flushed and every sign of being greatly excited –

"Come on, Jim! Come on! I'm on it – I've struck it – there's a pile. Oh no, certainly not! Hurrah!" From these unconnected words I was given to understand that he had touched it pretty fair, and accordingly off I went accompanied by our next-tent neighbour, a man whom we could trust. We took a bag with us to carry away the "glittering".

When we got into the drive, which was about twelve feet in, we lighted three wax candles on the uncommon occasion and commenced with fossicking knives. And there it lay, a feast more delightful than my most sanguine expectations had led me to expect! With trembling hands we dug the knives into the small but compact masses of the gold – "glittering gold – the yellow slave". We threw it round us in the drive and actually rolled in wealth. Oh, it was glorious! It was heavenly!

Double the amount made at the everyday jogtrot of business would have been nothing to that. It was not the amount, although that was something; it was not the luxuries it would purchase; it was not because we were greedy of gain. No, then what was it? Why, it was the way it was obtained! Now, just consider – we had obtained the precious from the bowels of the earth by our industry; we were the first men to touch the curious ore which would, when put into circulation, pass through the hands of so many different characters; would relieve so much suffering, gratify so many eyes, supply so many luxuries, cause so much crime, and influence the destiny of worlds. All these different things would be done with this useless-looking metal. And we obtained it, we worked for it by our enterprise, by our luck – call it what you will; was that nothing, was there no scope for the reflective man?

There we sat with our knives, the wax candles throwing a yellow glare upon our excited faces. Was this not a delightful study for the artist? We looked like demons intent upon some of our hellish practices. Occasionally a shout from one or the other would proclaim a richer discovery. The conversation went on in the following manner:

"Oh, my good God – Jim, look here!"

"Oh, that's nothing, look behind this stone."

"Ah, there's a big 'un – grab him."

"Ah, Dan, it lies in the blue clay – you see on this layer."

"No, I'm d—d if it does. Here it is in this red gravel."

"Well, but look at this rotten slate – there is a regular cake of it."

"The rock is rising – hit it with the pick."

"It will run out now I expect."

"That's it, Dan – lead me now and prise – heave ho! There you are – its only floating reef."

"Look the other side! Oh, oh, oh! By George it is thick!"

"Mind what you're after – you cut my finger to the bone with your infernal —"

"Well, I beg your pardon, Bill, but 'at such a time as this it is not meet, etc.'"

"None of your d—d quotations!"

"Here, lend me the pick – the driving pick I mean, stupid – I really think you've gone cranky – Look at him, Dan, but mind he does not bite!"

And there he was throwing the wash dirt about the drive and rolling in it.

"Hand here the crowbar and we'll have this big boulder out, and then we will go and have supper, for I'm getting peckish. Make a hole with the pick and enter the point of the bar. There you are – no you aren't! Yes, that's it!"

"It – I don't understand such an it as that."

"You've hit my eye nearly out with your humbug!"

"Well, never mind – let's have cheer, boys, cheer!"

"Very well – here goes – chorus, my hearties!"

"Don't make such an infernal row or we shall have the hole rushed."

"Ah well," said Bill, "Anyone that will come down this hole will have to be up to cleaning gaspipes out. Why the deuce don't you cut steps?"

"Oh, that's to keep fossickers out," said I, "and then you know I always heave Dan up and sometimes he has a try at me."

"Well, I'm blowed if I'd heave you up every day for your weight in gold, and what's more I wouldn't be hove up with *that* windlass on any account. You'll be carrying away the handle, coming down by the run and breaking your blessed necks."

"Ah well," said Dan, "it will only save the executioner a job if we break your neck."

And, by the bye, our hole was a remarkably small one, about one foot nine inches wide by four feet long. I was renowned for sinking a small hole, but Dan was the one for driving – he would beat any of the Cornish miners, although he had never been brought up to work. He was a very light weight and I could heave him out of the hole easily, but had to swarm up the rope myself. As the hole was thirty feet deep a person at the top couldn't see a candle in the drive.

We only picked out the thickest of it and put it into a small bag. The rest we mixed with the wash dirt scattered over the drive, and when it was all knocked up one hand went on the surface and hauled up the buckets by means of the windlass, having one bucket down whilst the other was going up. When all the wash dirt was up, the drive was carefully swept up with a grass broom, and then we commenced driving again. Who shall say gold-digging is dull work? And as for hard work, how can a man possibly feel tired when influenced by such exciting scenes as the one I witnessed this night. I would not have missed it for three times the amount in current coins.

Well, as I said, I put the precious in a small bag and carried up to the tent. It was quite dark but many of the holes in the lead were working, and I have no doubt that many of them were even more fortunate than ourselves. Several fifty-pound nuggets were discovered in this lead, but in our hole which was situated just behind the "Golden Age" Restaurant there was no nuggety gold – but it was all coarse and heavy, being about the size of peas. The heaviest piece weighed about two ounces. Wherever one gets large nuggets it will occur that there is little small – and, in the immediate vicinity of the nugget, none at all; but shotty gold keeps up the excitement, gradually getting thicker and more thick as one approaches the patch.

The place where we obtained this (and indeed all the patches) was on the lee side of a reef about three feet high which crossed the gutter obliquely, thus forming a kind of bar – not as might be naturally supposed, stopping the gold on the weather side, but apparently pouring over the reef and sinking down on the lee side. On most leads and gullies you find it in the same place.

Many a pound weight of gold we left in this claim – and it is invariably the same. Every good hole is left more or less good, no matter how experienced or sensible the party may be. This is the way it happens. If a man is getting a pound weight to the load, he thinks six ounces very small indeed and three not worth working for. If he is getting six ounces he thinks three very little and one and a half only fit to be cast away – and so you may go on until you get to dusts. It is the same with gold diggings as with every other thing, the more one has, the more one wants. Therefore if one gets less than one has been accustomed to one gets dissatisfied; and as somebody observed very wisely, "Nothing is either good or bad, except by comparison.".[36] Whoever it was matters not, but it is as true a sentence as was ever breathed, and conveys so much.

We carried the stuff to the tent, and you may guess that we did not enjoy ourselves this night, being so curious to see how much there was. Not that we feared being stuck up and murdered as anyone would naturally suppose we should have been, from the accounts in the papers. For verily I look upon papers as altogether bosh, although they are well enough for a lot of molly-coddles to talk about; but at the same time they often mislead the inexperienced youth. Let no-one ever be deterred from going to any place by the horrible statements of the press. Everything appears different in print from reality.

In the morning we bought eight buckets of water at one-and-six per bucket – one needs get patches to pay for the likes of this! Everything else was as exorbitant – flour a shilling per pound, sugar a shilling, bread five shillings the quarter loaf, and even meat eight pence per pound. But after this rush there was a reaction in the market at Melbourne in consequence of the sudden influx of goods, and one could get them for a song.

The squatters ruined the price of meat so much because on whosever's run a lead of gold might be, the owner had the monopoly of selling cattle. These are the men that made the money. But it is time they were done away with now, and I believe the Government do not grant any more squatting licences. If there were no squatters we should get better meat. The small farmer cannot afford to fatten cattle when the squatter has such an immense tract of land on which to feed his stock at a mere nominal rent. Besides, as long as that system exists the land will never be thrown open to the public at anything like a moderate price. That's the worst of the English – they are so very fond of a monopoly that there is no chance for the millions; not only is it bad for the latter but it injures the former, for anything that is injurious to the people cannot do good to the Government. It's like robbing Peter to pay Paul. If folks did but understand, how much the one ought to be interested in procuring the welfare of the other, they would act more in unison and have less bickering.

We washed the stuff in a large tub so that nothing should be lost, and it looked very pretty in the dish. It more than filled half a pannikin net. We took it to the Commissioner's and deposited it. There was ten pounds weight which was not so bad considering there was a great deal of it in the wash dirt. Jack's party had not yet struck, and of course we lent them something to go on with. But it was not long before they got two claims on Black Man's Lead, for the lead we were on had exhausted itself on the flat and had turned off and joined this Black Man's Lead which was very good. The gold was much more nuggety than in ours. The next hole to theirs was a German's, and very rich with several nuggets as high as eight pounds weight. Their claims were very fair, but they had so large a party that it was nothing when shared out.

We had no idea our washing stuff would turn out as well as it did, and we offered to sell it for four ounces to the load. Luckily for us no one would buy it. By the bye, we had two loads of the best of it stolen, for we had not taken it up to our tent – like asses. We suspected a mob of killers who lived just behind our hole, for we saw them take two loads out of the next claim, and they never worked anywhere. But we put a stop to it by shifting our tent and pitching it comfortably at the side of our hole. We also obtained a large dog, between kangaroo and bloodhound, and made him fast near the wash dirt; and gave our friends a salute every night by way of a warning, but they never attempted it again – bad luck to 'em!

We obtained several other smaller patches, and when we washed up the stuff averaged one pound six ounces to the load, which was excellent after all we had dry nuggeted. Suffice it to say that the total amount was about one thousand six hundred pounds worth. One of the Scotchmen offered us a claim next to him, which he had marked out, but unfortunately we delayed taking it until too late. There was seventy pounds weight taken out of it, proving how rich the ground was all over the gutter. Many little gullies were also worked about here.

We had a great spree when this was over, and never before or since have I seen money thrown away in such a reckless manner. If one happened to be walking the main street with two or three friends and met anyone he knew with some more friends, of course the first question after, "How do you do, Bill?" is in the same breath, "Well, what are you going to have?" You would stand one round and then no-one would think of leaving until all hands had stood a round. If you refused to take part it was considered as direct an insult as if you had spat in the man's face, and if one could not drink spirits one was obliged to take lemonade, or rascally stuff that was so called Egg-nog was much drunk here. Such a thing as twenty glasses bought at a shout, at the rate of half a crown per glass. Champagne was much in vogue and sold at one pound per bottle – so called from being made of bad cider inflated with gas.

Then there were various intellectual amusements, such as the theatre, a noble canvas building, the performance nearly equalling any penny gaff in London[37] – and if I remember rightly five shillings was all they charged. But the rifle gallery was as quick a way as any of getting rid of any superfluous cash. It was only sixpence a shot and then you could bet upon it, which was an easier way still. Then there were billiards and bagatelle, and, if one was very hard-pushed, one might perchance find a stray gambling house. Money *was* made about this time and no mistake, two or three hundred pounds being not an extraordinary thing to take in one day over the bar of some of the public houses. It did not require many months of this work to make a fortune.

We could not strike it again after leaving our old hole – which we gave away and the parties made very good wages out of it. Another party went into it and drove up the reef on both sides, and found it first rate. They took about as much out of it as we did. The whole lead was rushed again on account of this, and the reefs were found tolerably good all along. Nobody had thought of touching them before.

There was a rush about twelve miles off, and we took our blankets and left our tent, intending to come back if it was no good. And as it turned out so, we returned in a week and found our tent gone. But it was not far. Our old carter, finding us not returned, thought that we had hit it and was about to bring the tent; however we returned in time to save him the trouble. This old fellow had been out here some twenty odd years, and had lived principally in Gippsland. He was a very good hand at breaking in young horses, but it nearly cost him his life; for as he was returning across the Carisbrook Plains after having taken a load of stuff down for us, the horses took fright at something and bolted across the plains capsizing in the rut of the race course, the cart falling right on top of him. We carried him to our tent and kept him there until he got well. One of the horses slipped his shoulder so he was turned adrift. There are thousands of wild bullocks and many horses in the bush which have escaped from time to time. The former breed very rapidly.

One morning one of the young Welshmen, Davis, who had joined Jack, came to our tent and said that he was going home to Britain.

"Well," said I, "I don't see much doing now, and I think I shall go too."

"Alright then, and we'll hire a band to play us down to Melbourne!"

Now this was done without the slightest reflection, and we all set off together in an American waggon,[38] which having no springs nearly jolted our insides out. I was not right for a week after it. I would not go in another empty one even if they would pay me. We passed through Castlemaine, and took a fond look at the infernal old water hole. It was completely full again, the dam being washed away, and a miserable-looking place it was. I know nothing so miserable as a deserted diggings that one has known in its prosperity. One looks round for the well-known tents, such and such a windlass, and this or that tree, but he sees nothing – all is void and dreary. The holes did not seem to be in the same place; they had all been turned over again and again. The ground that had once been so rich, that had been prized more than life itself was all deserted. That old familiar ground in Diamond Gully where my tent once stood was the same as I left it – there stood the bark table, the forks of the stretcher and part of the chimney. The remains of the bark hut, wherein I had spent so many happy hours with the Scotchmen, were all exactly as they were. The holes around the trees were the only things touched. Verily I shed a tear on the old spot I felt so miserable. Why? I know not, for I was now comparatively wealthy and then I had a mere nothing and cared less. Those were the happiest days of my life. Folks say that one's childhood is the happiest. I don't believe it. It's only distance makes it appear so. Children have their little troubles and feel them as acutely as an adult. At all events, my childhood was far from a happy one. A great fool I was to leave the diggings. I shall never like them so well again, or have the chances I have now thrown away. Heigh-ho!

Must return to the waggon and soothe my mind with the infernal jolting. I sold my share of the gold on the diggings and got a cheque on the bank. We paid Tom Brice up, and made him a present of the largest nugget. But although we paid all our debts there was a great deal of money owing to us by different parties who did not have it in their power to pay. But I don't call it lost. I never lost anything yet by a loan or a kindness, and I don't believe anyone else ever did if they did it with a proper spirit.

We dined at Forest Creek the second day, but the place was almost entirely deserted except by a few old hands who knew the ground and still managed to knock out good wages. By the bye, Dan carried his gold down with him in the waggon thinking to get a better price in Melbourne – instead of which the gold was sixpence an ounce less than on the diggings. Nothing of note occurred on the road except standing rounds at every public we came to. The roads showed a little sign of improvement, but they were still very bad across the Keilor Plains and the Black Forest. There were a great many more accommodation houses, so called, but having tried them, I would sooner at any time sleep in the open air, not being partial to the little flat mahogany things.

Melbourne had changed in a most astonishing manner, North and South being quite new, together with most of Collingwood. Catherine Hayes gave several concerts at the Queen's, where she reaped a golden harvest.[39] She wheedled a counter out of me which I regret, for I thought nothing of her.

The Ballaarat[40] Stockade broke out a little while after this. I will relate the particulars as far as I know. The Eureka Hotel was kept by an old hand and frequented by very bad characters. Several robberies had been committed there, but the proprietor knew a thing or two and fed the police so largely that they took no notice of his house and allowed him not only to sell poisons but to keep open all day Sunday, about which the regulations were very strict. One night it went rather too far for, besides robbing a drunken digger (who resisting broke a pane of glass) the publican, his wife and another came out and clove his head in twain with a spade. No inquiry was made about it by the police and a verdict of murder was brought in by parties unknown.

Now the police had been tampering with the diggers for a considerable time and the licence question was considered by all to be a very rascally thing. But this act was too glaringly public to pass. Bills were posted by friends of the deceased which called upon the diggers to revenge his death and to reform the Government. A mob collected round the Eureka Hotel with the intention of hanging the proprietor, but he made his escape out of the house, and springing on a horse, galloped off, followed closely to Geelong. However they failed in catching him, for he got on board the Geelong steamer that was just starting and laughed at them. He was however taken into custody by the authorities of Melbourne who had got wind of it.

The mob vented their fury upon the house which was a very fine building and burnt it to the ground. They then turned their fury upon the "Traps". A regiment of soldiers was sent from town but before they arrived order was restored. Three men who had been active at the fire were taken and sent to Melbourne for trial. One of their names was McIntyre,[41] a friend of the "Wee Hairy Man" who had gone down to see me off. The proprietor of the hotel and his accomplice got three years – a very inadequate punishment for the offence – and the three men for the fire were reluctantly found guilty by the jury who annexed a rider censuring the authorities of Ballaarat.

I forgot to remark that La Trobe had been superseded by Charles Hotham who acted in a different, but no less reprehensible manner than the former. He was received in Melbourne with every appearance of great joy, and his first acts were good – but they soon had cause to execrate a martial Governor. He reduced all the government servants' salaries and under his management the enormous expenses were curtailed and vast improvements made in town and country – and the roads showed well up; he cut off a great many useless government servants, and all the wages he reduced except his own.

Things did not long remain quiet at Ballaarat. The diggers were goaded to the last extremity of forebearance, and at last things came to a head and burst. They all refused to pay any more licences, and refused to go quietly with the troopers as heretofore. They raised a militia, the stores were thrown open to them with the gunpowder, guns and other offensive weapons. The blacksmiths were all employed to sharpen pikes and make bayonets. And the only foolish thing they did was to throw up what they called a stockade, or barrier of trees, calculated to be musket-proof. Then they were enclosed like a flock of sheep at the mercy of the butcher; whereas they might have planted themselves on the road and picked off all the soldiers like a lot of pigeons in a trap. They had several leaders, principally Germans and Yankees, for Johnny Bull was a cautious bird and liked not to put his fat neck into a noose. When the soldiers marched up a few hundred stood their ground and the rest bolted as fast as their legs would carry them.

C. Hotham, instead of offering to enquire into the conduct of the government officials, declared his intentions of cutting off the rebellious ones – or as he himself said, "They'll all run away when they see the troops." He had made a slight mistake in the characters of diggers. They were not all an ignorant British mob, for in some of their veins as good blood as his own flowed. There were educated men among them who had been sufficiently long their own masters to have wills of their own, and cared as little for red coats on the side of tyranny as they did for a dead possum. *They* stood their ground manfully. Charley was right in his supposition in part, for there were many who had but lately arrived and had yet to learn the spirit of independence.

There were many heroes on that little day. One Yankee fought with such desperate valour that, although surrounded, he laid seven of his enemies dead at his feet with his resoluteness. The poor fellow was however overpowered by numbers and gave up his gallant soul. When they entered the Stockade the soldiers showed no mercy; they shot a poor old man, a blacksmith, in his tent and burnt him in it. The diggers lost men but the loss of the soldiers must have been large. They were taken down privately and it was never publicly known. The officer in command was shot.[42]

The other diggers were much enraged at the massacre for had they (the authorities) made the least concession it would have gone by without so much unnecessary bloodshed. Better would it have been for the diggers, and indeed it always is better, passively to submit to oppression than to provoke the wrath of the Omnipotent by going to war – than which a worse or more useless argument cannot be. However they gained their end – the licence fee was immediately abolished, and a tax of one pound per month called the diggers' right was levied, but it was not enforced. The greater part of the police were disarmed, and a short staff given to them instead. They talked of erecting a monument for those diggers killed in the Stockade.

The *Great Britain* was just about to sail, but the allowance for forty pounds was so bad that I would have nothing to do with her. The next one on the list was the barque *Chicora* – forty-five pounds in the cabin, and we paid a deposit for a passage in her. She was for

London, but she did not sail for about six weeks. We all put up together at the Crown Hotel. You may guess our time was pretty well occupied with sight-seeing, and every other possible way we could get rid of our money. There was no lack of ways and means in Melbourne at this time. The money soon dwindled away very considerably, and could I have sold my passage I should never have gone.

The town was full of Jews and rogues of every description. I went to sell some gold with Davis (we had previously weighed it) at the corner of Elizabeth and Collins Street. The Jewish scamp (Hyams) made it an ounce and two pennyweights short. "Put it back in the bag," said I. He did so and we took it to another man and got the full amount. We went back to the first one and told him, showing the receipt. But to our astonishment he swore point blank that there had not been a soul in his shop that morning, and that we were mistaken.

It was dangerous to go into a shop without someone with you. They were up to all kinds of swindles. I went into MacFarlane's[43] in Elizabeth Street to buy a silver snuff box which I was going to give to Dan, and I ordered him to engrave his name on it. He told me the price which I agreed to. I left one pound deposit, but when I called for it and was going to pay I found that he had doubled the price, and swore point blank that it was the same he asked at first. Of course I would not have it, but lost my pound. The gold buyers were up to every kind of dodge and roguery, such as long nails, false scales and weights and many other ingenious contrivances so that a man was never safe. The most stylish shops were usually the worst. The place wanted purifying badly, and things were just coming to a head – rents being so high and the markets so overstocked that folks were setting fire to their houses every now and then to get clear of them. The fires were very numerous, and the supply of water being quite inefficient, people were obliged to allow them to burn themselves out.

Many people began to turn their attention to agriculture, and the land for many miles round was bought with avidity at large prices. They do not cut wheat as in England close to the ground, but the ears and about a foot of the straw only is cut and the remaining straw ploughed in, forming good manure.

And now I think I have very little more of colonial experience to relate. They all went on board the *Chicora* to see me off, and when I was cooped up for good I wished heartily to be ashore again. The trip in the *Seppings* had given me a complete sickness of the blue briny and I am very glad it did. The film has fallen from my eyes and I see clearly the misery of a sailor's life. However much one may be affected by the beauty of the sea – for at times it is awfully grand – the startling change from clime to clime and the splendours of foreign lands – yet one cannot help remembering that one separates oneself from all the social and intellectual enjoyments of life, and lastly, forfeiting one's liberty, without which death were a boon; for who is a greater slave than a sailor? Who is more of a prisoner? There is only one path by which he can escape from his prison. It is by opening the gates of death – blue above and blue below – there are no back doors.

What a wonderful country is Australia! A splendid climate and everything mortal man could wish. The emigrant is more free from difficulties here than in any other new country. There are no warlike natives and no infectious disease. The land is uniformly good and not over-thickly wooded. About the shallow diggings the land is not so rich, being rather too stony. Cattle breed amazingly fast. Never was there a country discovered with so few disadvantages. If people expect to go to a new country and find every luxury prepared for as in an old one, of course they will be disappointed here. Many of them do go out with those and similar rotten ideas. Read the history of any of the new colonies, and you will find that this country has not had one tithe of the difficulties to combat.

Again I continually hear people say, “Oh, we might have done well there once, but there are too many now.” Did ever mortal man hear such stuff? Here is a country as big as the whole of Europe and about as many people as there are in London. People don’t know the riches of this land – not one-fifth part of the Island has been explored. Why even the coast 125° to 132° Longitude has not been surveyed. Then there is no end to the gold yet to be discovered. It’s found in the Sydney district, and the Ovens, and in different places over an extent of about seven hundred miles.

IV

CAPE HORN AND HOME

Passage in the barque 'Chicora' – Captain Alnack (George Allanack) about 200 tons registered (298 tons)[1]. From Melbourne bound to London, commences November 21st (1854).

November 21st, 1854. Went with Davis on board. It was dark and we were to get under weigh the next morning. The appearance of the passengers was anything but prepossessing, nearly all of them being in a disgusting state of fourpenny. Indeed that appears to be as necessary an accompaniment to a sea voyage as sails are to a ship; they usually begin the voyage with a drink, just a parting glass. Besides a couple of months in Melbourne does not improve a man's personal appearance much. There is such an endless nobblerising that would completely astound an uninitiated new chum. To refuse a nobbler when invited is considered a gross insult and a decided breach of etiquette. The publicans regularly coin money; a nobbler which is about a wine glass costs them about one penny, and they sell for sixpence in town, and a shilling and one and six on the diggings.

On sitting down to the supper table we had a good opportunity of scrutinising our fellow passengers; for it is a matter of some importance to a man to know what sort of characters he is going to be penned up with for four months. It's not like being ashore where if one doesn't like a man one can leave him, and I find it better to put up with a disagreeable fellow and be civil to him rather than to have an open rupture; for being continually thrown into contact with one another it's well to be friendly, but not too familiar. There were nine passengers which was one more than was bargained for, and it was a very close squeeze at the little table. One of them, who by his twang was a Scotchman, was very drunk and made some very funny remarks during supper. Next to him was a little blear-eyed fellow who had the delirium tremens to such an extent that it took both hands to raise his cup to his lips. [There were also] two Americans, Dresser and Allan, an old shellback who had been Bosun in the *Harbinger* (Captain Lone).

The first one I mentioned, McNaughton, was an awful lushington as was also his berth mate Lister. They were very seldom seen sober during the passage, and only came out of their berth to replenish the brandy bottle and then turned in again. I never saw such confirmed drunkards – and they were both well-brought up. Lister was not more than two and twenty and could speak six different languages; he was awfully bloated and as weak as a cat subject to fits. He was good company when sober which is not saying much. The former was a strong man, or at least had been, and a more-seasoned veteran. It is curious that all drunkards should be so fond of pepper. Almost every day at dinner the top of the castor came off into one or other of their soups, and I'm sure it was done for the purpose; for they never changed their plates but licked it down pepper and all. I used to wonder how they could possibly bear it.

There was a doctor – so-called. He got off paying some of his passage money. He was an Irishman, but like all ship doctors very little good – an amazing old cadge, he would take anything one offered him, but the deuce a cup he would ever offer.

The Yankees were not bad fellows on the whole; very ingenious, always making some kind of fancy-work out of wood. Dresser had bad teeth and was as yellow as a guinea. Davis who came down with me was far too much of a hypocrite to suit me. Myers[2] and the Skipper were two of the most decent men on board.

The man with sore eyes, who called himself Captain Garrett,[3] was taken ashore by the Police Boat whilst we were detained at the Heads with foul winds. He was charged with some swindling transaction – a very good riddance – but it was rather hard lines to be taken out of a warm bed when he thought himself so nicely off. Another five minutes of fair wind and he should have been out of reach of the land-sharks. Myers had lent him some money which was returned to him out of Captain G.'s trunks – rather lucky for the former that he was taken, and indeed for us all. I wish they had taken two or three more.

Altogether there were now eight passengers, the Captain, two mates and two stewards aft, and eight hands and the cook in the forecastle, making a total of twenty-two souls. The first mate was a useless whipper-snapper, a kind of young pup raised by interest; the second dicky was much older. He had had an accident with a pistol on the diggings and shattered his right hand which obliged him to have it amputated. He was on the whole a better sailor than the first dicky.

The Captain had raised himself. He had received an ordinary poor Scotch education, which is a little better than English first-rate boarding schools. He had been apprenticed to a ship's carpenter and had gradually raised himself without aid to his present rank. For navigation and seamanship and true politeness (although he was not a gentleman) I would prefer him to any captain I have been with. He used to place four bottles of wine on the table every Sunday although there was none allowed by the ship. And of course he expected us to do the same weekdays, but Myers and I were the only ones that brought it forth. Although the old doctor would take his fill of our wine yet deuce a drop would he put on – or indeed any of the others. But the Yankees never drank anyone else's.

We fared very well, and might have passed the time comfortably enough had they chosen to make themselves agreeable. But they were men of that peculiar kidney who have no spirit in them – dull, heavy men. The utmost one could goad them to was the unintellectual amusement of picking one another's pockets of handkerchiefs and making them fast to the masthead. Some of them would rather let them blow away than go up and fetch them down. And there they would sit like a jolly lot of old dummies talking about the price of congreve matches, and how a bloody war might be averted by lowering the price of stewed cabbage, and such like disgusting bosh. A four months' voyage is a miserable thing at the best of times, but more particularly so with such companions and in such a small ship. There is no exercise for one except the monotonous fisherman's walk of three steps and overboard. It is worse for one who has been accustomed to an active life. I have not written so much for a long time, and now I am only doing it to cut the throat of old Father Time.

I was in a four-bunked berth, the aftermost, a very close hole. I had one of the top bunks, Davis had the one underneath me, and the two Yankees were the opposite side. All the other berths were only fitted up for two. Of course we could not all rise at once so we had to take spell about. You may guess oxygen was a scarce article in this hole, and it was not till we were all ill that I could prevail on them to prise a hole in the door and pass a line through so as to keep it open and from slamming.

*On the 25th* [November1854] we weighed anchor and set sail from the Heads although the wind continued foul for getting out of Bass Strait and we beat from the mainland to Van Diemen's Land for a week without gaining any ground. If we could have got on shore some of us would have been off to the diggings again, for I was heartily tired of it already. But the first few days are usually the most tedious portion of the passage. On the 1st December the wind changed and took us through Banks's Straits, a small passage about a cable's length in width, to the Eastward of Bass Strait. Many vessels go round to the westward of Van Diemen's Land, thus getting more sea room, and no doubt we might have done so at the commencement of the voyage, with advantage, had we thought that the wind would have continued foul so long. We now steered away for the south-westward and the weather got considerably colder.

On the 20th [December 1854] it became so cold that the Captain thought we were in the vicinity of ice, and in the afternoon we sighted a large iceberg, about a mile in length and several hundred feet high – as near as we could judge in Latitude 57° 28′ South and Longitude 145° 43′ West. This was the first I had the opportunity of seeing. They are not usually seen. This is the most likely time of year to see them for the ice breaks up in the spring from the South Shetland Islands and always drifts to the north and gradually melts. Being in such tremendous masses must take some time. They are exceedingly dangerous and should a ship run against one there is little chance of escape. The *Madagascar* is supposed to have been lost in this manner.

It was a splendid sight and I would not have missed it for a good deal – rising in majestic grandeur from the deep blue ocean like a glittering citadel, its snowy whiteness contrasting strongly with the dark clouds behind. I never saw a more magnificent sight – the sea near it was green and was dashing furiously over it. We did not expect to see any more – the Captain would have rather not have seen that – but we were disappointed, and on the 29th saw another in Latitude 56° South and Longitude 105° West. After this we saw large numbers every day together with quantities of field ice some of which we hauled on board and found quite fresh. We passed through 2,700 miles – the whole of the distance the sea was studded with them – the last one was seen in Latitude 56° 39′ South and Longitude 43° 25′ West. Fortunately, at this season it is light nearly all night so with a good lookout we ran no danger. The weather was fearfully cold and blanket bay was the most agreeable place, there being no stove in the cabin.

On New Year's Day [1855] we had a great jollification. The Scotch do not keep up Christmas Day, but they pay much respect to the first of the New Year. The Skipper, Myers and I were killing time with cards for a bottle of wine per game and, as we imbibed deeply the generous juice, got very merry. The others, finding that sleep was impossible, joined us and we made a night of it – as folks say when they get into a disagreeable state of fourpenny.

We sang the old year out and the new one in with great gusto – and I, thinking that the doctor's sweet voice would add to the harmony, tried with exemplary patience to inspire him with a knowledge of how highly necessary it was for his peace of mind. But it was no; the Goth wouldn't have it. And so we made the best of our small party, and as for noise, had enough, for I'll defy twenty men to have made more noise. Davis sang "The Bay of Biscay", Myers, "Do You Ever Think of Me, Love?", McNaughton "Auld Lang Syne", Lister "God Save the Queen" and I, "The Old Woman of Rumford", and as we all sang at once the effect must have been delightful to anyone who appreciated it. Not that any of us was in a condition to judge, the criticisms being made by a neutral party.

I have some faint recollection of standing on my head at the cabin door and wondering what business it had there. Myers got under the table, and, after several vain attempts to find his way out, quietly resigned himself to his fate and went to sleep there without further bother. We all suffered pretty severely in the cranium the next morning, which served us right.

January 7th [1855]. We doubled the Horn and very glad we all were at the hopes of getting into warm weather; for the cold had pretty considerably doubled us up, feeling it the more acutely as we had left such a warm climate. We shot a great many gulls. The Captain was a crack shot and seldom missed. Catching albatrosses and Mother Carey's chickens[4] was also a favourite amusement – by Myers in particular, whom we christened the "Ancient Mariner". A large number of whales was also seen and had we been fishing we should have done exceedingly well.

With the doctor I was no great favourite and he predicted an untimely end by means of hemp. Our arguments were carried on in a very spirited manner. He was a great man for soldiers and Bonaparte was one of his particular cronies, and to say anything derogatory to him was equivalent to putting oneself out of the learned doctor's books. He dressed and deported himself *à la militaire*. He was very wrath at the loss or destruction of his best wellington boots which had fallen a victim to the sporting genius of some young squatters staying at Hockin's Hotel[5] with him, and who by way of doing a private injury to the lodgers had filled all the boots that were standing at the doors of the various apartments with their own liquid manure by way of making them go on easily.

Curious tales were told by the passengers. I will relate one told by Davis who was an eye-witness of it on Old Bendigo. The gully was infested by those pests who call themselves Tipperary Boys. The Scotchmen were working a very good claim and, the sinking being not more than six feet, the Tips got scent of the richness. One morning the Scotchmen found two of them hard at work in their claim, and remonstrating with them it came to high words, and from that to blows, and the Tips making use of their national weapon, the shillelagh, and the shovel, split one of the Scotchmen's heads open with the latter weapon. His mate went up to his tent and brought down a double-barrelled gun, and without saying a word shot the offender dead on the spot. A large crowd of Tips had collected by this time and instantly rushed on the former, who resolutely stood his ground and brought down another; and with the stock of the gun laid about him so lustily that he disabled two more. But he would soon have been overpowered by numbers had not the other diggers interfered and the fight became general. But the troopers having got scent appeared in time to prevent further bloodshed – and the Tips took to their heels and made their lucky escape. The Scotchman instantly related the case and gave himself up – he was taken before the Commissioner and afterwards acquitted. His mate and the two Tips who fell under his well-directed fire were quite dead, and were buried side by side near the scene of bloodshed.

Another yarn of a similar case was told by one of the Yankees, as it happened in California during his stay there. Two mates had been working a rich claim when suddenly one of them disappeared. His mate gave out that he had gone to San Francisco, leaving him to sell the tools and follow him. This rather astonished the friends of the missing one, particularly as the other seemed to be in rather a perturbed state of mind, and shortly after left the place leaving the tent standing without sale. They searched the tent and finding a bloody axe in a deserted hole near the tent confirmed their suspicions of foul play. The floor of the latter evidently had been recently disturbed and on shovelling the earth away they discovered the body of their missing friend – he having apparently received a ghastly blow on the head with the axe.

The hue and cry was instantly given and several diggers rode to San Francisco, fortunately in time to catch the murderer about to sail for New York. He was secured and brought back to the scene of his crime. He refused to look at the body and persisted in denying the murder. A rope was thrown over the bough of the tree and he was hauled up a few inches; but on making signs that he wished to speak was let down, when he confessed to having split his mate's head with the axe while he was sleeping and buried him under a stretcher. Being a Roman Catholic he begged for a priest, who attended him, and asked that some of his ill-gotten wealth which he had in his possession might be paid out for Masses for his soul – which was also granted. After his confession he was hauled up to the branch by the united strength of some twenty able-bodied men. The expense of burial was paid out of the money and the remainder was honestly remitted to the widow of the murdered man who was known to be residing in the state of Maine. So much for the Yankee yarn.

These and many other yarns passed away the dull days of a monotonous four months which in such a small ship is about the most tiresome thing under the sun.

February 9th [1855]. We shot a grampus[6] but as a breeze sprang up we were unable to get any good out of him. The next day we sighted the South American coast and passed Rio Sao Francisco,[7] a shallow river, but one of the largest in Brazil, a very strong current setting south west. We had a very light easterly wind which veered round to the northward thus making a foul wind for us. We had no south-east Trades – in fact they are little to be depended upon although sure of the north-easterly. Thus we were forced upon the Brazilian coast. The Captain had the idea of putting in for water which would have delighted us all, but for some reason he did not do so.

On the 12th we sighted Maceio[8] and passed a number of jangadas, or sailing rafts. Three men on board; they were catching flying fish. They are excellent eating and numbers flew on board us attracted by the light. They are much like a herring with long fins or wings. They cannot fly far as these wings require to be continually moistened. They are surrounded by merciless enemies – the albacores, bonitas and albatrosses all feed on them. The men on the rafts were mostly naked and entirely unprotected from the scorching heat of the sun and from the waves which made a clean beach over them. There were apparently a good many ships in the harbour before the fort, which is an open roadstead, protected on the east by a large reef of coral.

A large white house stood in bold relief on a bluff east of the town and a church to the left of it. The coast is in many places covered with cocoanut trees. I wish we had had a few of the nuts on board. In some places were spots of a red colour which could be seen with the glass but I couldn't make out what they were.

We signalised a ship sixty days out. She had carried away her masts round the Horn and had jury masts rigged. We encountered no gales and altogether had remarkably light winds the whole passage. Signalising a ship is a nice and exciting pastime after being so long alone. It is mostly all carried on by flags called Marryat's code of signals[9] – except when we pass near enough to speak with the trumpet.

We harpooned several porpoises but the ship was going too fast through the water and they broke away, sometimes bending the harpoon very much. At last we managed to get a small one on board. He was something like a pig and the flesh was red like beef. We cooked some of it and it ate just similar to a beef steak, though rather dry, as all deep sea water fish are. However we relished it much. We also caught several bonitos with a piece of red rag attached by a line to the martingale. They are very dry. We were much pleased at being able to catch one of those fish called dolphin. In its last struggles it displayed all the varied colours of the rainbow, but I think they are much prettier in the water. It ate something like the bonito, very dry, the porpoise being better than any of them.

The Skipper was a very agreeable man. He said that the vessel he came out in was a schooner, but he spoke of her sailing qualities as far superior to this one. He had enjoyed himself much in the society of a very nice girl who was so condescending and timid that she could not bear the idea of sleeping by herself. He spoke feelingly on the subject, so that I suspect the schooner had more attractions than her sailing qualities.

14th February, 1855. We sighted Cape St. Augustine and on the 16th passed by Fernando de Noronha,[10] a penal settlement of Brazil "where cries and sighs and groans that rend the air are made, not marked."

On the 18th February at 4.00pm we crossed the Line in Longitude 31° 24′ West, which was much further west than we should have been had we experienced fair winds. There was no shaving as we had all crossed it many times before, but we gave some grog to the men and they had a jollification on the occasion.

30th February. We sighted Flores and Corvo, two of the Azores or Western Islands; the latter is so called from its peculiar shape, like a duck. Spoke the ship *Switzerland* from Manilla to Liverpool, 115 days out. The wind now fell light and we were becalmed to the eastward of Flores. This continued for several days which was very vexing as we now considered ourselves just upon home. However on the 14th March we got a fresh breeze from the westward, and the Captain, being as tired of the voyage as ourselves, carried on sail to an extent that I have seldom seen before, almost burying the unhappy barque. We have to thank our stars it didn't carry away any gear, for as she was being sent to England for sale there was nothing to spare.

On the *19th March 1855* sighted the *Lizard*, much to the satisfaction of all hands. Among the sailors there was an old shipmate of mine in the *Lancastrian*. He had done very well on the diggings and was going home to get married and also bring out his old mother. He was not the only tar who had made money. Two others had between thirty and forty pounds weight of gold in the forecastle – more than I should like to carry in such a place. To our great indignation, for we thought Dame Fortune had persecuted us enough, the wind fell light shortly after we sighted the *Lizard* and gave signs of an easterly wind. It was very cold and we all cursed our foolishness in leaving the land – not of milk and honey – but the one that's got the money – and gets the blessed sun occasionally.

We spoke to a small fishing smack and from her we heard that Nicholas, the Emperor of Russia,[11] was food for the worms, but that the war was being carried on under the present turnkey. Now to give a slight notion of how distance magnifies anything; makes it both much better and much worse, and what bosh the papers are. We had great apprehension on account of this war.[12] We had heard that the chances were about ten to one that we should fall in with some man-o-war and get pressed, or else taken prisoners by the Johnny Doboroughs; instead of which when one got to England everything was just as quiet as if there was nothing going on at all. But it's always the way, and that's the very reason why a stay-at-home man is always prejudiced against every other country but his own. Every man ought to travel to form a correct idea of things and enlarge his mind.

Although anyone might think I'm cutting in too heavy, yet I will say it – that *every man* who has not travelled; *everyone* who has not seen both sides of the picture, been both in the depths of poverty and in the height of prosperity – I won't mince the matter, there are no two ways about it – that *every man* who has not done this is narrow-minded and prejudiced – the rich against the poor, because they don't understand their feelings; the poor against the rich, because they don't understand their temptations, and their feelings. Every man, to be just, should fully understand that truest of true maxims, "Circumstances alter cases." Everyone should say to himself,

"If I was poor, starving, cold, too proud to beg, unaccustomed to asking for work, if I got it unable to do it, perhaps, if such were the case, might I not be tempted to do what I now condemn so loudly? Might I not have done as that miserable object has, who is now in the grasp of that relentless official, and subject to the brutal jests of the heedless crowd, who as Bulwer Lytton says, – which ought to be written in letters of gold – 'Man sees the deed, God the circumstances.[13]'" Or again looking on the other side, "If I was as rich as that man who has never known hunger or suffering, might I not be as he is? And knowing that I had the means of gratifying every whim, every sinful wish, should I not do so? Turn a deaf ear to suffering and say, 'Oh, it serves the wretches right! Every man can get a living if he likes to work.'"

Verily this is altogether bosh.

But it was most infernally provoking to be dodging to and fro from one side to the other and not able to get ashore. But as luck would have it the Skipper stood close into Dartmouth and hoisted a whip in the ensign as a signal for a boat to come off. Six of us went ashore for ten shillings a head. The old doctor and McNaughton stopped. The former was too stingy and latter had no money. Lister had no tin either but Myers was fool enough to pay all his expenses, besides lending him some money on board which, as he might have expected, he saw no more.

We all stopped at the first public we sighted, and ordered all the good things that were obtainable, such as eggs, milk and vegetables. The landlady had six daughters who did us the honour to take tea with us. Very condescending young females they were. We all partook freely of eggs, and three of us were completely knocked up. I was very unwell all night and I could not advise anyone, as the saying is "to go in a buster to the good things of this life." After a long voyage it is very injurious.

Dartmouth is rather a pretty place, but my first impression was that all the people had left in consequence of some contagion, but on making enquiry of the Custom House officer who searched us we found that the town was considered rather full just now. It is a middling large town – that is to say there are a good many houses in it. But we only saw about twenty straggling males altogether.

The females appeared to us very numerous – I should think there were about four to each man. Everything was so directly vice versa to the country which we had left that we were much struck. It appeared as if the destroying angel had passed over this country leaving only a few miserable objects to bewail the loss of the better-favoured ones. By far the greatest number of the Colonists are young, strong and in full vigour, enjoying the delights of a salubrious clime, which bore a strong contrast to the puny pale-faced race which here met our view. The scenery was well enough of itself, but it required to be lighted up to be beautiful, and the sickly rays of the spring sun seemed wholly inadequate to penetrate the thick murky atmosphere which hung heavily over the snow-capped hills. And the manners are so different. Poverty meets your eye at every turn, and with it the cringing unmanly servility. We were nearly stunned by the clamour of some half a dozen starved wretches at the steamboat who fought tooth and nail for the honour of carrying our effects.

"Didn't you employ me, sir?"

"No, the gentleman called me!"

"Eh, sir!" "Oh, sir!" "Yes, sir!"

We scrambled a few sixpences for which the poor devils were very thankful, and we gave them the excellent advice – to be off to Australia as soon as possible. One of their answers completely stunned me – he said he should not like to leave Old England. There was no place like home! Poor, prejudiced, half-starved fool! Did ever sensible man hear the like before! And yet it's true enough – there are many who would sooner starve in England, helping to add to the useless magnificence and luxury of the few, than venture to a country where they could be free – where, as Russell says, there is "wealth in honest labour",[14] or Burns "a man's a man for a' that."[15] Heigho, such is life!

We landed on *23rd March* [1855]. This was quite an event in my life. It was like going on another tack. Libertas! I had been mixed up with men, my path in life had been remarkably free from the society of the softer sex. Ever since I went to boarding school I had seen little or nothing of women. Thinking I knew something of the world when I had only had the opportunity of judging half of it (and that half the roughest of the rough) I was now thrown in an entirely new sphere, and behaved very ridiculously I know. This half is harder to read than the other because society does not allow them to express their sentiments so freely, although they are easy enough to manage when one becomes acquainted with them.

But to return – in fine weather this part of the country must be very pretty, but as it rained hard during our passage in the steamer, was very cold, and we had no very warm clothing, we failed to appreciate it. We went by rail to Bristol, not venturing further that day. Some of the passengers by the *Blackwall,* belonging to Green, had just landed at Plymouth and were proceeding to London. They did not sail from Melbourne until a month after us and had therefore made a much better passage. We put up at the Saracen's Head at Bristol, a very nice inn and exceedingly comfortable.

On *Sunday 25th* [March 1855] we started for London by the parliamentary train and arrived there about five o'clock; and after paid the cabman some very exorbitant charge. Of all the places in London, we put up at Covent Garden Hotel – much to the astonishment of the good landlady who was at first doubtful if she could accommodate us. But on informing her we came from the

Land of Gold she changed her tune and found that she had plenty of room. We were all dressed à la digger – blue shirts and moleskin trousers. We ordered a sumptuous dinner – mock turtle, ducks and quantities of champagne – and seated ourselves independently in the coffee room, much to the alarm of some swells who happened to be there supping. One of them yarningly remarked that Australia must be a hell of a place. He was quickly answered by one of the Yankees, that it *was* a hell of a place and he would find that a hell of a people came from it. He replied not, but they took up their hats and decamped – to our mutual satisfaction.

Dresser was very unwell with yellow jaundice and stoppage. We took a walk together through the Strand. The streets were very dirty and, being Sunday night, all the shops closed. He expressed much contempt for our large city. On Monday Lister got some more money from Myers and went nominally to get a cheque cashed but in reality to get beastly drunk. On his return he came to us in the smoking room and spoke very ferociously to one of the waiters. We thought this very wrong, in our ignorance of the customs, and apologised for his ill-breeding. The waiter smiled benignly at our greenness and replied, "Oh, that's nothing, sirs – we're used to that!" which spoke volumes about the country.

I set about the very necessary work of rigging myself – called at Babb's and brought two coats for four pounds, and an Albert watch-chain for four pounds ten shillings – and thus fitted out went to Hay's, and found all friends well. Fanny was at Burge's, 1 Lansdowne Place[16] and I accordingly went there – met her in the street and accosted her. She scarcely knew me on account of the quantity of whiskers. We took a cab and went together to dine with Mr. Hay. I slept there.

Everything seemed very strange to me as if it was ten years since I had seen the place. Now, what a remarkable thing that is! Some people say time passes quickly; others that it is very slow. If one stays ten years in one place, having the same occupation every day, time slips away without one's knowing it; but if on the other hand one changes the scene every day, and with it his occupation, two years appears quite as long as the other one's ten. Thus it is that some are frequently twenty years ahead of others in wisdom – that is if he has good sound common sense and makes use of it.

Others are sixty years old and never get any wiser than when they left school. Why? Because they have no minds of their own. Their opinions, their ideas, every one they have do not belong to them – they have stolen them from others. You hear one say, "There's a clever man. Observe him." And what is he clever in? Why is he clever? In the same way that a parrot is clever. He has learned by rote other men's ideas, and now brings them forward, second-hand, not having one single idea to call his own. And yet how many do you find like this? How often do you hear one asked his opinion on such and such an author – perhaps he has never read any of his works, but it is sufficient that the press and leading men say that he is good. He, of course, endorses it.

Do you call a man clever because he knows such and such a language? Because he has learned Greek or Latin etc., etc.? Pshaw! If you took time with a good grey parrot it could do the same, and a learned pig could be taught Mathematics. If a man who can neither read nor write has but one single idea of his own he has got more true knowledge than a dozen of your parrot-taught clever men. Let the idea be ever so small, if original and put into practice, it will add more to the progress of the world than if he had learned all that ever man wrote.

Tuesday 27th [March, 1855]. I received fifty pounds from the Governor who, although he approved much of my sending it home, did not at all like the thought of my drawing it from him again so fast. I called at the Bedford and paid Myers twenty pounds. And

Dresser and Allan, having lost their trunk on the railway, were pretty hard up for ready cash, so I lent them ten pounds. Although when I told the Governor he said, "Lend Yankees anything! I would sooner throw my money into the sea. I never heard of an honest Yankee. You need never expect to see that [any] more."

I certainly did expect it, but such is the prejudice of the stay-at-home Englishman that it is very hard to make one of them believe there are any honest men out of their own country.

I took my things away in a cab into which my noble Lister would willingly have placed his effects. But he was stopped by the waiter who recommended him to leave his carpet-bag until his debts were liquidated. Myers was fool enough to pay them after all, but he never heard any more of it after he left London, although he wrote to his address in Liverpool several times. Now, by George, I would let a robber or a murderer escape punishment rather than him, if I was to lay hands on him. If he had only written to say that he could not get the money – but had to go away in that dirty manner – and he was what the world would call a gentlemanly and very clever man.

28th March [1855]. I had a sail with Frank in his yacht, the *Razor Bill*. A very pretty little model she was with a centre board. He belonged to the Thames Yacht Club. But as for sailing, I had had nearly enough of it to care a great deal for it – dull work at the best of times without a girl and a good bottle of wine. We only went as far as Erith – the banks of the river below the bridge are not much after the Tamar and Derwent. We got back at dark and I slept at Hay's, not yet having taken up my abode at my regular house.

31st [March 1855]. Received of Governor 35 pounds – then went on board the *Chicora* which had arrived at the London Docks. The doctor had gone ashore but McNaughton was there in a delightful state of fourpenny. I sent Myer's trunk to Cowes as he had gone home before, being naturally anxious to see his wife and boy, not having heard of them for two years.[17] I paid Captain Alnack seven pound for liquor and invited him to dine with me at the Queen's, but he was too busy and I have not seen him since. I believe he has got the command of an Aberdeen clipper. If anyone can make a short passage he can, if he has a ship that will sail.[18]

I now went to the Queen's Hotel opposite the General Post Office. I had been recommended to it by Burge, as being a cheap house, but he has very little idea of economy. The London hotels are the most exorbitant in the world. Why even in Melbourne in the dear times one could get a board and lodging for three pounds per week, and they think it very cheap here if it is no more. They charge extra for everything and the imposition of waiters is 1/6 per day, and they expect to be paid extra for any little civility – twenty-seven pounds six shillings per annum for nothing. One could live on that amount in any reasonable civilised country.

Sunday April 1st [1855]. Made an April Fool of myself by going into one of her precious high churches with Fanny. St. Stephen's I think she called it, in Lincoln's Inn Fields. We dined at Legg's and I met with W. Patterson[19] who used to be a chum of mine at Moore's parent-robbing den called private boarding school. A deuced fine fellow I believe him to be and would have been clever if he had been at the right school. But, however, I think that very few of those kinds of schools do any good. One can learn more in one year after one leaves them, than one does all the time one stays there. The system is so rotten that learning becomes a pain to the boy instead of, as it ought to be, a pleasure. Verily they are altogether bosh. Public schools are the best. I'd sooner send my sons (if I had any) to a charity school, and then there is no favour.

Patterson was born in Paris, and educated by his aunt Mrs. Powell, a rich widow. I hardly recognised the plucky, adventurous boy in the quiet, inoffensive dapper little foreigner who sat down at Legg's table. And I have little doubt he looked with equal astonishment on the uncouth, devil-may-care gold-digger.

April 2nd [1855]. Called at Burge's and went with Fanny to Hay's. Charley and Patterson dined with me at the Queen's[20] and we went from there to the Lyceum, a concert night with which I was much disgusted and would willingly have cut my stick – came out and went to the Cyder Cellars. Did not get home until three o'clock. There is a great deal in knowing how to enjoy oneself. It takes a man some time to learn it even when he has no other employment. Now, I never enjoyed myself at that kind of game, was out of my element, spent a deal of money and played the deuce with health.

3rd [April 1855]. Dined at Burge's, a small party there, but I wasn't at my ease, not I. Asked an old maiden lady alongside of me, Miss Knight, the names of all the ladies round the table, and then took wine with them consecutively, because I thought it was etiquette. Of course I made lots of mistakes. If one's in Rome, they say, do as Rome does – well certainly I didn't do as I should have done on the diggings, viz. taken out my jack-knife and cut off a junk of bread and stuck a bit of meat, and then sat down comfortably before the fire. But I daresay I did things which seemed equally barbarous. After dinner the ladies leave the room and the men sit over their wine and talk bosh; until they get half-screwed and then begin to talk sense. Join the ladies in the drawing-room and some stupid little cups of tea are handed round by some of the gents.

It is considered the acme of politeness not to allow the ladies an opportunity to move their angel persons from their seats. I was rather glad of this as it gave me a turn to move my joints which had grown stiff with long sitting. I handed round the bread and butter in the same style as one would carry a bucket – the consequence was a capsize. Several other little incidents occurred which I can't remember just now. We had cards after tea. I joined in a rubber and the ladies and others had a round game in which considerable money was won and lost. Mrs. Clark, a remarkably fine woman, must have lost much for she continuously saluted her unfortunate little husband with, "Tommas, your purse!" – which he reluctantly handed over.

4th [April 1855]. Called at Burge's at 6. Found Mrs. Stokes and Dean, her grandmother, friends of my mother's, at Herne Bay – remembered them perfectly. Mr. Stokes had slit his windpipe a short time back and she was in mourning.[21] There was a young heiress with them, an Irish girl, who was shortly to be married. I went with them to Exeter Hall but the only seats vacant were a guinea each which was above our funds. It was a Lind night for the benefit of the widows and orphans of the Crimea.[22] So we went to the Great Globe in Leicester Square. A humbug of an affair, well enough to teach the young the idea of geography, and they want it badly enough, for it's shockingly neglected at English schools unless the youth is intended for the sea.

5th [April 1855]. Dined at Hay's. Got a pound of cigars. One can't get them good here under thirty-six shillings per pound, so its like smoking gold; and there is not much good tobacco here unless one pays an exorbitant price.

6th [April 1855]. I accompanied Mr. Burge to his son George's at Rochester about thirty miles from London. He has some cement works there.[23] I dined with him – he had just got set up in a house of his own, having been previously living at the Crown[24] at an extravagant rate. Also falling in love with the landlord's eldest daughter.[25] The parents and sisters disapproved much of the match. A publican is considered, in this country, a very low man. George is a chap who knows particularly well what good living is – in which he differs not much from his father. He turned out an excellent dinner of mock turtle, salmon, etc. – and a good bottle of port.

7th [April 1855]. Called at Hay's. Governor had gone to Hastings. Took Fanny, Ellen and some more to the Polytechnic, but found it closed so we went to Madame Tussaud's. Some of the models were very good, but I was not so much surprised as I was given to believe I should have been.

9th [April 1855]. George and Dinely[26] to Teythen's – he was going to take a situation in a tasting-house in China. Took a cab to the London Docks and went over his ship the *Eagle King*, a very pretty clipper. Went up St. Paul's for the first time. I thought it was free on certain days, but had to pay considerably for fees. They all dined with me – mock turtle, salmon and ducks, but not knowing the custom did not have any meat. However we made up for it in a bust of wine. Joe Peters was there. He had been to school with me at Winch's at the Bay.[27]

We all got rather lushy and Peters gave us a long yarn about getting in the same way once before and nearly losing his watch. It appeared that he always told the same yarn, and, as those present had heard it some dozen times before, it afforded much mirth. We took cabs and went to Caldwell's, Soho. George and his lass fell down and hurt the latter's head, or at least she pretended, so he was obliged to see her home.

10th [April 1855]. G.T. breakfasted with me and we saw him off. Called and saw H. Whaley, another Bay friend – I should not have remembered him. I took a private box in the Olympic and took the girls to the theatre. Saw Robson in *The Yellow Dwarf* – he was excellent (and in the double role unequalled).[28] One of Tom Taylor's was brought out and entitled *Still Waters Run Deep*. It was also very good.

11th [April 1855]. Dined at Hay's – to Kilpack's, Covent Garden, and had a game at bowls. This is the only American bowling alley I know of in London. It is an exceedingly nice game and exercise.

From the way this one fills it is a wonder there are not more. They would be likely to pay well.

12th [April 1855]. Called on the Governor and got another twenty pounds. This was going ahead like smoke, but one must pay for experience. Saw Mrs. Reed, an old lady with a wonderful lot of small talk. Paid my tailor, Babb, seven pounds fifteen shillings for a suit of black clothes. That's another great expense attending this island. One must keep up appearances and tailors are so exorbitant in their charges. Spent the evening at Burge's and had a round game. A nice family, the Burges – not so stuck up as some of the middle class of this country. Mr. Burge, a clever man, a contractor, built Box Tunnel and St. Katharine's Docks.[29] He had once a large fortune, but he lost considerably by building at Herne Bay and other speculations.

13th [April 1855]. Went to the Polytechnic. It used to be a very instructive place and amusing, but it has gone off much – and every public place one goes to one continually has "God Save the Queen" dinned into one's ears, and the asses get up and take off their hats! They say every man has a right to his own opinion – but consistently knock off anyone's hat and thrash him who does not conform to their trash. In the evening I went to Love's – a mimic and a bosh – wished I was off back to the Colonies. There's no pleasure in this – having no home and no companions except those I pay for; and then such a suicidal climate. This is what's called Spring – it's as cold as charity and raining every now and then. Oh, for sunny Australia, land of gold and freedom! Heigho!

14th [April 1855]. Fanny and Ellen going to school to Mrs. Taythen's at St. John's Wood. Called at H. Whalley's – he had a sore throat and could not come out. Had nothing to do and no one to talk to, so went down to Rochester – looked over the Castle which is in ruins, nothing remaining but the bare walls. I lost myself in the town. Chatham is a curious old-fashioned place built anyhow – very low of course, as there are so many soldiers into it.

16th [April 1855]. Came to town. George and I had our likenesses taken just by London Bridge, a daguerreotype, which I gave to Fanny. We dined at Burge's, ten of us, and we played whist. I won 3/6 and gave the servant 2/6.

17th [April 1855]. Had a game at bowls with Dinely and George. They dined with me at Queen's and then we went to Crean's singing and supper rooms. Sharp sang some amusing comic songs and Ross came out in his far-famed parody of *Hamlet*, which he did very well. But those rooms are so badly ventilated that one can scarcely see across the room for smoke.

The man who takes the money at the door has a hole in the middle of his forehead. He is a great rogue and frequently overcharges, usually making the charge one penny or so above the sixpence. And then it's "Waiter, sir! Please, sir!" and away goes your change. The obsequious manners of these menials, who at the same time are picking one's pocket, is enough to disgust anyone – but they can be saucy enough if they find that you are not to be done.

18th [April 1855]. Saw G. to the London Bridge Station, and went to Hay's. Got ten pounds from the Governor. Dined there. I now took it into my noodle to learn farming and wanted the Governor to give me some money to get a farm, or to go and learn off some farmer. He very wisely refused to do the former, although he did not grumble at the latter. So I asked George to write to Glennie, who was farming in Scotland, whether he would take a pupil, and what were his terms.

19th [April 1855]. Went to Burge's. The Emperor of the French, Louis Napoleon, came over from Paris on a visit to the Queen, and was about to pass through London in state with the Empress.[30] The last time he came here he was in a very different plight. He was then called everything that was bad; now nothing was too good for him. It shows the little dependence one can place either on the Press or people. A wicked man is never looked upon as wicked unless he fails in his undertaking – and no-one is good unless he prospers. Pshaw, it is altogether bosh!

Having nothing else to do, I took Fanny to see them. Business was stopped by proclamation. We went to my tailor's at the corner of Wellington Street in the Strand. Both sides of the street were lined with people. Nothing pleases John Bull more than useless pageantry. When the Emperor and his wife passed the shouts were deafening for a man who a few years previously they execrated. I had a good view of the Empress, who sat on our side. She was bowing. It must be pretty tiring to keep on it as long as she would have to do. She was very pretty, fair with clear complexion, finely chiselled features and a beautiful Grecian nose. Her spouse is a forbidding-looking fellow, quite her counterpart. The police kept the streets clear with their staves, for their majesties' carriages to pass, beating the populous over the shins.

The thought of it is very disgusting to a right-minded man. It makes one think very little of human nature that the race in a great nation could not keep order until driven back with force, like brute beasts by staves and the swords of mercenary blood-thirsters. I myself believe it is only because they have never been tried. It must be a bad cause that requires so much force to protect it.

Fanny went from there to Hay's to go with them to the Crystal Palace. I went to the Surrey Theatre and heard Wright.[31] He is a favourite of mine, always the same and so very natural. He makes no exertion, but is not as good as when he was at the Adelphi. He is getting old.

20th [April 1855]. I called on Ann Fezemeyer,[32] an old servant of my mother's, a good soul, and had been very kind to me after the former died. She had made me a present of a box of instruments when I sojourned at Moore's. Wishing to make her a present, I went with Mrs. Burge to select a black silk dress at Meekings for which I gave three guineas. Ann seemed pleased with it, but did not appreciate the fineness of the quality.

Mrs. Dean had a ticket for a private box in the Strand Theatre[33] and wished me to escort them, which I was happy to do. We saw Dickens's old Christmas piece *The Cricket on the Hearth*. What a natural writer he is![34] Folks may talk about their clever men, but it's the natural man who takes with the millions – as somebody said: "One touch of Nature makes the whole world kin."[35] This is a very small theatre, and of course uncomfortable. It's the great characteristic of British theatres – no cushions no backs and no room for one's limbs, and last, not least, no oxygen. All these very necessary accompaniments to good acting can be obtained with very little more expense to the proprietors, and would much increase his profits. The charges in most of the good theatres are far too high.

Saturday 21st [April 1855]. Mr. Burge called for me at the Queen's and we took the train to Rochester – saw George. The scenery on this line – south bank of the Thames – is not so tame as the generality about this part. Kent is considered the flower of England. If so, I would not give much for the rest of it. There is rather a pretty place called Abbeywood. We took the bus first, Rochester to Canterbury, and a fly to Herne Bay. We put up at the Pier Hotel, a fine large house which had been built by Mr B. at great expense but was now let for nothing. It commands a fine view of the pier and bay. It is altogether a very pretty place – a fine beach and not far from the beautiful village of Herne, a heavenly place (in summer). I have spent many happy hours there birdsnesting with Mr. Richmond. We never destroyed the nests, although we sometimes stole one egg. It was delightful employment to watch the nests day after day as the process of incubation went on.

Who shall say that man is worse for these peaceful and, some would say, lazy pursuits? Is such a man idle? No, his mind is constantly employed. He reads the book of Nature than which none can be more interesting. He goes each day to a more holy church than any of those built by the hand of man. He worships the Almighty and loves Him, as he looks on his works. Verily that man is pious though he never enters a church.

The charges are as exorbitant at this hotel as at any of the London ones. The people belonging to the house are very obsequious.

22nd [April 1855]. I accompanied Mr. Burge to church. There was a little boy in his pew whom I afterwards found to be his son Fred.[36] We dined with Clift, Lister and Fred; a first-rate dinner and some good wine after. I never dined with Mr. B. when he did not have it good. He is very fond of good living. Clift[37] was a lawyer, a little stumpy red-faced bloated man, very fond of his bottle and I should say inclining to apoplexy. Lister was related to the inventors of the patent gas burners and was in the gas business. We passed our time very agreeably, and in the evening took a walk up the pier with the pier-master Captain Gardiner, a very great character.[38] He gave us a long account of his inventions called the Tripper and Annihilator; also one for spiking guns quickly. The Government showed bad taste in not adopting them.

23rd [April 1855]. We left and I paid my bill which amounted to one pound two shillings – considering I had only been there one day and two nights – it was pretty well. We came to London by the steamer.

I went on in this way until 4th May [1855] but this hotel work was too expensive so I tried to get lodgings at Ann's, but she happened to be full. She recommended me to Mrs. Gill's, a few doors from her, No 32 Jewin Crescent. This is nearly on the Old Roman Wall and an interesting place for the antiquarian. It is close to St. Paul's, which is built on the highest ground in the city. I only paid twelve shillings a week for the bedroom and sitting room. I used to pay nearly as much for the servants at the Queen's, and no comfort either, for one has no sitting room and has one's meals in the coffee room.

I took the young ladies to Sadler's Wells Theatre, once famous for the sea pieces. We saw *Jack Sheppard* – Mrs Keeley taking that part. She is an excellent natural actress. All her family are good on the stage.[39]

5th [May 1855]. I went sailing in the *Razor Bill* with Charles Hay and young S——s. We got down as far as Gravesend which is twenty miles, and put up for the night at Waite's Hotel. Sunday morning we set sail, fair wind, ran up the Medway and brought up at Rochester. I left George's coat. He was not at home so we weighed again and brought up at a miserable-looking hole called Queenborough. Slept there. Monday we beat up with a foul wind – got to the wharf about five o'clock tired of pleasure trips by water. Went to the Adelphi.[40]

8th [May 1855]. Called at Burge's and had a round game. Met Miss Hanley.

9th May [1855]. Took Fanny and Eliza to the Crystal Palace at Sydenham.[41] I was disappointed in it, but it was because the place was not yet finished and it seemed too large for the things they had in it. The provisions were very good and not dear. It is a magnificent building and when the grounds are laid out will be a nice summer amusement. We called and had tea at my lodgings.

10th [May, 1855]. Went to Hay's – had lunch. A draft of ten pounds from Dresser and Allan which astonished the Governor who said it was a wonderful instance of honesty in a Yankee. I fancy he had not had much dealings with them or he would have altered his opinion. I sent Davis's box to him at Newton in W. Wales, and removed my things from the Queen's to my lodgings. I gave all my dirty shirts which I had worn during the voyage to the chamber-maid. A voyage is more expensive than one would imagine.

11th [May 1855]. I received a letter from Mrs. Mather,[42] my digging mate's mother, a Scotchwoman residing in Hawick about forty miles from Carlisle on the River Teviot. He had sent fifty pounds by me to her. She was very grateful and hearing that I wished to learn farming she invited me to her house to see how it was carried on in Scotland, for they are better farmers than the English. I accepted her kind invitation and she promised to meet me at Edinburgh.

I took my passage in the steamer. It is twenty-one shillings – provisions not included. We were two days on the passage. It was not very rough, but some of them were very sick. They were not at all companionable or communicative – the stay-at-home Englishman seldom is, – and altogether I was glad when we arrived at Granton Pier. There were a few flies there but they were all engaged, and hearing it was some distance I had apprehensions I should not get my portmanteau up. The porter who passed it ashore indignantly refused fourpence which I offered, thinking it was quite enough for all he did – was told that they all had sixpence. They do not appear to be so anxious for a job here as in London, and not nearly so many poor are seen. They are well-informed and altogether a superior class. This is simply because education is so much more general. One seldom hears of a Scotchman not being able to read.

Fortunately a gentleman offered me a place in his fly. He had been to London with his invalid daughter. He did not go all the way, but told me that I need not fear any imposition, the drivers being more conscientious than those in London. I went on to Salisbury Street where I was to meet Mrs. Mather. She met me with unfeigned satisfaction, happy to see anyone who came from her son Dan. She was as much interested in me as if she had known me for years. The house, or rather floor, belonged to a relation of hers, who was very kind.

Most of the people here live on floors or flats, eight or nine families sometimes living in one house. The consequence is that very rich persons and very poor often live in the same house, the prices being regulated according to the flat. The ground floor is the most expensive and the upper one the cheapest.

Her friend's name was Henderson. She had two sons in a brewery, very well-informed young men. They much recommended ale in preference to porter which they say is awfully adulterated with bullocks' blood, liquorice, vitriol, etc. I think the taste for all malt liquors is an acquired one. I was very fond of it before going to sea, but being obliged to do without it there, I do not care a pin for it now. And as for London porter, I perfectly believe what they say, for whenever I take it at dinner it sends me to sleep, from which I wake up feverish and unrefreshed.

One of them showed me over the city which is very clean and orderly. The new town is beautifully laid out, in precisely the same manner as Melbourne, viz. the streets being wide and running at right angles. The houses on the old side are very high and built in most curious places, in consequence of the hills. There is a fine walk around Arthur's Seat giving a view of the city and country. A fine monument is erected to Sir Walter Scott near the Scottish Gallery of Painting. The admission to the latter place is sixpence. I was so struck with the very excellent collection that I went there several times.

Women of loose habits are prevented from walking the streets, or indeed from stopping on them, which has the effect of driving them to worse places. All these kind of preventives increase the number rather than diminish. There is only one way of putting a stop to it – don't encourage them. If there were no bad men there would be no prostitutes. He (my guide) wished me to go to the theatre where, he said, there were the keenest critics in the world. If an actor can pass these boards with success he can pass any other. The London favourite, Charles Kean,[43] was hissed off the stage – any trash goes down with a London audience. They prefer pageantry to good acting. I did not however avail myself of the theatre as there were some pieces acting there which I had seen before.

The old lady was very fond of seeing the sights and told me she indulged in a tour every year. Her husband used to keep an hotel in Hawick, but he was dead and she had retired from business with her daughter aged sixteen and her son, nine. Her two eldest sons were at the diggings. She had lots of cousins in all the towns of Scotland and she purposed going with me to Glasgow in a few days. We made sundry calls at different places. At all I was introduced – whisky and bread and cheese was placed on the table, the former handed round in wine glasses neat. They appear offended if you do not take a wee drop – which they call "taking a tile off the house". It is the practice to wish everyone good health before drinking which is a very annoying custom.

I can safely affirm that the English are prejudiced against the Scotch for what they call stinginess without the slightest cause. I met with far more hospitality during my short stay than I have during several years in England. If you call waste generosity why the English housewives are truly generous. Were an English lady to do the same as a Scotch one – viz. look after the dinner, children or other useful things, she would instantly lose caste. There is also much more equality here – caused by education. Clergymen and bankers of high respectability do not think it beneath them to sit to meals with mill girls or tradesmen; and as for hospitality, there was I, a perfect stranger in Hawick, invited to the house of Mr. Cathree a wealthy banker; to the owner of several large mills (the owner has an unpronouncable name so I won't try to spell it) and to several other highly-respectable people. I also saw several instances of true benevolence, of the rich visiting the poor and sick, bringing with them little comforts. The English may learn much besides farming from their much-slandered neighbours.

We only stopped three days in Edinburgh. There are two lines of rail to Glasgow. They run in opposition and the fares were remarkable. The fare was only sixpence, for this nearly fifty miles, the Edinburgh and Glasgow Line. The country is rather pretty at this time of year. We were not long on our journey as there was no stoppage. Like most manufacturing cities there is a great number of poor, and an immense number of mill girls. I was much surprised to see them without shoes or stockings – some very pretty ankles they have too! It appeared to me to be a very depressed place; much drunkeness was going on. It was different to Edinburgh.

The Clyde is a very fine stream and much picturesque scenery on its banks, but as we only stayed there two days I had not much opportunity of judging the town. I was not much pleased with it. We called at several houses. They live on flats as in Edinburgh and are very kind and hospitable.

We went by train to Hawick, took our tickets for the second class but were shown into a first-class carriage, and on taking them at the end of the journey they tried to make me pay again; but I refused and they let it pass. There was a remarkably pretty girl in the same carriage but she did not go the whole distance. Hawick is a very nice place, and some pretty walks are to be had on the banks of the Teviot. I had purchased a fly-rod at Glasgow and commenced thrashing the stream, but it is too much netted by the public to afford much sport near the town, and the trout do not run very large. I hired a fly very cheap and took some very nice drives to Galashiels, Minto Hills, etc. Had some shooting on Lord Minto's estate and did well – rabbits, hares, etc. The latter are very tough though.

The girls here seem most anxious for husbands, but the men are very scarce, large numbers having gone to Australia and America. The Scotch appear to emigrate much more than the English. Their prejudices are scarcely as strong and they are more enterprising.

Lord Wilton has a very pretty estate on the banks of the river but most of the landed property belongs to the Duke of Buccleuch. One of Mrs. Mather's cousins who had a large farm kindly showed me much of the farming business but at the same time advised me not to commence, as he said it was a very poor speck. I should be rather inclined to doubt it as he has made considerable money at it.

I stayed here nearly three weeks and was very much pleased with it. It has never been my lot to experience so much kindness from anyone, leave alone from entire strangers. Mrs. M. made me a present of a little black bull terrier, yclept Halp.[44] I took the coach to Carlisle, but had some difficulty to get the dog to stay on the box, but at last I let him run, which he did the whole distance. The country was hilly, but few trees were to be seen. It was scarcely so interesting as I should have expected from reading accounts of the Borders. The coachman was not communicative, but civil. We changed horses every ten miles. I had paid my fare at Hawick and was rather surprised by being asked at the end of the journey "to remember the coachman". Being quite unaccustomed to stage travelling I offered him sixpence which he indignantly refused, telling me that he always had five shillings. I was unwilling to submit to this imposition and, having made enquiries and found it was usual, gave him half-a crown but would not give a farthing more.

I put up at the White Hart and there made another mistake by going into the Commercial Room instead of the Coffee Room, thinking all public rooms alike; and as Halp came with me one of these Commercial snobs tried to expel him by force. But he would by no means submit to that, and made free with the gent's trousers, much to my inward satisfaction. I quieted him off, and the gent had the impudence to ask why I was in the Commercial Room, not being a traveller. I replied that I should not have come there had I known I was to meet a snob like him. He left the room in high dudgeon.

In the middle of the night I was awakened by loud cries, attended with barks and slight screams. On opening my door who should rush in but my noble dog Halp. He had been accustomed to sleep with his master and, having posted himself at the door, had prevented anyone from coming up the passage. The cries proceeded from the domestics who were endeavouring to expel the faithful friend. I tried to induce him to go downstairs, but in vain, so I allowed him to stay in, much to the satisfaction of the visitors of whom about a dozen were collected in various elegant night costumes, armed with chamber utensils and keeping close together with a view to mutual protection. I inwardly cursed the humbugs and returned to bed with my poor dog.

I took a walk through the town next morning but didn't think much of it – no scenery in the environs, streets dull and dirty. Took my passage to London – had to pay for Halp. I had a long conversation with one of my fellow passengers, a soldier. He was about to leave the army and retire on pension. He said he was deuced glad to get clear; that he had been misled like a good many others with the fair outside, but soon found it was quite rotten at the core. The puff in the papers of the brave defenders was all bosh – anyone would fight when urged on by the music and excitement. Put a rat in a corner and he would fight. If the English knew half the horrors of that system which levels man with the brute beast they would not be so fond of engaging in it for the veriest trifles. Thus spoke the veteran, and I doubt not he spoke the minds of many of his comrades who are thus made to prostitute their strength and health, to become hired assassins at every brute's beck and call, for the greedy ambition of the few and the folly of the many.

Very glad to get back again – don't like travelling. It's an infernal bore – humbugged about and kept no log – spent a good deal of money and got no pleasure for it.

July 7th [1855]. I found it impossible to keep the dog in London. Everyone is frightened of a little dog they could eat in half an hour. I was at last obliged to give it to George Burge at Rochester. Went down and put up at the Crown. George was enamoured of the hotel-keeper's daughter, H. Wilson. We dined there – had a first-rate dinner attended with curious blue. His dog went mad.

On Monday I came to town and led a dissipated life – had a spree in the Haymarket, mauled a policeman and escaped.

10th July [1855]. Called at Burge's – saw Mr. Matheson who looked very ill. I wished to give him two sovereigns but Mrs. B. would not. He said he had been discharged from the army and could not get into the police.

11th [July 1855]. Chiswick Flower Show. The girls talked of going but, as usual, it rained all day. Frank wrote to Captain Neatby and thanked him for advertising for me when I was on the diggings.[45] Went to the Olympic – Robson's benefit. Could not get a seat in the pit so went in the gallery.

I got the Governor to give his consent to my learning farming, and accordingly Cyrus Legg[46] wrote to a Mr Bolling, a farmer at Hassocks Gate,[47] and the Governor met him and settled to take me for a hundred pounds a year; one of those d——d impositions that people are accustomed to in this country. The idea of a man going to work on a farm and paying to be allowed to do so! I went down to see them and found his wife a fidgety, nervous lady. She offered me some bread and cheese, and being very hungry, having had to walk from the station about five miles, I was much in need of it. When she heard I had been to Australia she seemed alarmed and thought that their quiet house would not suit.

I saw Bolling but did not think much of him. As he was going to send to that station for some sacks he offered me a lift in his cart. I was to come down in a week. I wrote to him asking to take the dog with me, which he refused, so I broke up the engagement, telling him that as we disagreed in such a trifle it were better to part in peace. He answered saying that he was rather pleased as he did not like shady tricks, and I had scored the toll against him after he had been kind enough to give me a ride in his cart. This was true, but it was from carelessness. The gate had been passed unperceived by me, or undoubtedly I should have done so, but even allowing that, it would have been shabby if he had lent me the cart. One can scarcely think so as he sent for his own sacks and gave me a lift by the way. Heigho, it was one of those lucky misfortunes which have so frequently happened in my travels. We pursue the course we think best, and if we fail in it we think it a great misfortune; when at the same time the very failure is turning us from destruction to happiness. "L'homme propose et Dieu dispose." [48]

Thus ended my farming freak – another of my foolish bubbles had burst. It's not a bit of use pushing and fretting to get through the world. Don't swim against the tide. Get astride of a dead log and float quietly down with the stream, take everything as a matter of course, and ten to one if something doesn't bring you up all standing before long.

Fanny and Eliza got acquainted with a tall man with a black moustache in Hyde Park, and a flirtation began between Eliza and him. They introduced him to me and I, like a good-mannered fool, consented to introduce him to Mrs. Burge as one of my friends from Australia. Now I did very wrong in this business, but I at all events had one excuse – that the girls wanted it. I knew very little of women, or of the class that they mixed with, or indeed of the artificial society of this part of the world at all. But I had no excuse for mixing with them in deception and telling a lie to deceive a fond mother. I have been punished for it as all those who depart from the truth usually are. I got blamed by the mother, blamed by the girls, ditto by Sweetman and ditto by myself. I went to several places with them – to the Zoological Gardens, theatres, etc., and finally introduced him to get rid of the bother after we had dined together at Simpson's and I was merry after a bottle of curious blue. Whether Mrs. B. saw through the game or not I don't know, but at all events I made myself very disagreeable by objecting to every place of amusement which was proposed; sometimes saying I did not like one and sometimes another – for the truth was I wished to get clear of the blessed job after getting up to my neck in it. At last Mrs. B. got up in the stirrups and said in a positive tone, "Now I've made up my mind. You shall not go anywhere. No, oh no! That you shall not!" And walked majestically from the room.

Dear old lady! It always delights me when I get up to an excitable point, particularly in politics, and I think she agrees with me sometimes, in what folks call my radical humbug. Having now made myself thoroughly disagreeable to all hands I walked home in no very pleasant frame of mind. I usually go on at this game until it comes to sticking point and then I'm sorry for it. At this time, having no company, I used to muse over all the disagreeable occurrences of the day and curse myself for my folly, resolving never to do so again. It is a very bad plan and the resolves never come to anything. I have given it up lately and seldom muse over an unpleasant circumstance, such as doing something awkwardly or saying something foolish, and I find it an improvement to drive it from one's mind by force or some vigorous exercise.

This is the greatest and almost only evil of being alone and having nothing to do. Therefore endeavour not to muse on disagreeable subjects. It is this and this alone that is the cause of a suicide. He thinks and muses and dreams away over a trifling jar over his sensitive mind until the molehill becomes a mountain. He turns it over and over again until it is like rolling a snowball on snow. It becomes enormous and maddens him and at last he rashly plunges into that bourn from which no traveller returns.[49] A sensitive mind without delicate moral cultivation is a curse rather than a blessing to its owner, and until those feelings become blunted he is no use for mixing among his fellow men.

I have often noticed that those who feel a cut most are the least cautious how they inflict one on others. Speaking for myself (for I shall not spare myself), I often say things to others that I should feel much hurt if said to me. Now that is a strange anomaly in human nature, and it's the same in many other things. For instance, a captain tyrannises over his officers, the officers over the crew and the crew, instead of correcting their conduct by the folly of the officers, tyrannise over the boys; and when they get into office they are as bad as the others. I have often heard it said, "When I was a boy I used to have a good rope's ending when I did so-and-so, and therefore here goes into you" – and thwack goes the rope. When will the world understand that angelic saying, "Do unto others as you would they should do unto you" – not as they have done unto you?

They (the girls) still continued to meet him [Sweetman] occasionally, and in order to get out of his way I went to Herne Bay with George. Besides, it seemed as though they were making a fool of me, and anyhow playing second fiddle is not in my line. I had a kind of sneaking regard for Lizzie. A very nice good-natured girl she is and will doubtless make an excellent wife. Thinking that it would be better for all parties if these clandestine meetings were put a stop to,

I told George of the matter, knowing that to tell him was equivalent to telling everyone else. I had been to Sweetman's lodgings at Camden Town, and as he was a widower with two children and merely a life salary of two hundred pounds a year in the Post Office, it was anything but a desirable match for Lizzie. As I expected, George told Mama and she gave it to the girls and commended me for the latter proceeding. But on the whole, like the man who tried to please everybody I got blamed by everyone instead. Ah, well! One must pay for experience. But the worst of it is when one has to pay and at the same time derives no benefit, for the more scrapes I get into the more foolish I become.

Went to the Bay and put up at the Pier Hotel. George and I had some glorious swims together. He is as strong as a young donkey and is an agreeable companion when he pleases; but like most of the Burges he sadly wants application. Well, we are none of us perfect. We walked into curious blue together one night until it walked into us, causing us to commit sundry feats. Twelve o'clock found us on the pier (sailing the cars up and down) growing poetical.[50] We wished to rush into the waves by way of acknowledging their beauty. Went to Grove Ferry and Reculver fishing. We caught little, but it suited George who is a reflective man and will frequently stand stock-still in the middle of the road, with glass in eye, gazing vacantly at horse droppings.

These places were full of associations of my childish days although I fancy they are not altogether pleasing. One naturally thinks how much better one might have done. Still when anything is over how little it looks. I always try to impress that on my mind, when about to undertake anything new and of seeming importance, that when it's over it will not be of near the importance it is before it's begun. Things are very easy when one sets at them with determination, and obstacles are only bugbears to frighten children with. They vanish directly one charges them. Quickness and talent are all very well, but they are nothing without perseverance. With the latter quality a stupid man will go ahead of a wise one, and it is not a gift either because any man may plant it in himself. But of course it greatly depends upon the way one is brought up in childhood. I suppose the word "impossible" is in every language, and yet it's a most stupid one because there is no such thing. Verily, it's altogether bosh.

On leaving and calling for the bill I found the charges pretty high, and moreover my noble Steer had stuck all George's expenses down to me and pretended not to see it at all. But as I stuck out firmly against them, but offered to pay for the wine, Steer made the necessary deduction. I don't like underhand tricks and I had lent George a five pound note a few days back – and by the bye never had it offered me again. They thought the digger a fool, but were mistaken a trifle.

V

GREATER EXPECTATIONS

(A voyage in the clipper 'Red Jacket' from Liverpool to Melbourne. Martin Massey Milward, Commander, 2460 tons registered. Commences 20th September 1855.)

Came up to town and called at Hay's. He told me that he had made my fortune, having heard that I had an uncle in Maitland, New South Wales.[1] He was very rich, had farms and houses, etc; had been there upwards of twenty years and had lately made enquiries as to whether his sister had any children living, and if so he would provide for them. "Well," thought I, "This is indeed a chance," and although I want nothing from him, he may probably set me on one of his farms. Mrs. Hay had known him before he left the country and from what I could learn, (for she had, it appeared, promised the Governor to say nothing to dissuade me from going) she did not think much of him.

At all events I determined to go, and as I had had quite enough of small ships and their four month passages, I took my passage in as large a one as possible, one of the White Star Line of packets, yclept *Red Jacket*.[2] But as she did not start for three weeks I went down to the Wight with a view of spending a short time with my sister.

I found the Ancient Mariner, Myers, had taken a lodging house at 3 Pelham Place, but it did not pay so well as he expected and therefore he got a mate's place on the *Red Coat* a small brigantine bound to the Mediterranean.[3] I saw him off and he gave me a gold ring in lieu of the five pounds I had lent him. He did not seem to relish the idea of going on the briny after such a long spell of the diggings, but "needs must when the devil drives."

Fanny and I went sailing in a little boat, and being very rough we got wet through; but like most of the ladies when they catch cold and get seasick, she said she had a delightful sail.

I went back to London and found the Governor had gone to Brighton so I posted off after him. I could not bleed him for more than sixty pounds and got a good rowing for that. Finding that it would be insufficient, I borrowed another twenty pounds from Frank. I spent the last evening with them.

Sunday, 16th September, 1855. Set out for Liverpool at 8 p.m. Fanny and Mr. Burge saw me off. It was a night train and consequently a fast one. I arrived at Liverpool about three o'clock in the morning. A number of Irish quarrelled for a share of my luggage, but by dint of much determination got it all on one truck. Soon reached the Railway Hotel and ensconced myself. Another man came with me from the train. A little eccentric character, he stuck out that one shilling for the truck was too much. I found out afterwards that this little fellow was our doctor, it being his first voyage taken for the benefit of his health.

Next morning I went on board with luggage. The *Red Jacket* is without exception the most beautiful model I ever saw. I had taken my passage and I paid the remainder at Pilkington and Wilson's, Water Street. The first man belonging to the ship I made acquaintance with was Beckham,[4] a very stout handsome young man, who talked much and had been to the Colonies before. We went ashore together. I invited him to take a bottle of wine with me, which he did; and talking about Australia, we were accosted by an old gentleman, who we learned was a Sydney man. I asked him if he knew a W. Burgess of Maitland. He replied that he did, but that he was a great blackguard. The prospect began to darken. However I thought

RIGHT: The diary of James Montagu Smith. Collection: Jean Truebridge.

BELOW: James Montagu Smith, 1836-1888. Collection: Jean Truebridge.

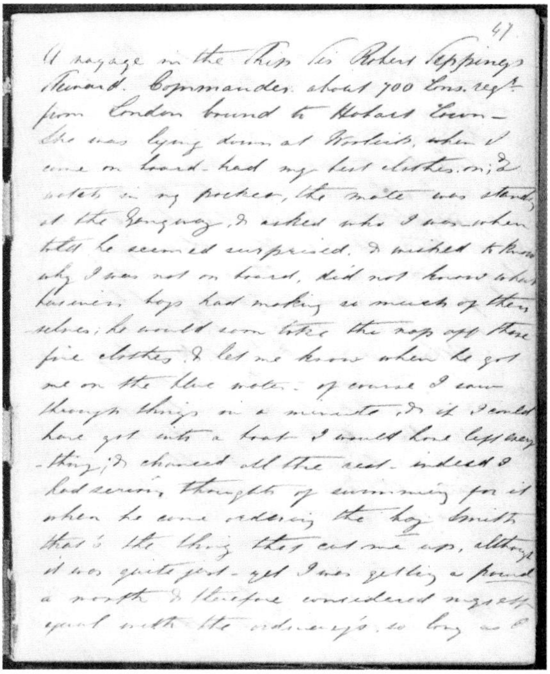
41
A voyage in the Ship Sir Robert Seppings
Renard. Commander. about 700 tons. regt
from London bound to Hobart Town —
She was lying down at Woolwich, when I
came on board - had my best clothes on; a
watch in my pocket, the mate was standing
at the Gangway, he asked who I was - when
told he seemed surprised. he wished to know
why I was not on board, did not know what
business boys had making so much of them
selves; he would soon take the nap off those
fine clothes, & let me know when he got
me on the blue water - of course I saw
through things in a minute, & if I could
have got into a boat I would have left every
-thing, & chanced all the rest - indeed I
had serious thoughts of swimming for it
when he came ordering the boy Smith
that's the thing that cut me up, although
it was quite just - yet I was getting a pound
a month & therefore considered myself
equal with the ordinary's. so long as I

Merchantman under full sail, 1850s. Collection: Barbara Cuffley.

1 Flying jib
2 Jib
3 Fore top-mast stay sail
4 Fore course
5 Fore-top sail
6 Fore-top-gallant sail
7 Fore-royal
8 Fore-sky sail
9 Fore-royal studding sail
10 Fore-top-gallant studding sail
11 Fore-top-mast studding sail
12 Main course
13 Main-top sail
14 Main top-gallant sail
15 Main-royal
16 Main-sky sail
17 Main royal studding sail
18 Main top-gallant studding sail
19 Main top mast studding sail
20 Mizzen course
21 Mizzen top sail
22 Mizzen top-gallant sail
23 Mizzen royal
24 Mizzen sky sail
25 Mizzen spanker

ABOVE: *North-East View of the Settlement of Port Arthur.* This pencil drawing by an unknown artist is dated to 1854, some two years after James was there as a sailor on the convict ship, the *Sir Robert Seppings.* Collection: Allport Library and Museum of Fine Arts, Hobart.

LEFT: James was imprisoned in one of the solitary confinement cells built as part of the foundations of Trinity Church, Hobart. This lithograph by Henry Melville appeared in the *Hobart Town Magazine* in 1834. Collection: Tasmaniana Library, State Library of Tasmania, Hobart.

BELOW: Royal Pier Hotel and St George's Terrace, Herne Bay, Kent, 1854. James lived at 7 St George's Terrace as a young boy. Collection: Harold Gough, Herne Bay.

TOP: *Melbourne Wharf looking South-West from Custom House Reserve.* This lithograph by S.T. Gill is dated 1853. James and his friends stayed at the Yarra Family Hotel, the three-storey corner building seen beyond the Customs House steps. Collection: Rex Nan Kivell Collection, National Library of Australia.

ABOVE: This view of Forest Creek diggings was engraved in 1853 by W.A. Nicholls for John Sherer's *The Gold-Finder of Australia*. James first saw this scene in July 1853, and would remember his time in the area as the happiest days of his life. Collection: Peter Cuffley.

CAMPBELL
TEMPLETON
LYTLETON
MOSTYN
FOREST
STREET
GAOL RESERVE
POUND
SEC. D. 8
SEC. D. 7
SEC. D. 6
SEC. D 5
SEC. D. 4
SEC. D. 3
SEC. D. 2
SEC. D 3
Winter's Flat
GOVERNMENT CAMP
Clinker's Hill
New Chum Gully
Dead Horse Gully
GAINSBOROUGH
LANDSEER
LAWRENCE
ETTY
MACLISE STREET
WILKIE STREET
Surface Workings
Lushington Lead
Lushington Hill
Diamond Flat
Diamond Hill
Diamond Gully
Old Diamond Hill
Preshaw's Flat
CAMPBELL'S CREEK
Tunnel
Seventy Foot Hill
CHINESE RESERVE
SEC. E
SEC. 4 A
Little Specimen Gully
Specimen Flat
Crow Gully
Johnny o Groat's Flat
Campbell's Flat
Cemetery Flat
LEMAINE CEMETERY
SEC. I.B.
White Flat
The White Hill
Little Poverty Gully
Poverty Reef
Cumberland Flat
Poverty Flat
The Five Flags
NATIONAL SCHOOL RESERVE
SEC. I. A.
Hill Lead

RIGHT: This advertisement appeared in vol. 1, no. 1 of the *Age* (Melbourne) on 17 October 1854. It was the paper's first paid advertisement. Collection: State Library of Victoria.

BELOW: The *Hobart Town Courier*, April 1853. Collection: State Library of Tasmania.

FOR MELBOURNE DIRECT.

THE well-known and favourite brigantine
SWORD FISH,
Captain JOHN CLINCH,
Now arrived will sail for the above port viz ten days from this date. For freight or passage apply to the master on board or to
C. LOVETT.
Franklin Wharf, April 13. 1222

SHIPPING ADVERTISEMENTS.

FOR LONDON Direct.—The barque CHICORA.
550 tons, is appointed to sail about the 24th instant. This fine vessel for strength is surpassed by none in Hobson's Bay, and her fast-sailing qualities are well known, she having been some time in the trade here.

Shippers will find this a most favorable and early opportunity to send home Wool, Tallow and other produce, which will be taken at low rates.

She can accommodate ten cabin passengers, who would find this a most desirable conveyance, where every care will be taken to provide everything to make them comfortable, and where greater quiet and enjoyment can certainly be had than when exposed to the annoyance necessarily arising from crowded passenger ships.

For further information and particulars apply to WILLIAM BARKER, 93 Flinders Street, West.
1 3t

OPPOSITE PAGE: Mining map of Castlemaine (detail), Mining Department, Melbourne, 6 November 1861. James and his mates were working on Campbells Creek, and cut bark in Diamond Gully. Collection: Castlemaine Historical Society. CMHS 1997-1502.

ABOVE: Originally drawn in 1852, this view shows a digger's hut of canvas and bark at Forest Creek. Sheets of bark were both waterproof and insulating. Collection: Peter Cuffley.

RIGHT (top): The *Argus* (Melbourne) 14 November 1854. Collection: State Library of Victoria.

RIGHT: The *Argus* (Melbourne) 8 December 1855. Collection: State Library of Victoria.

SHOULD this meet the eye of James Montague Smith, supposed to be at Mount Alexander, he is requested to communicate with Henry Nealby, Ship Vimiera, Sydney, New South Wales.
142 nov 18 d and b

IF this should meet the eye of John Burge, late of Herne Bay, his friends are anxious to hear from him, and if he would write to his old friend James Smith, George and Dragon, East Maitland, he will give him particulars from home. 329

RIGHT: This engraving of Old Neptune's Car was published in February 1855, just six months before James and George Burge junior would go 'sailing' up and down one midnight, 'growing poetical'. The upright figure with a light-coloured waistcoat is Captain Cornelius Gardiner, the piermaster.
Collection: Harold Gough, Herne Bay, Kent.

ABOVE: In this 1851 view of the pier at Herne Bay we can clearly see the tramline.
Collection: Harold Gough, Herne Bay, Kent.

Herne Bay Pier Company.

This is to Certify that Alfred Fowler of 73 St John St Clerkenwell London is a PROPRIETOR of one Share No [illegible] in the HERNE BAY PIER COMPANY, subject to the several Powers & Provisions of an Act of Parliament, passed in the 2nd Year of the Reign of William the 4th Cap 25, whereby the said Company was incorporated, and to the several Bye Laws made or to be made, by Virtue of the said Act, and that the said Alfred Fowler his Executors, Administrators, and Assigns, is and are entitled to all Profits and advantages, arising in respect of such Share.

Given under the Common Seal of the said Company, the twenty seventh day of May in the Year of our Lord 184[illegible]

BY ORDER OF THE BOARD OF DIRECTORS.

Clerk to the Company.

No. [illegible]

NB. All Transfers and Assignments of this Share, must be duly registered by the Clerk of the Company, otherwise the same will not be valid.

RIGHT:
Collection: Harold Gough.

ABOVE: The clipper ship *Red Jacket* carried James from Liverpool to Melbourne in 1855. It was one of the fastest sailing ships ever built. This picture appeared in the *Illustrated Melbourne Post* of 7 February 1863.
Collection: La Trobe Picture Collection, State Library of Victoria.

LEFT: *The Invalid Digger* was S.T. Gill's title for this picture. In mid-1856, James was similarly struggling with a sore foot. Engraving by W.A. Nicholls after S.T. Gill, 1853.
Collection: Peter Cuffley.

BELOW: Diggers carried as much as they could when freight was very expensive. This 1853 engraving has been 'borrowed' from an 1852 lithograph by S.T. Gill, with the main figures reversed. Collection: Peter Cuffley.

ABOVE: George Stansell Septimus Smith, 1886-1981. Collection: Jean Truebridge.

TOP RIGHT: Marion Smith (née Harmon), c. 1848-1920, wife of James Montagu Smith. Collection: Jean Truebridge.

RIGHT: Viola Smith, 1867-1940, with Viola May Fuller, her niece. Collection: Jean Truebridge.

LEFT: Smith family at Nulla Nulla, Hinton, c. 1900. Left to right: Marion Smith, Viola, Fanny, Harold and Reginald. Collection: Jean Truebridge.

of that very rotten proverb "a bad beginning makes a good ending" – which it never did nor never will. I gulped down my wine in disgust.

The owners of this line keep a man to show passengers where to buy their things, and also what things they want on the passage. This is a good plan providing the man is trustworthy. I went with him and bought some preserved salmon, sardines and meats, tin plate, pot, water can, slop pail, mattress, etc. This man, yclept James Sunderland, pitched a long yarn about wishing to get out to the Colonies as a gents' servant, and wished to wait on myself and Beckham; but we did not want him. He then tried to get up a subscription to pay his passage to America, and we were fools enough to give him a couple of pounds. He kept very close to me with a view of showing me about the town, but I began to see through him – that he was a downright sponge.

I spent a good deal of money at a kind of dress house and became acquainted with a lady by name Stanley, from the Isle of Man; and she knew, or pretended to know, an old mate of mine, Jack, and wished much to take a passage in the *Red Jacket*. But it was too expensive, and my cash had run pretty small.

I went on board the night before she sailed and slept in the house on deck, but found the bunk so small that together with Beckham I determined to transfer into the cabin or fore saloon. Beckham got a berth and Wilson promised me one; but as I was to have the one at present occupied by the third mate, I had to wait until he moved.

We set sail the next morning, 20th September, 1855. A tug took us clear of the land. Wilson left in the tug. I paid my extra passage money. It was thirty pounds for house on deck, and thirty-two for fore saloon, and as one wanted nothing in the latter, all my extra provisions, mattress and tin ware, was useless. I subsequently gave it to Seater, a man I knew on the diggings who had gone home for his wife. He was a native of the Orkneys.[5] We had been on board some time before he recognised me.

The saloon was fitted up in a splendid style, all painted and varnished white and gold, two large mirrors at each end. The after saloon was carved with mahogany with a library at each end. The difference in the accommodation was nothing and we dined off the same table. It is more fitting for single ladies and that's all.

The provisions were excellent. Breakfast at eight – eggs, milk, hot rolls, fish, cutlets and pastry every morning; luncheon at twelve, usually salmon, herring or oysters and bread and cheese. Dinner at three consisting of all kinds of soups, poultry, fish, meats and pastry; tea at seven, of which only a few of the passengers partook. Some again had supper but it was not a general thing and only to be obtained by getting around the steward.

Wines, ales and spirits were to be procured at a moderate price of the purser. If one required any you only had to ask the boy for a card, write on it what was wanted, the date and your name. This was sent to the purser who in return sent your wine, which, after drinking as much as you thought proper, was labelled and stood in the swinging rack over your head so as to be handy for the next time. At the end of the week all these cards were sent you together with the bill. I am sorry to say that my bill frequently came to far more than I could at all afford. Nearly all the passengers in the cabin were great lushingtons and we used to sit for too long over our bottles. They gave you no trust if you did not pay your bill at the week's end. The purser would dishonour your card altogether. It is an excellent plan and much better for all parties than the wines and spirits being found you, and although sold cheaper than they could be bought ashore, duty included, yet the price was sufficiently large for the retailer to gain a good profit.

In each berth were two bunks, my companion being the second

mate, a very rough Jack Tar of the old school, but a good seaman. Had I been a landsman I should doubtless have experienced much inconvenience, and as it was I was occasionally roused up by the boy of the mate's watch, a cunning young shaver under the patronage of the first mate. He used to open the door quietly and see all clear for a run, [then] sing out, "Mr. Ballomono, hallo, sir – not up yet? Why it's eight bells, eight bells! Turn out! – the mate says he shan't wait any longer!" – The bells had gone about a second before. The only answer he would get from Ballomono would be, "Humph, humph!" but this would not do for the boy, who would walk softly in and suddenly give B. a good shaking, repeating the former dialogue. Up would start B, and out would go the boy in the twinkling of an eye. A volley of oaths, and perhaps boots, would be answered by a slight chuckle in the distance.

Down would come the first mate, a very eccentric Irishman, yclept O'Halloran, not much of a practical seaman, although I doubt not a good theoretical one.[6] He had received a college education and had risen to his present station through interest. He prided himself upon being much of a lady-slayer and had one or more sweethearts every passage. He would willingly pay for a child, to be honoured by the name of father. Ballomono said that he was paying half-a-crown per week for a couple, although as he shrewdly added, "I wouldn't like to swear as how they were mine for a' that."

Well, O'Halloran would appear at the door. "Mr. B., Mr. B. Oh, I see you're rising. Happy am I to see it, for I was about to turn in, tired of waiting for you."

"Now, just look here," replied B, "if you don't tell that d——d boy of yours to call me in a proper manner and not pull me half out of the bunk I'll break his cursed young neck."

"Oh, if that really is the case I will punish him severely. Here, boy. Did you pull Mr. B. nearly out of bed at eight bells?" said O'Halloran, winking at him.

"Lor, no, sir," replied the boy looking very innocent, with a slight smile playing upon his lips, "but when I comes and calls Mr. B. it ain't no use, sir. It ain't indeed – and then I just touches him and he flies up and swears awful and shies boots at me."

"There, there! I thought so. Now you can turn in."

"Well," said B. petrified with astonishment, "Did you ever hear such a d——d young liar!"

"No swearing if you please, Mr. B., and do me the favour to come on deck. The ship may be lost whilst you take so much time to put on your trousers. – Ah, Mr. Smith, how are you tonight? Has the noise awakened you? There's a light breeze sprung up from the northward."

"Oh, I'm glad of that," replied I, "but I wish you two would not make quite so much row when you relieve watch. Will you take a drop of this?"

"If you please, and I daresay B. won't refuse," said O'Halloran.

"Oh, no!" replied B. who had now recovered his good humour, "but not that infernal sour stuff. I'll have a little of the real stingo."

"Ah, that's your sort – good night!"

This kind of thing frequently happened. Indeed I was lucky when I got off so easy without getting a long lecture on Astronomy from O'Halloran, that being his favourite science on which he got very prosy.

These ships are most comfortable, the cuddy being built like a house on deck with an alley running round it so that one can always have one window open without being flooded with water as in the flush poops. It also affords good shelter for the steerage passengers in bad or hot weather. The monkey poop is a nice smoking room. There are three bathrooms, but the gents' had been broken by some mismanagement, so in the hot weather we usually got up early and shied a few buckets over each other which proves very refreshing;

although it is requisite to have a wash in fresh water afterwards or one is so sticky, the deep sea being very strong, and much more so than one finds at the English bathing places.

In the hot weather we had an awning over the poop and quarterdeck, and a variety of games such as quoits, made of rope grommets, gymnastics and others were played. Dancing was carried on at night with much spirit, some Germans in the steerage forming the band, being paid by subscription. The cabin gents, after a little while finding the poop ladies' society every night tedious, took to the quarterdeck where there was more excitement, being more numerous. Others played cards or draughts, read, wrote, etc. At half past ten the lights were usually put out in the saloon, but one could burn the lamp in one's cabin as long as one liked; and although smoking in there was prohibited yet one could open the window and smoke at pleasure. Ballamono seldom turned in without his weed.

Prayers were read every Sunday on the poop in fine weather and in the saloon in wet. The little doctor frequently read prayers and the Captain gave a short sermon. The latter was a very worthy man, and one thing I particularly liked him for – he paid even more attention to the steerage than to the cabin passengers. He went through the 'tween decks every morning and inquired after their health and had a word for everyone. The officers called him an old woman because he was too fidgety about the sail and did not carry on enough. Ballomono and he had a civil growl occasionally, the former being a great swearer. The Skipper remarked, "Mr. Ballomono, can you not carry on work without swearing in such an awful manner?"

"No, Captain," replied Ballomono, incorrigibly, "I'm d——d if I can, for if I don't d——n the men they'll see me d——d first before they'll work."

The cabin passengers were mostly young men going out more for a spree than anything, few of them having a settled course to pursue.

Having just enough money for a good start if taken care of or for a good spree which would about last until they got there – and then much repentance would follow. They were all young men of a good education, and who had moved in easy circumstances, unaccustomed to hard work or to depend on their own efforts.

The ladies were nearly all country girls, one West Indian, one a widow and very pretty and engaged to the editor of a paper in Melbourne. She however changed her mind and fell in love with an Edinburgh man yclept Burgess, who had been in the Customs but had lost his place by his irregular wet habits. Much cooing and billing was the result of this flirtation. The widow did not give Burgess much trouble for she did most of the courting herself. In the evening the order of things was reversed and he was frequently discovered reclining in her arms and resting his weary head on her bosom.

The West Indian lady was also a widow but with one encumbrance and not so pretty as the other. Feeling naturally lonely and envying the seeming bliss of the other couple, she made love to Beckham who we familiarly called Jack Falstaff – and indeed he was the image of honest Jack. He certainly was the biggest liar that it has ever been my luck to fall in with, and there was withal something so extremely ridiculous in his boasts that one could hardly find fault with him. He was very generous whilst his money lasted, but it could not be expected to last long with his extravagance – and when gone he would borrow from you whilst you had a shilling and never leave you while there was a drop underway. He had letters of recommendation to the Governor Hotham from Lord Palmerston and others, but they were unfortunately of no use as Charley Hotham died shortly after our arrival. Alas, poor Beckham! Thou wast indeed a glorious character – would that I had the pen of Dickens to describe thee as I ought.

But Taylor was my favourite, and strange to say I'm peculiarly lucky in the choice of chums. A right good fellow was Bill, albeit a jovial one and easily led into temptation, a reflective man, very good-tempered and with a sincere pure love of the beautiful.

Then there was Collier who, with his sister, came from West Wales, going out to their brothers who were well-to-do. A young man of excitable temperament, fiery, but nothing in him. His sister was coarse, sensible, but with bad teeth.

Then there was glorious little Book; German, a magnificent musician and linguist, a strange eccentric little toad, but one in whom I would put no trust. Talked much of his wife whom he described as a fine woman, taller than himself. Showed her picture – her qualities as a bedfellow he spoke of in glowing terms. His courtship when described by himself was most amusing, but would lose its beauty were I to repeat it.

Walker, with his wife and the latter's sister, had been out before. He had returned to his native Yorkshire where he had married this farmer's daughter, and her sister had accompanied them nominally to attend her sister during sea-sickness, but in reality to ensnare the unwary eligible.[7] Both had bad teeth, thought themselves pretty, very thin. The sisters wore curls. Both good-tempered and amiable but silly; might do well with sensible husbands. Walker was a conceited pup – thought that everyone did wrong but himself and was disliked by all. I did not dislike him, but pitied him. When at dinner he seemed to have an idea that if he did not make haste and force his and his wife's plates into the corner he would lose by it. It seemed an understood thing among the party that the Captain or doctor ought to be done out of their dinner entirely, so whenever they carved everyone would take a fancy to that particular joint, and none other would they have.

"I'll trouble the doctor!"

"Yes, if the doctor pleases!"

"I think doctor has my favourite joint."

"When the doctor's at leisure." etc.

Poor little doctor! He was a shocking carver, and by the time the last one was served the first was ready for a second help until the poor fellow got so bewildered he would splash the gravy over the cloth, break a glass or so and finally throw down the knife in despair and retire from the field. He was withal a nice, good-tempered little soul, and frequently have we had a yarn upon the cause of sterility and other equally interesting subjects. He was the most unsophisticated simple man I ever saw, quite a Vicar of Wakefield.

There was F. Mason, son to a past captain in the navy. He had an after cabin to himself, had been to Sydney before and was going out to marry a Miss Jones, daughter to a rich brewer. He showed me her picture – she appeared about old enough to be his mother, and ugly to boot, but he said that was the fault of the daguerreotype – (most likely). He was a sterling fellow, generous and upright but with an infernal bad temper like myself. He was handsome, tall and thin and I should say would go out like a match someday; consumptive. The Colonies is the only country he could hope for health.

Miss Jones in the after cabin was going out to her brother, a squatter in Gippsland. She was good-looking, young and sensible, but she had a fault; and who has not? She knew too much. Some would say that one cannot know too much but I say that a woman can be too learned in certain things. Great flirtation went on between her and Book, albeit they were both too knowing to be led into anything worse than a flirtation. They danced better than anyone on board.

Then came S. Lowe, a stout man, in years too *old* for me. It was said that he went out to collect a debt of seven thousand pounds. Petrie, an agreeable man of good address, was a lawyer going out on business – politeness will cover a multitude of sins. Ah! And did I indeed forget my noble Griffiths, a green Irish boy from the bogs direct, going out on a speculation to some well-to-do relation in

Melbourne who would probably kick him to the devil in a week. He was made quite a butt of – and a useful thing a butt is, particularly for many folks who have not sense enough ever to be that itself, and who think themselves clever in showing off the other's simpleness. And Bullock will make all worth mentioning I think.[8] He had a command in the Indian Army, had nominally sold but in reality been kicked out. My noble Bullock was very lucky at Vingt-et-un and strange to say always won. I used to play at first, but finding that I seldom rose without being a loser of one or two pounds I abjured the card table in future. Bullock being the only winner, cards gradually fell into disuse.

In the warm weather claret came into large demand and as I showed myself handy in the manufacture of that delicious beverage yclept claret-punch, it was my duty to make a bucket full of the same every evening. Together with much singing it dissipated the time.

This ship is indeed a sight for a seaman. It is wonderful to observe how noiselessly she glides through the clear, blue water. In a calm one can see her whole copper and such a beautiful model has never been surpassed. Few but those who have seen it will believe that she can sail seventeen knots per hour with the wind abeam, and so little motion that one could stand a glass of water on the capstan head without spilling a drop.

Go into the head when the sun is up and you will indeed see a lovely sight. Two fountains are continually playing, the spray forming a magnificent rainbow and the snow-white foam as it roars angrily from the bow of the gallant barque contrasting grandly with the deep blue ocean. Gaze on this for a short time and one loses oneself in ecstasy. It appears as though one had left the busy world, with all the noise and bustle of the main deck, to enter another and more beautiful sphere. And one is usually awoken from this delightful dream by a violent slap on the head which knocks your cap off. Dismally you raise your head thinking – there goes my last cap. But you are agreeably disappointed by seeing the laughing figure of Bill, as may be, with the cap in his hand.

"Hallo, Jim! I've been roaring out for you the last half hour, and the deuce a bit could I find you. Just left the man on the wheel who states that he saw you go over the side, schooner-rigged. Come, man, and have a turn at chess."

"Oh, d——n the chess! Leave me alone, – but ho, what is that sound I hear?"

"Eight bells! It's lunch time and I can go a bit of salmon. Will you have a glass of champagne, etc?" Thus passed this anything but dreary voyage; the only thing I was sorry for was that it was over so quickly, for a pleasanter seventy-three days I have seldom spent, and if I had known the hardships in store should no doubt have regretted it more. But it's one of the beautiful dispensations of Providence that the future is veiled from our eyes.

There was a great spree on the event of our crossing the Line. The weather had been unfavourable to our progress for some time past and dead calms attended by hot weather. No shaving was allowed. Indeed I believe it's all but entirely done away with now. It's one of those foolish old customs that one doesn't regret much – pity more of them were not done away with. However in lieu of the Neptune's physic we indulged with such zeal in curious blue of all sorts and sizes that the two B's, Burgess and Beckham, got full of wind, and the former was nearly coming to grief, for, as after our potations we had adjourned to the head to watch the fountains – some growing maudlin sentimental, others sparring with handspikes, singing, dancing, etc. – Burgess began to lecture on the extraordinary brightness of the rainbow, and got so excited by his theme that he determined to go over and see the rights of it. I prevailed on him with much earnestness to postpone the proceeding till the breeze died away, but he, becoming excited by a doubt being expressed of his having seen a dolphin, sprang out on the jib guys with the intention, as he said, of going "Down, down to hell," and telling 'em as how I sent him there! And he assuredly would have gone there had I not caught a turn with his coat round a guy and, with much difficulty, held him up until assistance came and dragged him in.

How I managed it goodness knows, for I felt as though two Burgesses and myself were having a spree on the tight rope. Suffice it to say that the Captain in a long yarn complimented me on my presence of mind which had been the means of saving a fellow-creature's life. Others said I did it first rate, and not one of them had the remotest idea that I felt myself quite as bad as Burgess. Yet such was the case, and although I remembered everything perfectly, yet I seemed to myself as a being of another world gazing on the folly of mankind. Nevertheless I meekly took the praise which I deserved not.

The remainder of the evening is scarcely so distant. Faintly do I remember making punch in two buckets and Jack Falstaff coming out with scoldings. Bullock mistook Miss Conway's berth for his own which of course was very hurtful to the Miss's feelings, as other women saw him there.[9] On the whole the evening ended in a peaceful manner.

On *1st November* [1855], in Latitude 35° South, we saw the first albatross on which sundry bets were lost and won. These large gulls are seldom seen in North Latitudes. They grow to an enormous size but are easily caught with a hook and a piece of pork. The feathers are fine and the down very soft, but they are usually infested with a black louse and therefore disagreeable to keep.

The next day A. Guillim (Boatswain's Mate) fell overboard from the main yard whilst bending the main topsail, with the yard hoisted. He was standing on the main yard shackling on the topsail sheets. It was a foolish thing to do and indeed a dangerous way of bending sails. The clew struck him from the yard, and overboard he went. I was at lunch as the awful cry thrilled through the ship. I rushed on deck in time to see the poor fellow astern wildly throwing his arms about for help – where none could come. The lifebuoy was within a few yards but he could not swim a stroke – 'twas his last dying kick.

"Hard down with the helm!" Shouted Ballomono. "Cut away the lashings! Jump into the boat! Lower away!"

All these orders were done quicker than I have ever seen them done before – almost as quick as it takes to scribble this – but alas, although the boats were out pulling about for nearly two hours the poor fellow was seen no more. He was a fine young man, about four and twenty, a smart fellow but very quiet and inoffensive. He had married two years before and had a fine boy.

In throwing the ship aback she got stern way on and carried away the iron work of the wheel. She must have gone pretty fast astern. She worked beautifully however, and the yards would spin round faster than the hands could haul in the slack of the braces. We instantly got up a subscription for the widow and by striking the iron whilst hot we got together upwards of eighty pounds. Less than that sum is better than a bad husband, but I doubt if any sum will make amends for the loss of a good one, although it will soften the blow in either case.

We carried away the main topgallant yard through not having the braces kept taut, which is a great fault when a vessel is before the wind, as in that case the whole strain is on the lie or centre of the yard causing it to part amidships.

14th November [1855]. A little "Red Jacket" was born, and red enough it was surely. It was the first I had seen so young. It was covered with a kind of white down being, the doctor said, a seven months child. The mother was not married and was rather a nice-looking girl. We of course crossed the kid's hand with silver. There was also a miscarriage brought on by seasickness. I can scarcely forgive the doctor for damaging the body before I saw it. However the head was perfect, and not bigger than a small nut.

We saw an iceberg in Latitude 47°. These are the dread of all captains, but withal they are a magnificent sight. Everyone got up to see the first one, but as it was so far off and the morning scarcely broken, they were hardly recompensed for leaving their snug berths. We saw three others the next night, but though they were nearer and much better worth seeing few of the passengers turned out for them. From the Longitude of the Cape of Good Hope to Melbourne (albeit the last run ever made by poor Captain Milward[10]) was a run altogether unparalleled in the annals of good passages, being barely twenty-five days. It was indeed flying over the waves and all the time scarcely any motion to speak of and every sail set.

People have a foolish idea that a clipper ship is under water half the time, and that there is no comfort in a fast ship or with a captain who carries on too much sail; but I can assure them from experience in both fast and slow – what some call the trashy American fast boats and the strong frigate-built English – that the clippers are by far the most comfortable, take in the least water – for during our whole passage we seldom had a wet deck – and I must also declare that there are more ships lost by not keeping on enough canvas than by carrying too much. For instance, when a ship is before the wind you can scarcely carry too much, for your object is to go faster than the sea. If the sea catches you the consequence is a pooper. Ships have foundered in this manner and at best there is a wet bed and skin which is anything but comfortable.

The crew, having got some liquor from the passengers, some of them got drunk and when a sailor is drunk he must fight; and so fight they did, one of them drawing a knife. But fortunately no other injuries were received but bruises.

25th [November 1855]. We held a meeting in the after saloon with a view to present a testimonial to the Captain, and although I do not approve of the system of paying a man either for doing his duty or for civility, yet I readily subscribed two pounds five shillings for this. We raised fifty pounds which considering it was only among a few was very liberal. It was to purchase a piece of plate. But I believe the Skipper thought just as well of those who did not subscribe as of those who did. The meeting ended with a champagne lunch. The general expectation was that he would give a grand dinner in port, but they were disappointed. I daresay the poor fellow was too unwell. At all events there is not much generosity in giving a dinner that one does not pay for, as some captains do – it all goes to the owner. We had a farewell ball among ourselves, in which I did not join, not being very well, and caring little for those things. I smoked the calumet[11] over the bows and thought and dreamed sweetly. Much flirting went on, but not being present I could give no account of proceedings.

On the *3rd day of December* [1855] we came to an anchor in Hobson's Bay and fired two guns for the mail. We brought the first news of the fall of Sebastopol,[12] although a false report having been circulated before, there was very little rejoicing here. In fact very few seemed to care if it was taken or not. I subjoin the Latitude and Longitude with the distance run each day and, although ten days becalmed on the Line, we had made up for it by fair winds from the Cape.

N.B. Captain Milward died on the passage home off the Horn. He was not well when he arrived and no doubt the sudden change and the probable cold round the Horn hastened his death. Peace be to his ashes – albeit he was buried at sea and therefore one can hardly think they will have much peace unless quickly nipped up by some shark. He was a good seaman and what is still better, a good man, and no respecter of persons, which is much to say of a captain. This was intended for his last voyage, he having made a nice little competency, but there is an old saying about "the pitcher", etc – in this case it has come true. O'Halloran took the command but Ballomono could not agree with him and therefore left.[13]

Day to Day Log – Voyage 'Red Jacket' – Liverpool to Melbourne

Days Out	Date 1855	Latitude	Longitude	Knots travelled	Remarks
	Sept.				
1	21				
2	22				Exchanged signals with the 'Sir Colin Campbell'.
3	23	49° 32´	9° 30´	147	
4	24	46° 43´	11° 55´	192	Capt. & owner of 'Emerald Isle' from Gibraltar to the Mauritius came on board & exchanged papers.
5	25	44° 26´	13° 58´	164	
6	26	41° 34´	16° 50´	200	
7	27	37° 48´	19° 0´	248	
8	28	34° 47´	19° 20´	186	Spoke the 'Miles Standish' from Liverpool to Calcutta.
9	29	30° 56´	18° 22´	256	
10	30	28° 48´	19° 31´	142	Caught a small dolphin.
	Oct.				
11	1	26° 58´	20° 21´	119	Spoke a French barque bound to Bordeaux.
12	2	24° 36´	21° 26´	134	Caught a shark.
13	3	22° 39´	21° 42´	178	
14	4	17° 42´	21° 26´	237	From Liverpool to the Line calm & light winds.
15	5	15° 30´	21° 17´	154	
16	6	13° 55´	21° 47´	100	
17	7	12° 20´	22° 40´	111	
18	8	10° 12´	23° 16´	133	
19	9	8° 44´	23° 13´	88	
20	10	6° 58´	22° 43´	108	Weather warm. Calms and light breezes.
21	11	6° 54´	21° 49´	60	
22	12	6° 15´	21° 25´	40	
23	13	6° 6´	21° 37´	15	
24	14	5° 39´	20° 35´	66	
25	15	5°36´	20°9´	26	
26	16	5°0´	20°12´	36	
27	17	4°20´	22°0´	109	
28	18	3°8´	24°38´	172	
29	19	2°57´	24°4´	36	Calms & light breezes.
30	20	1°44´	26°24´	161	
31	21	0°2´	29°0´	183	Crossed the Line.
32	22	2°14´	30°40´	171	
33	23	5°53´	32°0´	233	Stiff breezes.
34	24	9°46´	34°0´	258	Carried away main top gallant yard.

Days Out	*Date 1855*	*Latitude*	*Longitude*	*Knots travelled*	*Remarks*
35	*25*	*13°22´*	*35°50´*	*249*	*A. Guillion Boatswain's Mate fell overboard – lowered boat but no tidings.*
36	*26*	*16°43´*	*37°30´*	*221*	
37	*27*	*20°0´*	*36°54´*	*197*	
38	*28*	*22°57´*	*35°58´*	*182*	*Raised subscription 80 pounds.*
39	*29*	*26°9´*	*34°10´*	*223*	
40	*30*	*30°2´*	*32°0´*	*260*	
41	*31*	*34°23´*	*29°10´*	*300*	*Saw the first albatross.*
	Nov.				
42	*1*	*35°31´*	*26°35´*	*144*	
43	*2*	*35°34´*	*22°8´*	*218*	*A small "Red Jacket" born.*
44	*3*	*35°45´*	*20°30´*	*73*	
45	*4*	*36°2´*	*20°22´*	*13*	
46	*5*	*38°42´*	*17°49´*	*199*	
47	*6*	*42°9´*	*13°50´*	*250*	
48	*7*	*49°9´*	*9°34´*	*221*	
49	*8*	*45°20´*	*5°0´*	*206*	
50	*9*	*45°35´*	*0°25´E*	*204*	
51	*10*	*46°15´*	*4°28´*	*173*	*Saw an iceberg at daybreak.*
52	*11*	*47°0´*	*10°47´*	*256*	*3 other bergs in sight.*
53	*12*	*47°15´*	*16°10´*	*215*	
54	*13*	*47°41´*	*19°6´*	*127*	
55	*14*	*47°38´*	*24°35´*	*229*	*Fine stiff breezes N.W.*
56	*15*	*47°57´*	*30°20´*	*233*	
57	*16*	*47°27´*	*36°27´*	*220*	
58	*17*	*48°8´*	*43°10´*	*270*	
59	*18*	*47°36´*	*50°0´*	*256*	
60	*19*	*47°17´*	*56°20´*	*257*	*Stiff breezes westerly.*
61	*20*	*47°10´*	*61°20´*	*240*	
62	*21*	*47°3´*	*62°10´*	*238*	
63	*22*	*47°39´*	*75°0´*	*290*	
64	*23*	*46°48´*	*82°12´*	*300*	
65	*24*	*46°25´*	*87°30´*	*230*	
66	*25*	*46°15´*	*93°36´*	*249*	*Meeting in after saloon – raised subscription for Captain.*
67	*26*	*45°57´*	*100°23´*	*273*	
68	*27*	*44°34´*	*106°43´*	*310*	
69	*28*	*42°9´*	*113°10´*	*298*	
70	*29*	*41°31´*	*118°25´*	*240*	*Sighted land. Grand concert.*
71	*30*	*40°39´*	*123°45´*	*237*	
	Dec.				
72	*1*	*40°0´*	*128°40´*	*243*	
73	*2*	*40°0´S*	*133°6´E*	*299*	*Ran through the heads and took Pilot on board. Came to an anchor – fired two guns for the mails.*
74	*3*				

Through my foolish extravagance on the passage I had run through my little bit of money and was therefore obliged to borrow. The best way to prove a man's friendship is to attempt to board him for cash – then comes the tug-of-war. However I had no sooner thrown a hint to Bill Taylor than the money was in my fist. I took ten pounds, thinking of course I could borrow enough to supply my wants from my well-to-do uncle. Poop, poop! I had yet much to learn. Bill and I went ashore at Sandridge and up by the train. It is only three miles distant from Melbourne, yet this line cost an exorbitant sum of money. It is the only one at present finished in Victoria.[14]

We put up at the Yarra Yarra Hotel at the corner of Market Square and close to the wharf. It is a nice building erected by the late proprietor, McGloulin[15] who made an enormous [amount of] money in the little grog shop which used to stand there. The hotels in Melbourne are numerous, good and cheap. They are mostly all on quite a different principle from English hotels. The bars are very large and covered with decanters and glasses; the waiters, usually Americans, are very sharp and almost before your last word of an order is out of your mouth your liquor stands before you, decanter and glass; for the plan is to help yourself and I have no doubt that they find it pays better than measuring it out – for it being the custom on meeting a friend to ask him to take a drop, which it is not considered friendly to refuse, although at the same time the friend would rather not, therefore they merely wet their glass and the ceremony is completed. Of course there are exceptions, but the barman is usually awake to them.

Melbourne appears to me much improved since I left. Many buildings have been built and are in the course of erection. One complains of bad times but it appears that they were recovering from the last year's crash caused by overstocking the market.

The Wilsons put up at the Yarra for the night.[16] They were a family in the steerage, well-behaved enough, from the north of England. He was a blacksmith; had three daughters, one married.[17] I had a slight flirtation with the youngest, but like a good many more it came to nought.[18] Now I was quite in earnest and would have made an ass of myself by marrying the girl and would not do anything dishonourable; but like all the fickle fair they can't bear to be treated well – the more you slight them the better they like you, for all the world like spaniels.

It is all very well to talk about the undying love of women in novels, and it's right to a certain extent, but this is my opinion about it – that women being the passive – viz. having to wait till asked, or in some countries where the heart is altogether out of the question and the parents settle the business – that God, who provides all things beautifully and "tempers the wind to the shorn lamb",[18] has so ordered it that a woman seldom loves until beloved, and after marriage her love for her husband grows with her marriage and strengthens with her strength. (That is to say if he behaves as he should). The first story a woman hears she believes before all others and with love she thinks on an object; she ponders over him and at last loves him, but if there is no connection this love becomes obliterated by his absence, if too long, and sometimes by seeing too much of him. Therefore if one wishes success one must steer carefully between the two extremes, and however firm her love may be care is required in not trying it too much. We can none of us bear temptation therefore leave her not for too long a time.

The only case in which woman's love is stronger than man's is after having made the impression of his image on her virgin soul. This is a beautiful dispensation, for were it not for this the whole social world would be in an uproar and marriage would not be binding. After all that is said about the freedom of choice I think it would be better for the girl if the parents were allowed, as formerly, to give away their daughters without an appeal to the latter. But it would not be so well for the men, because if parents thought the young man ineligible he would not be so softened by swain's entreaties as maidens would in all probability be, if he had a good gift of the gab. And if a man truly loves it is not so easily effaced as in a maiden's slight impressions.

Well, after all that bosh I can make nothing original out of it, for as some wiseacre has said, "Marriage is a lottery". One may marry for love and live miserably, another may marry for convenience and live happily, or may marry for money and live lovingly. One may think oneself very wise and think one knows how to pick out a mate of suitable disposition, and at the same time one doesn't stand a whit better chance than if one picked out a mate blindfold. Verily it is altogether bosh, bosh, bosh!

But it appears that I'm digressing. Wilsons slept at the Yarra Yarra. The old man was in a great stink about getting conveyance to Bendigo where it appears his eldest son, who was married, was working at his trade and doing very well. I met Jack Forster, an old Californian, who came down with us last time and he was kind enough to put Wilson in the way to get a waggon, and the girls were to ride on top altogether. I advised him to send them by coach. They set off the next day. These waggons are usually drawn by very fine young horses belonging to a company of Americans in North Melbourne adjoining Conway's Royal Hotel, and they take up goods very reasonably. The horses took fright at something and broke the pole of the waggon so they were detained until evening, and in the meantime Nell and I had a loving walk together. At last they got off safe, but I had much misgiving for the remainder of the passage, for they had overloaded the waggon.

Bill Taylor had seen his friends, the Turnbulls, or rather his father's friends, for they owed him considerable money, and he had sent his son out to them thinking that they would at least set him up in business with a part of the owing capital; but although they professed much at first, and also lent him as much money as he could spend, telling him to see a little of the country, yet it was only with a view to putting him off. He carried on a rare game whilst the money lasted together with the honest fat man Beckham who borrowed from Bill liberally.

Mrs. Love quarrelled with the intended, the editor. Burgess, when the money was done, quarrelled with her and there was some talk of her bringing an action for breach of promise, but it all went off quietly I believe.

I knew that if I stayed here long it would soon eat up my passage money, and so having taken my passage for Sydney in the *Telegraph*,[19] I started on Monday, 10th December, 1855. She was a fast boat, there were few passengers and we made the run in forty-eight hours. A very bluff coast it is, quite iron-bound. In some places the cliffs rise six hundred feet perpendicularly and run right down into deep water. Therefore if an unfortunate ship beats on there is not the slightest chance for a soul on board. I had many misgivings on my reception by my Nunks [uncle] for I had a pretty good idea as to how relations are usually treated. It is usually "Do as I do – I had nothing when I began – You must depend upon yourself." But still I hoped that on my giving him proofs that I should receive some gold on my attaining the age of twenty-one, that he would lend me some on account.

We arrived at Sydney on Wednesday [12th December1855] at three o'clock and my sensations on passing through this magnificent bay, the finest harbour in the known world, passes description. It is indeed a lovely sight, a Garden of Eden. The almost perpendicular rocks running down into lovely inlets of clear water deep enough to swim the largest ship. Not a puff of wind can disturb the harmony of ships that load and unload alongside the wharves. And then as to scenery, who can look at the Domain or the entrance to the Hawkesbury without acknowledging its beauty – his soul must indeed be dead. I cannot describe it as it deserves for I had not time to go about and see its beauties, but I hope to do so at some future period.

The Domain is a beautiful place – there is very little art in it, it owes its beauty principally to nature, but I have never seen anything to compare with it in England. Species of every flower and shrub which adorn the gardens of Britain are here, besides every tropical tree and flower. The view is grand, the climate is delightfully warm, the air is clear, the deep blue sea without a ripple on it is cool and healthy – fountains, weeping willows, seats under stupendous rocks – all, all tend to make one look into the azure vault above and glorify the Maker of all these bright and glorious things. Don't talk to me of a dusty, dirty church where men and women collect together for vanity's sake – there is no religion in that compared to this. Can a man gaze on such a sight as this harbour presents and be irreligious?

A nice shady carriage road goes outside the Domain and out to the point of this bay, for the beauty of this harbour consists greatly in the irregularity of the sides which hang in festoons, each point forming a bay. This drive winds out to the point and then back through a township called Wooloomooloo – but after seeing such delightful sights as the bay presents it is impossible to look with patience on brick walls and dusty streets. And by the bye, perhaps this is the reason why some people do not like the town of Sydney. Ladies especially who are forced to live in the town give an awful account of its misery and privations.

I must own I did not think nearly so much of the town as of Melbourne. The roads are not to be compared with them and the streets are not nearly as wide or regular. Pitt Street and George Street appear about the best. The news of the fall of Sebastopol caused more rejoicing here, or perhaps it was sorrowing, for I found all the shops shut and the town apparently deserted, so much so indeed that I could not even get a clean shirt or a place to wash. The place appeared miserable enough to me, an entire stranger and alone.

I found the Hunter river boats left every evening and I accordingly started off at once and arrived at Newcastle at the mouth of the Hunter early in the morning after a rather boisterous passage, some of the passengers being seasick enough. The rocks at the head of this fine river are rather imposing. Newcastle is famed for its coals. It's a dirty, miserable-looking hole enough, as indeed are most all the new settlements, in consequence of a fashion they have of cutting down all the trees without distinction. It ought to be put a stop to and the finest left to beautify and cool the town.

Farms are occasionally seen on the banks – some parts are very bushy, others from the bushfires the trees have become blackened and withered offering a wretched appearance. And the whole is rather level as far up as Morpeth where I landed. After this it became hilly and about the Blue Mountains very grand. The banks are frequently visited by tremendous floods which sweep everything before them, and although they enrich the soil on the banks, yet are much dreaded by the farmers of the flats or low grounds.

Morpeth is a small town about three miles from Maitland by a very bad road. I went up in a coach and arrived safe and sound at my respected relative's. It was a beautiful, clean house of one storey covering much ground, the rooms large and lofty. The verandah which kept the house nice and cool was so clean that it would puzzle the most careful housewife to find a piece of dirt about it. The kitchen is built detached from the house behind, which is a good plan for a warm climate as it keeps the smell and heat of cooking clear of the rooms.

I met my aunt, a tall and has-been very pretty woman of about forty-five.[20] She welcomed me kindly and instantly brought refreshments, always the first thing thought of in this country. Soon after my uncle made his appearance and professed himself very glad to see me, and instantly saw a striking likeness to person or persons unknown. Mrs. Burgess saw a likeness to him. He was a tall stout man and had been very strong. He was much affected when talking of his sister, my mother, and surprised that I should not have brought a likeness of my sister or any other tokens from England. He promised many things about putting me on one of his farms, for he had some fine land on the Hunter and begged me to make his house my home; but I did not like the dependency and he said he could not put me on a farm until next December. I wished him to lend me some money and I would try my luck at the diggings until then. He did not seem very ready in bringing out the blunt, and at first offered ten pounds, but that was no use as I owed it.

He lent me twenty pounds and his wife pressed upon my acceptance five pounds. She was exceedingly kind and got all my things washed and mended. She was a Sydney native and had been married before to a Mr. W., by whom she had three boys. The second one, Jack, the only one at home, has an impediment in his speech; a shingle short. The youngest had gone to California about seven years ago and, not having been heard of since, is supposed to be dead.[21]

My uncle does not do a large trade now. Indeed he does not wish it, and the house is more like a private house than an hotel.[22] His house is in East Maitland, the government township laid out at right angles. The roads are in a very bad state. The West part is the best. It is a long street, the main road to Mudgee and Wellington. It appears to be in a flourishing state. The coal pits are about a mile from East Maitland, only about from thirty to sixty feet deep. A railroad is in contemplation to Newcastle and will no doubt much improve the place.

On the *20th December* [1855] I left here taking with me only a few shirts and my much valued opossum rug, my constant companion. Now had I been economical I had money enough to last me for some time on the diggings with luck, but I had yet to be taught sense by some very severe lessons. On arriving in Sydney I found that the boat did not leave until Saturday, so I had to put up at some hotel for the time being. The Sydneyites have a decided objection to taking in boarders as they think that preparing a bed is too much trouble for the return they get, quite overlooking what lodgers spend in their houses. It is a practice to make answer that they have no room. It is sometimes with the greatest difficulty that strangers can get accommodated. Not so at Melbourne where they are very civil and obliging.

Considering that the sister colonies are occupied by the same country people and the same Government it is wonderful to observe the difference in manners and customs. I must certainly give preference to the latter, putting aside the wonderful progress Melbourne has made in the last few years, and it even now ranks before Sydney in population and commerce. It will quite soon throw the latter in the shade.

Sydney is more like England. It has the worst kind of aristocracy, that of wealth; also a class termed exclusives who pretend to be select and keep clear of prisoners or prisoners' descendants, as it were making an abortive attempt to place a mark on the unfortunate who has stepped aside from the paths of honesty; and thus, although he has fulfilled the punishment awarded by the authorities they endeavour to punish him forever, and not only him, but his innocent offspring. This stupid attempt, I am happy to say, only brings the exclusives into well-earned contempt and makes themselves miserable.

In Melbourne society is very differently constituted. There is a general equality, and wealth in honest labour. Everyone is busy and stirring and a glance assures one that it is full of business. Nothing is at a standstill – the go-ahead principle is uppermost. Thousands are flocking to its shores and the natural consequence of so many eager money hunters is an occasional stagnation in the labour and provision market; but they soon sift down and come to a level again.

But to return; after much trouble I succeeded in getting lodgings at the Skinner's Arms (Turner). The waiter, was a Chinaman who could speak but little English. They frequently take situations as waiters and they work for less than Europeans. My room was a four-bedded one, and very little sleep did I get for mosquitoes. For it was not like my uncle's – surrounded by mosquito curtains. They have a very pretty effect being made of white, blue or pink muslin covering the whole bedstead and reaching the floor.

Turner proved to be one of the exclusive caste for when I enquired for an hotel near the wharf he haughtily answered, "I know nothing of the people of this place – a lot of old lags. We keep to ourselves and mix with none of them."

He had been keeper of a small beer shop in London and I told him that albeit he was very high in his line yet that hardly justified him in looking with contempt upon so many much better and wiser men. This brought up much argument on the merits of the country, by which he proved himself to be not only a narrow-minded man, but a half-witted one. His wife caught poor Foki at the bottle and threatened him with imprisonment.

VI

HARD TIMES IN TOWN AND COUNTRY

(Melbourne, the Victorian goldfields and labouring to survive – December 1855 to August 1856.)

I was not sorry to get away from this place and left on the 22nd [December 1855] in the *City of Sydney*,[1] a screw steamer – not so fast as the *Telegraph* – and did not arrive in Melbourne until Christmas Day. Made an acquaintance with a young man called Green and I introduced him at the Yarra. Bill, Burgess, Prouse and several more dined together and a great jubilee – that's the way the money goes. I paid Taylor the ten pounds but finding that without it I should be short I borrowed it again. Prouse joined me. He was a new chum at diggings though he had been out before. One could stand quite as good a chance by oneself as with a new chum. This was not the only folly I committed, for we took a coach which pulled out another five pounds and we might just as well have walked.

We went by Cobb's six-in-hand stager, an American affair, got up on first-rate style, fine horses and the way they drive is something wonderful considering the state of the roads.[2] There is a wooden bridge at Keilor, built something like the suspension bridges and just wide enough for a coach both sides and no more. Now they drive through this at full gallop, the wheels grating against the post on either side. It makes one wince when not accustomed to it. We changed horses every ten miles and arrived at Bendigo, a distance of one hundred and twenty miles, at six o'clock – not bad work considering the stoppages and also the bogs of the Black Forest and Gap. Catherine Hayes[3] arrived at Bendigo by special coach at the same time, about to honour the diggers by easing them of a little superfluous gold.

We put up at the Shamrock,[4] a comfortable place of the kind, but too expensive for us; so on Monday we purchased a calico tent, eight feet by ten, and pitched it at the head of New Chum Gully – bought two stretchers, put up a table with tools; which made a pretty hole in my funds. We were tolerably comfortable if we could manage to knock out a living. The place looked so shockingly dull that I had small hopes of it. However Jack Forster, who had taken a billet as cook at the Victoria Hotel,[5] (he was a first-rate hand at it as he had kept a restaurant in California) had promised to lay me onto a piece of ground where he hoped to find a bit of gold if the run that he had worked on continued.

We found out Wilson's[6] at the junction of Iron Bark and Long Gully's – the old man had commenced blacksmith work and said that he was doing first-rate; but like all men who make money faster than they have been accustomed, he was wearing himself out and was as stingy as possible. "But", said I to myself, "Hold on a bit – he'll kick over the traces by and bye, and then be fifty times worse than one who has never been reined in tight." Strange, yet so it is! After all there is nothing like letting things take their course. It's no use a man's pushing and sweating and getting excited, as I have said before – float down with the stream. Lord bless you, haven't I been trying and doing and building castles, getting enthusiastic, and what good has it done me? And then again, I've let things go on quietly and been able to see advantages which otherwise I should have missed.

Now this is always the way – I wander away from the subject. Well, where's the harm? I'm only writing to amuse myself. It passes away the time and perhaps instructs one a little. What can be more instructive than to write down one's everyday thoughts and actions and then to read them over, and observe what bosh, what nonentity in man's proudest, man's best endeavour. But then, if one is reflective one can just con over the old newspapers. Now then, just take last year's and look at it just for the fun of the thing, and see what bosh it seems; its high-flown language, its praises and its blame. And yet some folks will read a paper, today's for instance, without making the necessary allowances, and then they misjudge.

Read a police case. A poor wretch is sentenced to seven years' transportation for which perhaps he could not help. Perhaps he is not guilty. Perhaps it was starvation that drove him to it, the biting pain of want. But then of course he must be guilty. Just look here – the evidence is so clear. The judge says he is sorry that these cases are increasing and he must put a stop to them; and that is a very sad case, and the prisoner is quite the hardened villain – he shows no remorse. There you see! The judge says so – the learned judge – and therefore the man must be guilty. And yet, perhaps he may only repeat what he has learned by rote like a parrot. The words he speaks he has said to thousands before. He is quite callous, and the suffering he inflicts he thinks not of. He does it all in the way of business. The fact is that to be able to judge one must have been judged; and the man who judges by impulse is just as likely to be right as the one who judges by appearances. The same kind of red on the brow may indicate many things – what one may call the blush of guilt may be that of modesty or that of indignation. The hectic flush of consumption looks much like the bloom of health. Then again, a man's brow turns pale – some say he is afraid. Be wary – provoke him not – for the fiercest passions may rage beneath a pale brow.

Well there; don't judge by appearances. "Well", says you, "What are we to judge by?" And now you pose a man. I guess to be right one must do as the Bible says and, "Judge not at all."[7] That's the ticket.

Where did I leave off? That glass of ale has played old Nick and made me wander.

I saw the Miss Wilsons[8] and found them well after their ride, and getting as brown as Aborigines.

1st January, 1856. Commenced a new year. The last one has passed pleasantly enough but I learned little enough in it; spent plenty of money, so one may say it was an unprofitable one. I had sanguine hopes for the next year. We commenced sinking today for luck – but it proved a dead shicer. We continued sinking until the end of the week and they all turned out duffers, and my money began to run very low.

Green called. He said he had had much trouble in finding us out, but as he could not get a situation in Melbourne he thought he would come up and cook for us, or go mates. One new chum at a time was plenty, but how to get rid of him I didn't know. Told him as plain as one could that I did not want him and was badly enough off for money, but he didn't take much notice, and remained with us until Thursday. And what made his company more disagreeable, his feet were moist ones and used to stink one almost out of the tent. At last was obliged to tell him that he must go, for I had not more than would last me another week, and Prouse was not the sort to lend any.

I wrote to Uncle asking for the loan of some cash at the usual percentage because it was little use on these old diggings without a little capital; but receiving no answer and not getting any gold, we thought of looking for some kind of work. And there is little doubt but that if I had been accustomed to that sort of thing I might have got it, but I had not cheek enough to ask for it.

The fact is that, though, I have heard much talk among folks, who have never been obliged to work for a master, who say when they hear of anyone starving, "Oh, they are lazy, and would sooner starve than work. There is plenty of work if they like to do it." And then how often will you hear the men who have plenty of money say "Those that won't work deserve to starve. I know that I would sooner work than be idle." I should very much like to see them penniless in a strange place, and no other chance of getting a livelihood but by hard manual labour from daylight to dark. They would alter their tune, I'll be bound. I've seen men row very hard for pleasure who would think it very hard if obliged to do so.

The weather was raining and we wandered about sometimes trying another hole, looking for work, and occasional love-making. The money running low, although expecting a supply from Maitland. By the bye, it's the worst thing in the world for a young man to have a friend to fall back upon, because one doesn't put sole reliance in oneself, who is the only person who ought to be trusted. As the saying is, "When one draws the sword to go through the world, throw away the scabbard." I did much better the first time without a farthing from anyone; and now, through dependence upon my uncle, I could do little or nothing. Besides, these old diggings did not suit me, having never been a fossicker; and it was well known that one could not get a pile here, if indeed one made a living, for almost all the ground that was rich had been worked out two years ago.

16th [January 1856]. I got a letter from Maitland enclosing one from Fanny, the former having many good wishes, but none of the more needful. Fanny's gave me the address of John Burge, requesting me to find him out and lend him some money if he was hard up.[9] I wrote to him and received an answer; so as I was hard up and thinking there was a better chance of a start in Melbourne than here, and I also wished to see John, I was about to start.

However I saw an advertisement for men to work at a puddling machine so I thought I would try what it was like. The wages were four pounds per week. The boss was an Irishman and the whole party were the same. Although I had a vain idea of my powers of work yet I could soon see that they were trying to work out the Englishman. It is a thing frequently done; a number of Irishmen working together, and when they get a stranger among them, they instantly begin to work as hard as they can and if they see him flagging they redouble their efforts remarking, "Sure, and I'm not going to do all the work for that lazy devil – I say, mate, if you don't work you'll get no pay."

"Faith then, Pat, and didn't I say he couldn't work, etc."

This was a gang of the same kind. I determined that they should not work me off until the day was out, so I worked away, in these long days and the sun blistering my arms and back until I was ready to drop with exhaustion. It came particularly hard upon me, having been nearly two years without doing anything – and as for people saying that they would sooner work hard than be idle, I'll never believe them until they have done a day's work, from five in the morning until seven at night with a very heavy pick under a burning sun, without cessation. They'll say with me that their night's rest will be the most peculiar one they ever had – for I could neither sit, stand or lie with any degree of comfort. Every bone in my body ached as though beaten with many stripes. The skin peeled off my face arms and neck and it was as sore as a boil. Of course I worked there no more although I got my well-earned 13/6 for that day.

Now, let me swear – I'd sooner starve than work like a brute beast from daylight till dark, just time enough to eat one's necessary food and when at night one's labour ceases, too tired to read or refresh the mind, can do nothing but sleep – no time for reading or any other intellectual pleasure – why starving were a thousand times preferable to it – and I speak as one who has a right to do so, for I have tried both. Sooner would I expire under the questions by water than live such a dog's life.

If a nation requires those sort of labourers never educate the people, but bring them up to it from their earliest infancy, for then you will succeed in your end, by keeping them even lower than the beasts in the field. For I'll answer that you'll neither get educated men nor any men but those brought up to it from childhood. Eight hours a day is quite enough for mortal man.

There are no greater slaves in the world than Britons on the average. They go to extremes – some work worse than any slave in the southern States, and live on worse food than dogs, and others are so lazy and useless that they cannot even dress themselves, that the slightest change of wind lays them up with cold, and a damp dinner napkin gives them rheumatic fever or sudden death. As Solomon said, (I'm not sure it was that wiseacre) "Give me neither great riches, nor much poverty, but a kind of half and half."

Jack Forster, directly he heard that I was hard up and going to leave, forced me to accept a couple of pounds, and pay him when I had an opportunity. Fine-hearted fellows those diggers are! Poor Jack got an awful cutting up a few days back from a party of those blackguards, Tipperary Boys, who had come into the hotel with a view to make a disturbance, and began by pitching into the Governor. But Jack rushed in and would have made very small work of them had not the Governor turned tail, so he was overpowered by numbers, who beat his head and face to a mummy and would have finished him had not the by-standers interfered and secured them. Poor fellow, he was nearly killed, but he gave some of them a lesson that they will not easily forget. The Tips, and in fact all quarrelsome men, are great cowards, and never fight singly or without being the largest party, and always with sticks and murderous weapons. They are only fit for soldiers, which is in amount about the same as saying that a man is not fit to live, it being about the lowest grade.

I left my things at Wilson's together with stretcher and set off, my sole companion my opossum. I wish I could make numbers and I should certainly write some lives on it. If I ever get to be a rich man it shall be placed in a glass case in my drawing-room. Off I set to Melbourne. The weather proved fine and I was in good condition for a long walk. It was a beautiful shaded road and I was as free as a bird. What cared I for poverty as long as I was free. But by the bye, rainy weather is not so pleasant in the bush. Passed the far-famed Porcupine,[10] and sat down to dinner about five miles beyond. I ate my frugal dinner consisting of a loaf, a box of sardines and some tea, which one seldom goes without in this country, as the water is so warm in the sun and likely to give dysentery. A glass of pure cold water is indeed a luxury here. It can be easily obtained if one is stationary, but my wanderings of course depend on circumstances. Having eaten my meal I had a smoke, a five minute nap and off again.

I got as far as Sawyer's Gully[11] the first day, which is excellent good walking with a swag on one's back. I ate my supper, lay down by the fire and turned into the 'possum with my trousers under my head for a pillow. I was awakened by something slimy crawling over my legs. I guessed it was a snake by the feel, but I had heard how to fix 'em, so lay quite still and let him settle down between my legs comfortably enough; then placing my hands on the ground behind me I suddenly threw my legs open so as to let him slip beneath, and sprang to my feet. I soon put an end to him with a stick and found him to be a small diamond snake about eighteen inches long, black and yellow.[12] I am told his bite is very poisonous. If I had not been careful not to irritate him no doubt I should have felt his fangs.

It was just breaking day, so I turned in no more, but made up the fire. The dead tree against which I lit my fire, having burnt all night, as likely as not the snake had been driven from or under it by the smoke. I had finished my breakfast and got under way again before sunrise, for in bush travelling we not only steer by the sun, but regulate all our actions by it – breakfast about sunrise, dinner when it's on the meridian and tea at sunset. I have no doubt in my own mind that if one wants health one will get it by living in that manner.

I caught up with a man who was travelling in the same direction today. In the course of conversation I found that he had been about nineteen years in the country, so I put him down for an old lag; but as I have always found them a good deal better chaps than new chums I did not part convoy on that account. The sequel proved that I was right for, my tea running short, he pressed a share of his own tea and sugar on me. He was on the look-out for work himself and therefore could not be very flush of money, and deserved the more thanks. He left me at Kyneton in order to see if there was a job to be got at splitting or fencing.

On the third day I overtook a bullock dray apparently stuck, but on examining I saw the driver sitting on the ground on the other side looking very pale. He told me he had a young pair of bullocks and in yoking them he had received a stroke from one of their horns which had torn up his shoulder, and he was very faint from loss of blood. He begged me to yoke up the other two and drive him on to Keilor. I tried what I could do, but as I knew nothing about talking bullock, made a bosh of it. So having helped him into the dray I drove the four that were yoked, and after nearly capsizing two or three times I managed to get into Keilor. He asked me to have a glass with him, which I did and then left.

I arrived in Melbourne that night, making three days, which was at the average of forty miles, faster than ever I walked before, or intend to do again. I put up at the Western Dining Rooms. They charge from twenty-five to thirty shillings per week for board and lodging, or a shilling per meal; which by the bye is very reasonable. It is also very good; a good deal more than one would get in London for the same money, and never any charge made for waiters here, or at any other hotels.

I left off making notes now. It is a strange thing, as Bacon says, that when men are at sea they usually keep a diary and when ashore, where there is so much more of interest to be seen and recorded, one neglects it. Yet so it is.

I called at the address Fanny had sent me but John had left. I found that his last residence had been the Tam-o'-Shanter,[13] but that he set out for Bendigo three days ago to see me, so we must have passed each other on the road. If we had met I expect we should not have recognised each other, for we are, I suppose, much altered since we last met.

I called on Whitlaw,[14] an acquaintance of Uncle's, who had left Maitland for debt, and had been here in a billet as fireman. He was staying at the cottage of a shipmate in North Melbourne near where John had been living. The shipmate had gone to the diggings and, like a good many more, had locked up his cottage, not being able to let it. Numbers of houses that were knocked up in West and South Melbourne at the first rush of immigrants are now deserted, and one can buy them for a mere song. Whitlaw, being hard up, had taken possession of this cottage and in order to save I came and lived with him. My money soon ran short feeding two mouths.

We used to go every day like soldiers looking for a hard day's work and praying to God we might not find one. The first thing in the morning I used to go to the *Argus* office, and many were the eager faces waiting for the first copy to by placed out on a board. They all rushed to the advertising sheet and happy the one who found a job to his taste or capabilities. Few indeed answered to mine. I was no tradesman and I knew it were useless to apply for a place of trust without testimonials – even for a porter's place they were required.

Eager with hunger have I rushed to some place of the kind. A cold answer perhaps, that they were full, would satisfy me, and often they would question me. Oh, how my blood turned to gall to be obliged to answer some of what I considered their insolent questions civilly, and after a close investigation, which often went on thus –

"You advertised for so-and-so, sir?"

"Yes, I did. What can you do?"

"Everything that is necessary."

"Oh, indeed. In what place were you last?"

"I have been to sea, but never worked at anything of this kind before."

"Oh, well! You had better call again about twelve, and then we shall probably settle it."

"Good morning," said I, and went away thinking – sure of that anyhow. Call at twelve. No-one at home. The master gone out – didn't know when he'd come in. Called several times, and at last found him at six o'clock.

"Oh, you're the young man who called this morning?"

"Yes, I could not find you before."

"Where are your testimonials?"

"I have not got any."

"Not got any! Then you won't suit me!"

At this point I culminated. I had been pressing down my rising wrath all the time that I was being examined like a brute beast, until I was like to burst, which I did thus,

"You dirty snivelling upstart! Why didn't you tell me this before. I told you that I had never been in a place before, and yet you keep me hanging about you, losing my time, for your infernal pleasure!"

"Young man, what do you mean by speaking to me in that manner? Do you know who you're speaking to?"

"Know," replied I, "no, nor don't care, if you were the Governor it would make no difference."

"Be off, you scoundrel, and don't be making a disturbance!"

"If you call me a scoundrel," said I, now fairly up, "I'll give you a lesson in politeness. I'm your superior in everything, you dirty counter-jumper!" and at this interesting stage I made a stride towards him. He bolted out of the room and called to someone to go and fetch a policeman. I, not being anxious to see that functionary, walked out.

Many other incidents occurred whilst looking for work. At one place there were a good many applicants and an old man obtained it, not because he was more fitted, but because he was a Freemason. I determined to join that institution when the opportunity occurred for I have several times seen the benefit of it. I wandered about Melbourne for three entire days without any regular food. A piece of mouldy bread that I picked up under the wharf appeared a delicious morsel. I found that chewing a bit of tobacco occasionally alleviated the hunger much, but I was obliged to be sparing even of this luxury. Whitlaw was better off for he got a feed from some of his acquaintances in the town.

One morning I saw an advertisement for six labourers on a farm at five shillings per diem, with food, at the Salt River;[15] so I walked out there and obtained a place. It was to heave straw away from a threshing machine, getting first-rate grub, meat and tea at every meal. We slept in the straw. I worked away at this for about ten days and left sooner than I otherwise should in consequence of a row with an Irish workman who, being regularly on the farm, considered that he had a right to order the hands about, but I would not have it, and had I not been firm, should have got a poke with his fork. However he crawled round the Governor and I was paid off.

I found Whitlaw in much about the same condition as before. He was waiting for his money from the Fire Office. I found a letter from my uncle with many good wishes, but no mention of the needful. I shared what I had with Whitlaw. We went about looking for jobs. There was plenty of pick and shovel work on the road, but besides it being too hard, it went against the grain. I applied for a job at Fulton's Foundry[16] and was engaged; and on coming the next morning there was a pick and shovel for me, a regular kedge-anchor. I took it as desired but seeing that they were working on the roads in King Street, I threw down the tools and, without saying a word, walked off. I daresay they thought me a rum fellow, but I'd sooner starve than work like a nigger. I was never made for it.

A captain known to Whitlaw gave me a billet in a lighter at eight pounds a month, a drunken old fellow. I went on board in the Bay and used to wash decks, row him ashore, and do everything else necessary. One morning when we had put him ashore at Williamstown, he told us to go on board and went away to Melbourne in the steamer. With me was the cook who was a tailor and knew nothing whatever of the water, so could not row. It was blowing very strong from the northward and therefore dead ashore. I tried to scull her off, but it was no go against the wind, and we drifted on to the rocks, and only by letting go anchor we managed to keep her from getting a hole in her bottom. Having no money we could get no tucker and all we could do was wait till he returned, which would not be until six o'clock.

At about five o'clock the wind made one of those sudden shifts common to this climate. A hot northerly wind blowing furiously making it difficult to breathe and in a minute it ceases and blows as strong from the southward, but so cool, so delicious that one can scarcely believe one's in the same country. It's one of the greatest luxuries I ever enjoyed. Your spirits rise with the wind and one feels as strong as fifty men. We got the boat alongside the pier now and could have gone off to the ship, but did not think it worthwhile before the Skipper came back. It came on a sudden squall with rain and a sloop sank at her anchor. Several ships drifted foul of each other, the bay being pretty full of shipping. When it cleared off we could see nothing of our schooner, but the Captain arriving soon after, we said nothing and pulled off. To his astonishment we could find no lighter. The old man was in an awful state and nearly capsized the boat with stamping and swearing. But on enquiring of the next vessel to us we found she had drifted towards Leardes Beach,[17] and on pulling there we found her as near shore as she could be without grounding. The Captain blew us up for not going aboard when the wind shifted, and paying out more chain; but if we had done so he would have blown us up for leaving him, so it's all one in the long run.

Two or three days after he got a job to take in freight from the *Sir Colin Campbell*,[18] and to my great chagrin he informed me that I was only to be paid from the day we began to take in. I didn't like this, and tried talking him over but it was no go. We took in general cargo the next day, and the old fellow, being a little sprung, was very fidgety about damaged gin cases. The two hands who were passing over cargo, thinking themselves witty (the same complaint is frequently seen among very stupid people) were very funny at his expense, and he naturally vented his spleen upon us. Oh, what a thing it is to be dependent and obliged to bear everybody's bad temper!

We did not knock off until ten. The cook was working with us, therefore no supper was ready. No matter where one goes it's all the same. What a number of rows and disagreements would be saved by having good cooks and never taking them from their work, and always having meals at regular hours in spite of every obstacle. Men ought to endeavour to preserve their presence of mind in such a manner as not to be disturbed from their meals even though the world was just coming to an end. What a jolly world it would be if everybody was good-tempered; and if they would have their meals regularly and well cooked it would go a long way to bring about this.

The next morning turned to at four to stow the hold – nothing regular – had not enough hands, everyone in a bad humour. Skipper had been walking into the gin cases. We worked hard until twelve o'clock, the cases coming down a good deal faster than we could stow them away, there being only an old purser, so fat he could hardly move, the cook and myself. We did not go to dinner when the hands aboard the ship knocked off as we had to stow away. Having no dinner ready, we had several broken gin cases there and had a draw now and then to keep us going. My temper is not excellent at the best of times, but having to work hard on an empty stomach "I carried in my belly a spark of fire" which the Captain like a fool fanned into a fire, for he came down and began swearing about the cases not being stowed away quick enough. I instantly told him to do it himself, and that I was going to dinner, which I did. After much fuss, finding nothing in the galley, I went into the cabin. But being also unsuccessful there, and the grog on an empty stomach together with not being accustomed to it, the excitement began to get into my head. I determined to go ashore and commenced casting off the boat for that laudable purpose. The Skipper interfered and would not let me go.

"Well," said I, "Give me some grub then!"

"Well," said he, "Just come and stow these remaining cases away and then we will go to dinner."

But as I had once kicked over the traces no concessions would now quiet me –

"Give me my wages from the time I first came on board," said I.

"I'll see you d——d first!" said he.

"Then let go the boat's painter!"

He refused, and we had a scuffle for it and I carried it off. He made a rush at me with a handspike, but stepping aside I let him have it in the eye and dropped him like a hot spud. He was up again and running on like a mad bull, but the hands from the ship came down and separated us. The mate decided that I had no right to go ashore, and in the meantime the ship had hoisted the flag for the police boat to quell the disturbance.

Now if I had been quick it would have been right enough, but I am such a fool and the more opposition I get the more I persevere. So I determined to get ashore and went on board the ship [from the lighter]. Seeing a shore boat alongside I made for it but the boatman, not wishing to be implicated, shoved off. And so as Dibdin says "Being half seas over, overboard I went," and struck out for shore. But the police boat coming up kindly offered to give me a lift, and hearing I was so determined to go, they took me ashore and locked me up at Williamstown. I was wet through. Having a couple of blankets given me I stripped, hung up my clothes – or rather rags – and turned in on the floor. Dirty enough it was too. But the police here are not such demons as I have before seen on a similar occasion to this. I was precious ill during the night from having swallowed a quantity of the briny.

In the morning I put on my rags again, which were nearly dry, and found that this was a decidedly superior lock-up, for they gave each of us a large hunch of brown bread and as much water as we liked, very nice water. I was precious glad when the time came to be brought up, being anxious to know what I should get, for although this place was all very well in its way and a piece of brown bread better than nothing, yet one would sooner starve in freedom.

To tell the truth I expected a fortnight, for I richly deserved it for my obstinacy and bad temper. The purloining of liquor is of course looked upon as nothing in the sailor's prayer book – but it is somehow a strange thing that when one deserves it one seldom gets it, and vice versa. Yet it is so. Now although I say it, in the *Sir Robert Seppings* business no person deserved reward rather than punishment more than I did, but I was punished heavily and unjustly. Now in this case I really did deserve it, but I did not get it. The charge was disorderly quarrelling and refuses duty. The sentence twenty-four hour imprisonment, and I did not even do that, for one of the police, about an hour afterwards wanting some water pulled up, asked me to lend him a hand, and he then told me I might go, which I did taking my remaining brown bread with me.

It's a long walk into Melbourne and as I had no money to pay for the steamer and not cheek enough to run the passage I was obliged to walk. What a glorious thing cheek! It's as good as a fortune to a man. It was dark before I reached the punt at Salt Water River. As I had no money to pay them they were obliged to take me for nothing, and no thanks to them, for I didn't tell them until we got over. The fare is fourpence – exorbitant enough to take a few over for nothing. I lost my way and wandered about the fields for some time in the dark, got into a ditch and being very tired, wet and miserable, was glad enough to find the embankment of the railway from Geelong to Melbourne, and by continuing on this I at last reached West Melbourne.[19]

I found Whitlaw looking better on it, having got a new rig-out, and on asking him the meaning of this change for the better, found that he was going to Anderson's Creek with a friend who had a horse and dray, and was going to set up a bit of a store. I told him the long and short of it, at which he was much surprised. He had some money. Being a cockney he was immoderately fond of porter, and if he ever had sixpence would prefer it to bread; now I differed and preferred my mutton chop, so to cut the matter short we had both.

I was in a worse state now than ever I had been before, but fortune had got partially tired of tormenting me. My trousers were completely done after many patches. Everything else but my shirt had long since been done. As for shoes, the uppers were fairish but the soles were entirely gone and I was walking on the ground. As Whitlaw was going away he would be obliged to lock up the cottage and then what the deuce was I to do? But "God tempers the wind to the shorn lamb"[20] – about the truest saying that ever was written. For you'll hear many folks say, "If I had to go through anything like that, die I must." But horrors fade away when one gets pretty close to them, which proves that there are few things impossible, and the greatest undertakings lose all their supposed difficulties when one grapples closely with them.

Whitlaw was to set off the next day, and he lent me one of his blankets, for I had not even my old and valued friend the 'possum with me now. It had gone up the spout some time ago for one pound. He had also kindly given me an old pair of moleskins which were a great Godsend, for one can't look for work if one's got nothing on. You may be sure I was not in very excellent spirits at losing my companion in misfortune. It's cheering to have one, although he was differently situated than myself; perhaps better off if anything. He would sooner have lain in that house and starved than he would have gone down torn, ragged and dirty. Now, there was the difference between us. I didn't care about my back so long as my belly was full; but I'd sooner starve than submit to be spoken to or, as I foolishly said, be made a slave of. It was a false pride in both of us. His was the best because mine had much of obstinacy mixed with it. Bosh!

The next morning he went off, and after much looking for a job, I slept under the Post Office, a place much resorted to by poor immigrants before the town's people saw the necessity of doing away with such an abomination as a poor wretch having no roof. Accordingly orders were given to take up all vagrants found sleeping in or about the city, and give them a lodging in jail with a week or a fortnight's hard labour afterwards. Very kind of them, was it not? Now such a law appears to me in all its naked deformity because I've been one of the sufferers.

The idea of locking a man up, treating him like a felon, for what – because he has no money. But it's no use saying anything against it – few people suffer by it, and it's human nature, so that if it adds to their comfort and does not hurt them they won't care. "Why, what a fool I must be; every country punishes vagrants, and what everybody does must be right."

In order to avoid being locked up I did as others did. There were about a dozen there tonight, some walking, some sitting and all wretched. I sat me down under the verandah, wrapped myself in my blanket, supporting myself against one of the pillars. I was soon asleep. "Happy low, lie down." I was awakened by talking and in the moonlight was a policeman about to take off one of my late bed-fellows – he had incautiously lain down and gone to sleep. Another policeman came and remonstrated, saying to the other one, "How would you like to be took up if you was hard up? You might be some day. It ain't so long since you was at the bogs feeding on praties." On being thus remonstrated with, the bog-trotter let the delinquent go with a caution, "By Jasus and don't yer be ater doze'n' agin, or sure and I'll lock yer up intirely." And I inwardly blessed the kind-hearted policemen, who although uneducated, could not be hard-hearted enough to execute the fiendish laws of their sleek, well-to-do brethren.

I was unwilling to chance the balmy air any more so I got up, felt very cold and had a brisk walk to the corner of Swanston Street, where a man stood with hot coffee; and Whitlaw having given me sixpence I had a cup of hot water and a bun. Having been down to the *Argus* office and finding a lemonade bottler wanted, I called, but found a man there before me. But the master, a Yankee, spoke civilly and told me that although he was obliged to take the first one he should be happy to give me one tomorrow if I should call. Be as saucy as you like to those equal or above you in fortune, but always be polite and condescending to those inferior or dependant on you. Otherwise you hurt their feelings, which one should never do, as much from one's own interest as from right.

I went on board the lighter in the afternoon with a view to trying it on to see if I could get anything out of the Captain; but he would not have it, but was civil and held out hopes when he got paid himself. They were discharging cargo and much gin was being made away with. I got a good feed in the forecastle from the original fat Jack, who was about half-slewed. All those lushingtons are kind-hearted fellows. The only folks they do harm to are themselves.

I went in the evening to a man who had a billet in a store, who lived near W—— and he told me that they would want a hand tomorrow as some casks were coming in, and if I came round at 9 a.m. he would let me know. I slept in the forecastle of the lighter tonight by way of indulging myself in a little luxury. And the next morning he engaged me at De Pass Store at ten shillings per day.[21] All I had to do was stow away a few casks – there was plenty of wine to taste. We turned to at nine and knocked off about five. But it was too good to last long and the fourth day finished it; but good luck never comes alone and as I was going to dinner as merry as could be at the prospect of a good plate of flesh I met my noble Taylor. We were both overjoyed at the meeting and he was much surprised at my appearance, which actually brought a tear to the eye of the best fellow in the world. He would on no account suffer me to go and have my shilling plate, but persuaded me to go to Willion's and have a good dinner. He had been into Gippsland with his brother and had tried at the Omeo diggings but without success.[22] He had returned with more experience, but it would take much indeed to sour that benevolent heart. He was living with his brother-in-law. The Turnbulls had done nothing, but still amused him with promises.

I now took up my abode at the Australian Boarding House. It is a capital house in North Melbourne entirely free from those two great nuisances, bugs and mosquitoes. The latter are to be found in great quantities by the side of the river even in the best hotels. This place had been built at the time of the great influx of emigrants. The berths, private rooms, are all round the house and a large hall runs through the centre on just the same principle as the saloon of a ship. Everyone can, if he likes, have a key to his berth. The meals are laid out on these long tables at stated hours. For ventilation, health, and economy it is the best plan I have seen and I wonder it's not more generally accepted.

Soon after this I met old McMillan,[23] the old fellow who used to cart our stuff and got hurt by his horse at Maryborough. He seemed very glad to see me, but had not seen any of the old mates for a long time. He saw I was hard up directly and instantly offered to lend me some money and go up with him, as the last place he had seen Dan was at Creswick's Creek. I was of course much obliged, but I hardly liked to take the money, seeing no chance at present of repaying it; but he pressed it saying that it was only what he owed me for attendance when he was laid up from his fall, so I took three pounds ten shillings, enough to get my opossum and a pair of boots of which I was much in need. Thus equipped we started from the Royal Hotel, North Melbourne,[24] after much delay in consequence of two other drays going with us – one of the carters being on the spree. He had to take up a large chimney for some engine on Ballaarat and was very nervous and in doubt that it would not safely reach its destination. However at last we got off.

McMillan was at his old game again of breaking young horses and had a colt first time in harness with him. He is getting too old for this kind of thing. Besides being lame he has received several severe hurts from them. I took the driving now and then – was getting quite an expert carter. A man has to turn his hand to almost anything in this country, and indeed in every other one. There is no harm in learning for they come in useful some time or other.

The road to Ballaarat was worse than ever I had seen – no road at all is better than a bad one. The Government had marked the road out and fenced it in without doing anything else, thus more harm than good; for a carter could pick his way of a space of some dozen miles, but now he was obliged to keep within the fence, continual traffic having kneaded the road into a kind of pudding about a foot deep making it a pleasant walk!

The first day the colt had torn all the skin off his shoulders but on the whole he behaved himself pretty well except on one occasion being stung by ants. The next day it came on to rain, making everything very miserable, and in the evening it poured in such torrents that it not only put out our fire but wetted our blankets and everything through before we could get on the tarpaulin. After it abated we, with much difficulty, got a fire by breaking up a dry box in his dray. Two of the dray men climbed in the chimney and got a fair night's rest. I managed to get up a tremendous fire and laid down before it to dry, for it's the devil's job to carry a wet "possum".

Next day we came to the crossroad for Creswick's and I left them, they being bound to Ballaarat. I had fifteen shillings in my pocket and a loaf so I had to be very sparing, but I knew that if I could find any of the Scotchmen I should be all right. I arrived at Creswick's Creek that night. It looked a most miserable hole, as every deserted diggings does. A few holes were working on the Black Lead with horse whims. They bore to a great depth. There was also a rush on a hard hill – sinking not deep, but through an ironstone crust. I visited all the places where I saw signs of life, but could find no-one I knew, so pitched outside and had a frugal meal of bread and water – rolled myself up in my possum and retired from public life.

The weather was beginning to get cool and signs of wet than which nothing can be more unpleasant on a bush journey. It seems wonderful that a man can sleep out in the open air on the wet ground, no other comfort than a blanket, no other pillow than his boots and trousers, live on the coarsest fare, walk twenty or thirty miles per day and still keep his health, strength and spirits. Few of the well-to-do old-country men would believe it. But the fact of it is the climate. I don't think I could do it in England.

The air of Australia, on the average, is without exception as fine as any in the world; and although denied by some young ladies because they would be ashamed to state the real cause of their dislike, which is that there are not people enough to do homage to their finery and they are obliged to make themselves ordinarily useful; they think it unbecoming in a lady so to do. A man must have a great mind indeed who can compare England with this country to the disparagement of the latter – as Old Moore used to say, "Ossa like a wart; and elephant like a louse – there's a mind for you!"

I got up the next morning as fresh as a daisy, ate my bit of bread, rolled up my possum and off before sunrise on the road to Daisy Hill.[25] At dinner I made a fire at the foot of an old box tree just by way of having a smoke and it quickly ran up into a blaze. I carelessly watched the flames as they leapt and crackled up the rotten branches, and casting my eyes aloft I saw a possum on the highest twig. The smoke had driven him forth. The branch soon fell and down came Mr. Possum. I was on the alert with a stick and brought him up, thankful my luck had brought me a supply of fresh meat.

I skinned and gutted him, toasted him that evening on the ashes and found him very fair feeding but rather gummy. Hunger was a good sauce and he went down slick. The aborigines do not skin them, but get some stiff clay which they carefully roll over the entire possum, then make a hole in the hot ashes and cover him up. When the clay becomes hard they break it; the skin and fur adheres to the clay and the animal comes out as clean, white and tender as a chicken, and with the above-mentioned sauce, makes a good meal.

Arrived at Daisy Hill with no better success. Few people were there but it looked very different from when I saw it last. There appeared to have been a large rush. I set off for Maryborough. I came on to a rush at the bottom of Possum Gully, the very place I lost myself looking for once, before Simpson's were opened.[26] Much change had been effected since I saw them last. A large diggings was at work called the Alma and the Adelaide Lead, both of which I hear were rich.[27] I sank just at the bottom of the flat, fifty feet deep and never bottomed it. The fact is I left for England at the very best time and if I had persevered when I had that good hole in the main lead ... No doubt it was "the tide",[28] but as I neglected to take it at the flood it did not lead to fortune. I saw a large number of tents and apparently they were doing well, for they were working hard. I went round and enquired much for Jimmy Barr[29] or any Scotchman. I was directed to several mobs of the latter but they were unfortunately not the right ones.

I lay down beside an old tree, lit a fire and, having added a bit of bacon to my store, was just finishing up by looking for some water for tomorrow; was weary and dispirited by repeated disappointments, and wondered where all my old acquaintances had got to. Being camped close to the road I saw three men coming along and I went up to them to ask if they knew where it was likely to find some clean water. One of them answered and looking closely at him I found that it was Harry the Cornishman who had kept the kangaroo dogs. He was as hard up as myself – had engaged in a quartz reef which had cost him about £800. He did not know where any of the others were but thought the Avoca a likely place.[30] He wished me to come to the tent and have some tea, but as it did not belong to him I refused, being very comfortable where I was. He said he would come in the morning, but he not making his appearance I did not wait, but trooped off to the Avoca. There was also a rush there and it looked very busy, but I don't think there was much gold-getting, the water being very high and few holes on the lead getting bottomed. I slept down by the Post Office on the banks of the Avoca River. The Pyrenees are close by and on the whole this is a very pretty place. Gold has been found in large quantities on the Horseshoe Lead.

I could find no signs of Campbell's Store and having looked round at all the tents I suddenly fell upon Jack Long. He was surprised – thought I was in the North Countrie – told me of Dick, my old shipmate of the *Lancastrian* working on the lead. He was mates with G. Davies, Dick's brother. Dick was very pleased to see me. He still had my dog Smut who had grown a splendid creature, but did not seem to care much for me. Dick offered to return him according to agreement but I thought that would be hardly fair, and besides I had few scraps wherewith to feed him. Dick was hard up. (I did not expect much else.) He was sinking on the lead and had been down for the last three months to the water and there he stuck, together with a good many more.

Tom Berman, the chap who was hocussed at Campbell's Creek, was also there, working away with a son nearly as old as himself. Seater and his wife[31] were working on a quartz reef. I searched for him all next day with Dick but could not find him. We got a man to show us his tent. Mrs. Seater was very pleased to see me – a good little woman she was. They both belonged to a religious community.

I had tea with them and knew I might have had money for the asking but I don't like asking these good sort of folks.

I set off for Maryborough intending to go on to Castlemaine and get a job on the roads. I camped there and had not a shilling to buy a loaf. However when things come to the worst they are sure to mend. I went next morning to look at the old hole out of which I had taken so much precious. I could scarcely find the place, it was so turned over. There were a few stores along the street and I found a melancholy pleasure in gloating over the place where I had spent so many happy and prosperous days. I walked slowly along and when I least expected it my eyes met "D.K. Campbell and Co., Store".[32]

I was delighted. I had made Tom Brice a handsome present when I left and I felt sure that should at least get a feed on tick. He was in the store and when he heard that I was hard up he spoke to a very pretty girl, about twenty, apparently quite a lady, who invited me in to a comfortable back room and set before me a plentiful breakfast – talking to me at the same time in the sweetest tone I ever heard with a slight Scotch accent. I spoke to Tom when I went out – "Why, Tom! What a devilish fine girl you've got there. Cunning fellow – been getting spliced, eh?"

"Oh no! That's my sister," said Tom, "She's married to Campbell!"[33]

"Oh, oh!" thought I, "Lucky old man! Old enough to be her father. What a fine widow she'd make!"

I helped them to get in some bags of flour, and heard that J. Barr was at Buninyong[34] together with some others of my acquaintance, so thither I determined to direct my steps. Tom lent me a pound to continue my journey with. I set off quite merry, for, thinks I, with care this will last me a fortnight at the rate of a two pound loaf per diem and an occasional piece of bacon to slip it down. If the fine weather, which had hitherto been tolerably favourable, had continued

I should have got on pretty well, but a change was perceptible in the sky and with dread I looked forward to a rainy night.

I selected a place for camping early in the evening and got a good fire under way, and lay down under a fallen tree tolerably sheltered from rain. I was awakened in the middle of the night by something cold running under me and on putting out my hand found to my great astonishment that I was lying in a complete pool of water. It was raining hard and I had over-looked the place I lay in being a hollow, and although sheltered from the drops, had completely been filled up by a running stream. I found the fire, luckily, not quite out, and managed to get a good one up, covered myself with the possum, and there I sat dozing in the falling rain.

At daylight it cleared off a little and wringing out the possum I rolled it up and shouldered it; but it was like a lump of lead, and I was wet, weary and tired. To add to my luck it mizzled rain all day. There were no houses or signs of habitation on this road and I began to think I had missed the way. However it proved all right and after two days' misery I arrived at Ballaarat, as dreary a looking fellow as needs be. There was a large township, but it required a pair of very high boots to walk through it. I passed a very hard place, yclept Sebastopol Hill, from the gunpowder wasted on it. I looked about here a bit, but might as well have looked for a needle in a bundle of hay. I pushed on, passed the Magpie and came to the Chalk Hills,[35] with a township running through the midst of the holes – a most dangerous road for man or beast.

I halted here, very miserable, wet and cold. Went into a grog shop and had a glass of poison, yclept brandy. I lay down on a form and had a sleep for half an hour until disturbed by a drunken man who mistook me for the Emperor of Russia. But I was ill-disposed to be funny and having stood his nonsense some time he began to be pugnacious, so I knocked him down and walked quietly out hoping that he would run a knife into me – for I was tired of living. "Oh, what a glorious lesson this will be to me," thought I, "and how I will profit by it when I am once more prosperous. Catch me fooling my money away again? Nobody cares for one when one's without." How easy it is to make resolutions; but how difficult to adhere to them. Still I do not consider these few weeks ill-spent. I shall at all events know more about the value of money and the folly, nay the wickedness of extravagance. Extravagant men are always mean.

Walked along – did not care much what became of me. Hated the world when I should have hated myself. If anyone had offered me work and rest I would have cursed him – did not want it now. Walked through the diggings – they were very different from when I went to England last. It came on to rain again and everyone stared at me for walking through the rain so quietly, and it chafed me to be the cause of observation – I would leave the haunts of men altogether. I went up to several of the tents with the intention of asking for a night's lodging, but I was in such an infernal bad temper that somehow I couldn't do it; so I camped under a tree. Tried to light a fire, but everything was so wet that I found that impossible. Fell asleep for a little but the water running into the hollow made by my body roused me up. I tried to make a drain for the water to run round me but it would not do so, so I got up altogether. I was all of a cold shiver and kept up the double shuffle for half an hour before I could feel my feet. Longed for daylight – and then one could at least see to die comfortable.

I saw a fire twinkling at some distance and thought I might just as well kill myself trying to reach it as to die here – so off I went. And after having nearly broken every bone in my body over rotten trees, having got quite close to the object of my desires, I plumped head over ears into a water hole. It was luckily only up to my waist, but as I could not see, and thinking that I might get into deep water, I sang out. And after some time came a voice from the fire, “Who’s there? Speak or I’ll fire!”

Answer from water; “It’s only me. I’ve got into a water hole. Come and lend me a hand out.”

Voice: “I’ll see you d——d first. I’m not to be taken in that way. Get out the same way as you got in.”

“Well, this is pleasant,” thought I, “he takes me for a sticker-up, but his advice is not so bad either,” so I slewed around and paddled about; but having lost my reckoning I got a little deeper. I heard another voice from the fire saying, “Why, I’m sure there must be somebody in the water hole. I’ll go and see – there, don’t you hear the splashing?”

“Well,” said the other voice, “Go if you like, but I’m d——d if I’m going to get a knock on the head. It’s only a stall.”

I could hear no more, but was much delighted with that and soon I heard, “Who’s there?” close to me. I told him that I, being attracted by the fire, had wandered into the hole. He told me how to get out and conducted me to the fire which proved to be close to a tent. He gave me permission to stay there if I liked, adding that I should go into the tent, but that his mate was such a funky cove. I cursed such hospitality from my soul, thinking how different would have been my reception with any of the old diggers of the Long Water Hole, Campbell’s Creek.

Day soon began to break, and I then found that these benevolent gents were new chums just come out green from England. I told them a bit of my mind after I had dried my clothes a little, and hoped they might learn better before long. They were camped a good way outside of the diggings just on the banks of the creek, which accounted for my misfortune – I coming from the opposite side. I rolled up my possum, wet as it was, and carried it with me a short distance; but it was drenched and as heavy as lead. I left it in the care of a tent, went into the town and bought a loaf, and having regaled myself took a turn round the diggings.

It came on to rain again very heavily, having cleared off in the morning, and I and several others took shelter beneath a large tree. By the brogue of one of them I found him to be Scotch so I entered into conversation and asked him, though with few hopes, whether he knew anyone yclept Jim Barr, well-knowing that personage would be known sooner than any other. I was quite astonished when he told me that he was there, pointing to a wee hairy man boiling a billy on a fire before a dilapidated tent.

I was overjoyed and ran up to him. He stood aghast – he thought I was a spirit, I have little doubt, looking so thin and fairy-like. Found Welsh Tom in the tent asleep. He had been on the night-watch. Beef-steaks and onions, bread, cheese, butter – everything was brought out instantly and Jimmy jealously watched the slightest diminution in the contents of my plate – but there will be an end to all things, and so there was to my appetite and I had to finally declare off dead beat. Jack McGuiness came home soon after and we were much pleased with each other. They were all surprised to find me back so soon. They were sinking on the Black Lead and, being divided into parties, were sure of one hole at least on it.

Dan Mather and Anderson were also there. The former had made away with his little money as quickly as I did, though without going sixteen thousand miles to do it. After I [had] left, Yankee Tom, Dan and J. Barr went to Melbourne, and after much spreeing managed to get rid of all their little monies; came back after some road-working quite hard up. Of course the burden came upon poor Jack who doubtless had more pleasure in spending his money in their relief than if he had squandered like they did. Dan, who was with a party, had just sunk a hundred-foot duffer. He had a tent on the Magpie, which, as it was not convenient to take with him on his various expeditions, he had left with all the things to take care of itself; and as a proof of the honesty of the diggers, on the average, we found it untouched, save by the winds and rain which had torn the fly. That was all the damage although left for fully ten months with valuable things inside.

I removed it alongside of Jack's and put it up whilst Dan was busily engaged in drawing the slabs of his shicer. Jack, knowing my infirmity, and although as I afterwards learned, but poorly off himself, pressed upon me five pounds; and they also laid us on to a thirty foot hole which they had driven along a small lead, getting good wages, for upwards of fifty feet. They had eventually left it with a view of getting something better. They had done very well on New Bendigo[36] – they always found it easier to get than to keep.

The parties that struck these small but rich diggings had worked there for some time on the quiet and had gone to town to get provisions. On one of these excursions one of them got drunk and let it all out. There was a tremendous rush of diggers instantly, but to little purpose, for the dense scrub in that vicinity, called Mallee scrub, made travelling very difficult, and several parties were lost therein for days. But Jack went on a wiser course, by hiring some aborigines who guided them direct to the spot, and they proved to be the first party who found it. Consequently they got the next claims to the prospecting party. They had been at Creswick's Creek at the time of the Stockade and therefore had not opposed the sanguinary designs of C. Hotham. Yankee Tom had vanished to some unknown region and poor little Joe died on the Alma of colonial fever. A person buried in these regions may be truly said to have a golden coffin. Peace be to his ashes.

They appeared to have much more aristocratic ideas now and talked much of the high honour there is in being a deep sinker – a Ballaarat man. The shallow sinkers were now designated "Shallow-minded coves" and unenterprising. For all that, commend me to shallow sinking for comfort and gain, and if one gets as much gold as from the deep sinking so much the better for him. Shallow ground has been quite as rich as deep, but as the saying is, "Distance lends enchantment."[37]

Dan and I went on with this hole on the Chalk Hills[38] with little success – the lead appeared to have dwindled away. However we got a little. I now received a letter from my uncle containing a draft for five pounds which appears to have arrived there shortly after I left. Tom was going into Ballaarat which is about seven miles distant and offered to take it. Although I knew how careless he was of money I gave it to him, and he, as duty bound, put it in his jumper pocket full of holes and lost it. Jack with much presence of mind stopped it at the bank and I sent for the record of exchange.

In the meantime a large rush broke out at the Green Hills,[39] a most likely looking flat, quite a basin, gold having been struck in the gully above. The sinking being about a hundred feet, we could not resist the temptation of trying out in such a lottery wheel – which, as usual in such cases was represented as all prizes and no blanks. So we intermixed and humbugged ourselves into several parties with a view to stretch across the entire field to intercept any run which ventured to come down it. The thing was to cut slabs that no time might be lost, so leaving one hand in each claim to secure them we set off to saw down and split. Jimmy and I, quite unused to the work, split a hundred, as we modestly thought, quite specimens of art. Got well laughed at for them, making us very wrath.

A shicer being bottomed on the reef at thirty feet by an enterprising party who had determined not to be like the "rest of the lazy devils with their shepherding" caused all the holes on one side to be apparently thrown out, and a great rush took place on the opposite side. But after a day or two shepherding they found the reef on the surface and accordingly off they went to the other side. A hole bottomed on this side utterly bewildered us and made us doubt if there was any gutter at all. If any, it must be a very narrow one and accordingly claims on this line were at a premium.

Welsh Tom in the meantime, having nearly lost his hole on the Black Lead, by a nervous man and a running drift, at last succeeded in getting to the bottom. The hole proved to be a good one, but the best of this ground had been driven out by some chaps who had had little or no drift in the next hole. The Commissioner was sent for[40] and then the surveyor, the complainants having to pay two pounds to ensure their attendance. After a considerable delay, which gave the robbers time to make off, the Commissioner condescended to make his appearance and then the surveyor drew out a plan of the two claims, thereby showing an encroachment on Tom's party, which at the lowest calculation would be valued at five hundred pounds. The Commissioner approved it and proceeded to punish the defendants and order restoration; but it only amounted to threats for they, of course, by the delay of the Commissioner had wisely made their lucky escape. Tom was in a towering rage and expressed himself – "By Gold-n hur, no more Commissioner for me, hur will shoot the next b——r that touches my property."

Jim Barr, in the meantime, bottomed on the edge of the gully at about ninety feet, just missing it, and the next claim got it good in the wall. Jack and I were supplied with slots for an eighth share – it means that the man who goes to the expense of furnishing the hole with tools and all other necessaries receives in return a sleeping share if it's any good. If not of course he gets nothing but his slots again.

We sank down here, but the gutter was slewing again and in consequence of a hole, getting the black clay which is in Ballaarat considered the sure sign of deep ground. This clay is most peculiar stuff, only found in the gutters, it is much like charcoal. Trees are frequently found at the depth of one hundred and eighty feet, and many other very curious specimens. In fact these diggings differ materially from any of the shallow sinkings. The scenery about here is rather romantic; country very mountainous and consequently very rainy – more rain during my stay here than I have ever seen in this country before. Buninyong, a small township at the bottom of the mountain from which it takes its name, is increasing and will at some future period be a flourishing town.

The time which had been consumed in this shepherding and deep sinking had pretty well exhausted all our capital and to retrieve our broken fortunes we turned to the Chalk Hills to try the fossicking in old holes. But we found this a stale game on these infernal deep sinkings, for the holes fall in and get filled with water. Diggers are not so careless as they used to be and leave very little ground for fossickers.

At this time a tremendous rush took place at Sebastopol Hill; fabulous amounts of gold were said to be taken out of one claim called the Newcastle Hole. The sinking was three hundred feet deep with ninety feet of solid honeycomb rock through which they had to blast. The lead had been traced down from the Magpie right under the bed of the creek into the monster hill of solid rock. Brunel's Tunnel[41] sank into the shade before their great undertakings – marvellous they were.

It is an easy matter for a man sipping his choice wine with his legs under the mahogany to employ men to do his bidding, and pay for machines with a stroke of the pen. He only gives the capital and knows little of the hardship and anxiety of one who invests both labour and capital, thus risking both life and fortune. It only shows what man can do with perseverance. It was wonderful to see these men, the educated and uneducated, the rich and poor, on an equal footing, uniting their strengths and intelligence – most of them altogether unaccustomed to the kind of work – bringing forward a thousand little ingenious inventions to surmount the obstacles that were continually arising.

To sink a deep hole in ground that will not stand without being entirely encased in timber or slabbed, is in itself no joke. When the hardest rock was added, and when blasted, leaves hundreds of pounds of loose rock and large holes in the sides having to be stopped up. Add to this a continual rush of water which if not baled incessantly would soon rise above one's knees and render work impossible – I call some of these diggings monuments to the skill and perseverance of private parties; men who, had it not been for the diggings, would have lived and died in indigence and never known an original idea.

All inventions, all great designs, come from the masses, from the workmen – and woe unto those who, living without a want, looking down with scorn on the so-called rabble, and when spoken to on the subject say, "Oh I like them well enough. I daresay they are very good honest men and all that, but then you know one must keep one's station; and as for calling them brothers and associating with them, why that's all twaddle." Let him go to the diggings and see how those very men have persevered through incredible difficulties and manfully conquered them. There are many wise, good things to be learnt from even uneducated men, and all the education in the world can't put an original idea into a man's head, let him be ever so quick.

Of course we were all mad to enter upon these holes even without the wherewithals and agreed to divide, half of us to fossick and knock out a living for the other half who were to take out a claim on the lead by ballot, frontage claims[42] being allowed here in consequence of the great risk: viz. as there was a gutter in which the gold lay each party of twelve was to take an unlimited claim across, being numbered, and to ballot for these numbers. Some parties having already got good positions were unwilling to give up their work for a risk, and these were called the pirates. A surveyor was employed to go down the last hole bottomed and, by means of a compass, to find out the way the gutter ran; then come on the surface and stick a flag over the spot as a guide for the next hole. Many did not wait for this, but rather chanced it.

One hole, having touched the reef at one hundred and fifty feet, drove in one hundred feet and then sank another shaft over which they placed another windlass, sending the stuff into the primary shaft by means of tramways, and then heaving it up to the top. They bottomed the second shaft at one hundred and fifty feet, and after the most wonderful undertaking ever accomplished by any party in which capital and labour were so happily blended, were, I heard, well-rewarded for their labour and perseverance, although I could not ascertain the amount.

Now all this was done by men on a perfectly equal footing, all masters or all servants, which ever you like. Is not such heroism as this as well worthy of a monument as the many which are erected in honour of men who calmly witnessed the slaughter and misery of thousands of their fellow men, who dress in blue and scarlet and keep their delicate hands for human blood. The world does not think so. It sees a hero in nothing but stalwart fighting men. When will it get over its cowardly foolishness?

But I am wandering again.

We found that the "knocking out tucker" was not so easy as we had anticipated, and Welsh Tom cried indignantly, "Hurm not going to starve. Tucker be d——d. Hurl stache this!" Which he did, and went on half shares with a Welsh cobbler of his acquaintance, the cobbler giving him thirty pence per week and his grub until the hole was bottomed in return for being a sleeping partner and receiving a half share. This sort of thing is often done at Ballaarat but I never heard of it on the shallow diggings.

North was one of our party. Also a chap from Leeds, he was a rare original cove who, although uneducated, had more sterling ideas in his head than those who had education. Physiology was a favourite study of his. He proposed going to Fiery Creek[43] or to Mount Ararat with me at which place there was a rush. But we tried a hole on the hard hills before leaving a fifty footer through hard gravel.

Jim Barr and North were down driving and I was heaving up on the windlass. We had bottomed on the reef and they were trying to get into the gutter when all of a sudden a burst came like thunder. Out came Jimmy in great excitement. "Lower away – let go – hell – come on, Jack, haul up – let go – heave away!" was his almost jargon. He sang out to Jack to lay hold of the rope and never mind the tools. If he had done the former the windlass would have carried away and probably the roller would have killed the pair of them. But North, more collected, sang out to lower the rope and told Jim to go up first, which he did readily and Jack came up afterwards. I got the assistance of two men and we quickly got them. Jimmy was in an awful state of excitement, but he could not bear to be told of it. (But which of us can bear to hear our little failings?). Before North was up, the hole was full. We had burst into an old drive of which we had no idea. The fact was that someone else had been following this small vein for some hundreds of feet on the quiet, and no doubt doing very well.

This was a complete disappointment to us; we had so set our minds upon getting a bit out of it, but I was getting kind of used to these little disappointments and looked upon nothing as sure. Everything is visionary and uncertain. We were all pretty hard up now. Dan Mather had joined a large party at a whim hole on the Gravel Pits, thus there was but Jack McGuinness, Jimmy Barr and North.

The latter was always growling in his original way; cursing the place as a starve-gutted hole, always about to make a move but never doing so. He had a vile, thin and cadaverous-looking collie. When he had worked pretty hard for nothing he would always have a confidential chat with his tyke. "Come here, you stinking wretch!" That was the name given him by his master. "Come here, wretch, to your fond master, and we'll leave this here starve-gutted hole we will, off like b——y Arabs, and go to some jolly diggings where he shall have his wretched guts filled with gold; yea with fine gold so he shall, like that jolly old rip Croesus – bad luck to him – off like Arabs."

He was the best comedian ever I saw. He would make one laugh without intending it even in the gravest times. A rare cheek he had for asking tick. He made sure of getting it from our butcher of whom we had had many a pound's worth. But on asking he was told that he would not trust, but if he wanted a piece of meat he might have a piece for nothing. North was very much offended at this and was going to be off like an Arab, but didn't. He subsequently got a job with the Welsh cobbler at Ballaarat.

We had a good chimney and were tolerably comfortable, and no doubt we might have lived pretty well on nothing, as many other folks do who require more luxuries than we did; but one is never contented, always craving after something.

Experience is a deuced hard, stern school-master, yet one has to be a long time under him before one learns anything for all that. Just see what hard times I had had in Melbourne, and yet I chose to set off again, and in far worse weather than before, being very cold and wet. Jimmy Barr did all he could to dissuade Jack and me from it, but he was an interested party. He did not wish to lose the run of so excellent a mate as Jack; for doubtless it was hard to find one like him. His fault is one which is seldom found away from the diggings – he was too generous; his heart was open on an instant to a tale of distress – a nervous temperament, but as brave as a lion.

I don't wonder at Jimmy valuing him; he was very generous too, but it was from a different motive. He wanted the glory of men, and he had his reward. He liked not anyone who either doubted his yarns or was a bigger liar than himself; a glorious character he was nevertheless, and you could do as you liked with him if you played your cards well. His great failing was a love of praise; it was the food he lived on. When he was down in a hole you had only to say to someone at the top – "Jimmy can throw out more or higher than so-and-so," give the other a wink to doubt it, and you might get him to keep down there all day. No doubt he was a very hard workman when he liked, and as Welsh Tom used to say (who was the hardest worker ever I saw), "Jimmy's the chap, d—n hur man, he beat the devil for work."

But Jack was determined to go, and as I had hopes of getting my draft from Reid,[44] a draper's friend of Dan's, and who had not answered my letter, for I had enclosed the draft asking him to cash it, and we thought of getting some work. At least Jack did, for I swore that I would sooner starve; and as he had never tried the pick and shovel business under a master I knew that he would not last long. North was sorry to lose us; he raised us a few shillings on some tools at that glorious old bargainer who is well-known to all old Forest Creek diggers, and Tarrengower. I mean McTaggart.[45] He divided the money and our whole stack amounted to six shillings.

Off we went leaving poor North in an agony of grief with his stinking wretch, making up his mind to be off like his friends the Arabs, but his mind was too large and took so long to make up that the cobbler got him at last. We went down the Geelong Road, that being the nearest way, and soon came to the patent plank road. I have never seen it before, although I believe it to be common in America. To add to our luxuries it came on to rain in the evening, and rained in torrents all night.

I was always happy when on the move, but this kind of wet bliss did not suit me at all. It was little use to think of lying down, so we tramped on although it was pitch dark. We came to some kind of public house, or farm house, and here the road widened and spread into a thousand tracks, and very bad it was. No light was to be seen, and after several ineffectual attempts to rouse someone – we dare not go too near in case of dogs or balls, for at night one must needs be careful, for they send a ball through a man without warning; and dozens of curs lurk about with a view of laying hold of luckless travellers' calves – so we thought we had better toddle on, for they would have less respect for us on finding that our pockets were so very light.

But shortly after this we lost our road entirely and waddled about up to our waists in mud and water. Oh, it was glorious fun! We tried in vain to light a fire, everything was so wet. Having found a more beaten track we pursued it until daylight, and weary and worn we arrived at a few straggling huts; but neither of us had the necessary amount of cheek to go in for a cup of tea and a warm. We wanted one of those we had left behind us. What a glorious thing that cheek; it's better to be born cheeky than lucky. We managed to get a fire and boil the billy; a cup of hot tea did us all the good in the world although the rest was little good in the rain and we walked on again; saw some signs of working men, but had not cheek to ask for a job.

About four o'clock we arrived at the Separation Inn.[46] It was blowing from the southward, cold with rain, and a miserable plain this was. Lor, how I hate these plains. After holding a court martial we decided that, as we were nearly dead-beat, having been on our legs two days and one night, wet through and properly miserable, also having three shillings left (we had had a nobbler of spirits for we thought that we were in the regions of sixpennies, but were deceived into shilling nobblers) and knowing now that it was sixpenny nobblers, we would go in, have a nobbler and ask for leave to sleep in the hayloft – making sure that no objection would be made. But what was our astonishment, to be told that he did not allow anyone into his loft, that we could walk for three hours yet.

"We have been walking two days and a night, and are very wet," was our reply.

"It doesn't matter, you shan't sleep here."

"Why you crawling cur," said Jack, "It's the likes of us that keep the likes of you lazy wretches. You might be hard up some day."

But it was to no purpose. It gave us a good lesson though, and Jack and I made a vow never to spend another foolish sixpence among any of them; and with bitter, very bitter feelings, we tramped on.

"Well," says Jack, "one crime can't be laid at my door. I never turned away a hungry, or weary soul from my door, no never." And I firmly believe he spoke the truth. We went down a steep hill into a township and luckily espied a stack of wheat under which we ensconced ourselves; and although it rained a little we had a very comfortable night of it.[47]

We rose in the morning very stiff and tired but it turned out a fine day and very glad it made us. The stack was full of rats and we purposed making a meal off them but could not catch any. We had a good wash in a running stream hard by and took up our swags like giants refreshed. We had a job to get any grub as it was Sunday. Englishmen don't allow for people eating on that day of prayer. Oh, oh, if a man can't live by bread, I'm blowed if he can by prayer! At last we got a loaf from someone more charitable than the others, or perhaps he wanted money more – who knows? This finished our store, and as we made the plains the next day where we slept, had nothing to exercise our jaws on.

Jack was sanguine; a good-hearted fellow himself, he thought well of others.

"Oh surely," says he, "everybody's not like the landlord of the Separation. They'll give us a bit of bread anyhow."

"Try it on, my noble," says I, "Try it on. I have tried it and found out how kind and hospitable folks are. If you come across an old lag's or an old digger's house perhaps you might, but as for a new chum, he'd sooner shoot you."

"Now you see, man," says Jack, and accordingly went to a house with a large garden to it. "We are hard up and going across the plains. Can you lend us a bit of bread and we'll pay you presently?"

"Haven't got any," was the cross reply, and slam went the door in his face.

I thought I should have died to see his woebegone face; laugh I must or burst.

"There now, I told you what it would be," said I, exulting over my superior knowledge of human nature.

"Well, the devil seize 'em," said Jack, "They might have been civil anyhow. I'll starve before I ask anyone else."

Soon after this we came up with a boy in a small cart and he gave us a lift. When he left us we followed the telegraph wires. This plain runs from Melbourne to Geelong thirty miles, a most dreary desolate place. Ten miles seem no distance to the eye but to the leg they appear double as far. In summer time on a plain you get no water or protection from the burning rays of the sun; but we had not this to contend with, for we were up to our ankles in water oftentimes. In the evening the clouds gathered and it looked much like a wet night. Seeing some of the tents of the workmen on the line we determined to make out a night's lodgings, let what will be the result, and as luck would have it there was an old mate of Jack's in this very tent, yclept Tommy Roundhead, a shipmate of Yankee Tom's. We were welcome, the billy and the mutton under way directly. Tommy had heard of me before for he had worked in my old hole on the

Maryborough diggings. As may be imagined we slipped into the mutton and had a nice warm bed into the bargain.

They were working piecework blasting the rock out of the cut. This line had been tremendously rocky and must cost a mint of money. We were told that hands were wanted a little higher up at day work, ten shillings a day, but we were bent on getting the draft first, and I was very unwilling to set to at the pick work at all. They made us take some tucker with us the next morning and directed us the nearest way. Tom had no money as they were paid once a month and got their rations from a store of the contractor's, who stuck it on awfully.

We got to Melbourne that day precious tired, and took up our abode at the Western Dining Rooms. My first act was to shove the possum up the spout, but I only got fifteen shillings on it this time. The rain and wear had knocked off five shillings. I met Bill Taylor; he was hard up. I got my carpet-bag from him in which there were some flannels and shirts; both I was much in want of; also my great coat. I found that Reid had sent back the draft to Buninyong. As the first of exchange had been stopped the bank refused to cash this one, so that fell to the ground. We looked out for some job without success, and as the fifteen shillings was all done the second day I put my coat up the spout, thus getting ten shillings more.

Burgess was in town. He had been dredging out the Murray,[48] and having finished this interesting job had got a billet as barman next door to the Lyceum, a place which suited him to a T. Bill Taylor expected to get some tin from Turnbulls, and then he purposed going to the diggings with us; but the tin was long forthcoming. All our ten bob went the way of all flesh, and we were obliged to walk out of town every night and sleep under a haystack.

The first night it was pitch dark when we wandered out and as the country is all cultivated it loses its freedom. It was a long time before we found a convenient place to drop down. Jack luckily found the remains of a haystack in which we made a hole and slept warm and comfortable enough. There are many worse places than a good haystack. These old ones are not so nice – so many crawlers about. You see I had no blanket or coat so there were only two thin ones between us.

As a last resource we went about work on the roads, but even that failed us now. There was too much water to give contracts. We set off to try navvy work on the Geelong Railway.[49] Near Melbourne they were all full, and as it came on to rain towards evening we turned into a deserted hut about ten miles from Williamstown. The pigs had taken their abode therein and were much disconcerted at our turning them out.

We made a fire by pulling down the door and flooring. In the remains of a garden we found several turnips. This was indeed a feast, and with one of the suckers would have made a dinner for king; but unfortunately we could not easily catch one, for they kicked up such an infernal row we feared they would alarm the public house the other side of the creek; so we were fain to make a meal of the turnips. We had boiled turnips, baked turnips, semi-fried turnips and raw turnips, a glorious feed.

Plenty of straw being in the hut we made a comfortable bed before the fire, but we had not lain long when we both sprang up. Oh, don't mention it! I never felt anything to beat it. I had felt a disagreeable pricking all the evening but now it was like a million pins pricking one all over. They were pig fleas. The place was full of them. There is no other flea to compare with it, although it is so small. No more rest that night, and precious cold it was too, so we revenged ourselves by burning the straw, which eased us a little. The blankets were so covered that they appeared like a mahogany board. Ah well! I'd sooner get wet through a dozen times than go in there again.

Cold enough it was the next day as we traversed that dreary plain. I don't like this business in the winter time and a man feels twice as cold with his belly empty. "Never mind, my worthy friend Jack, a good lesson for you – take care of the baubees." Well, I must say that it's all my own fault entirely. It's either a feast or a famine with me, and there is no pleasure in extremes – the medium is the acme. The only truly wise man is the one who knows exactly how to do those things which will make him happy, and to avoid those which are disagreeable. Now it takes a great deal of experience to find that out; some men never arrive at it. I think the best way is to be contented, and never to allow anything to put you out. Take it easy, that's the rub – not even pig fleas or starvation shall disturb my equanimity.

We fetched up at Tom's tent and very hungry too. Jack was very ill after the turnip feed although it had no effect on my more-seasoned stomach. Tommy told us that he and his mate Jack intended to leave old Ben, the other mate, at the end of the month, and then, if we liked to join them, well and good. In the meantime we had better try our luck at day work. They wanted hands at the Duck Ponds so we went there and were engaged at ten shillings per day. Jack was set at a harrow and I at the pick. This was about one o'clock on Saturday, entitling us to half a day's pay and enabling us to draw provisions. The overseer, a Scotchman, remembered me; he was an old digger and we got on well together. The work was not so hard as the puddling machine, but it was constant enough. He was a fair man and did not wish to kill a man for his benefit; but by the bye, he was not interested in the cut, but received wages which perhaps made all the difference. Who knows?

We had to turn out in the dark and then half an hour only to breakfast, to cook our own grub, then knocking off after dark and having to cook one's tea. If you want a man to work not only is it requisite to give him grub, you must also have it cooked; aye, cooked, I say – not humbugged to death the way half the food is done in this badly-cooked world. The next world would not be a heaven unless they passed the candidates through a preparatory school to learn to make food eatable.

There were about a dozen men in this, our tent, all lying on the wet ground, and when asleep they looked like so many Egyptian mummies in an embalming tomb. Selfishness and uncharitableness is catching. The worse a man is treated the worse he treats others. Two poor devils came from Geelong, hard up, cold, wet and miserable. Some of the men in that tent had plenty of blankets and clothes, and those were the men that cried out loudest, "We will have no more men in this tent. There are too many here already." Had it not been for Jack they would have had to sleep out in the rain without a rag to cover them. Those who had tried to keep them out, cowed before that noble fellow's indignant glance. We shared our small blankets with them, gave them bread, meat and tea, and as Jack said, "Let me see the man who dares to object to them," they were silent, ashamed of themselves.

But as I had before imagined we were not suffered to go on long without a little bullyragging; man is so fond of tyrannising over his fellow-labourer – and McDonald, a sandy-haired Highland man, a petty contractor, came to superintend and show his authority by driving men like beasts. Those who were beasts of course submitted, and, as the majority of mankind are beasts, only a few kicked and those few were kicked out. He began at Jack who instantly down with his harrow and told him to roll it himself and would willingly have chastised him; but the "crate pig he rabbit, would ha nought to do we' vie crike fiery bairns" and drew in his horns. But Jack was discharged at the end of the week, with but nine shillings per day. I demanded mine as well, but he wanted me to stop, offering me eleven shillings per day.

I would not stop of course. Indeed I knew I could not stand it long anyhow. So we started off to the paymaster seven miles up the line; getting there he refused to pay us, stating that he had sent the money to the Duck Ponds.[50] Therefore we tramped back again, and, as we could get nothing to eat along the line, precious hungry we were when we arrived; and not one of them offered us a bit of anything to eat, no, not even the men we took in and fed; and we were too proud to ask. I cursed those plains, the men, my luck and everything; I was so tired and hungry. How easy it is to talk; how difficult to practise.

Old McDonald cheated us out of several shillings more when he paid us, and told us that he knew nothing about it; he did not make out the bill; we must go to the paymaster. We went back again to him and he said that he knew nothing about it – we must go to the overseer. He was sipping his brandy and water and we heard them laugh heartily as we went away. Probably it was not the first time and proved that it was not the last; the fact is that it was a regular practice, and nine out of ten of the men who were paid off were cheated out of a few shillings each.

What could we do if we had taken out a summons? We should have starved before it could have been served, and as the old saying is, "One must have a long spoon to take soup with the devil." So we let it pass until the great Judgement Day when all those trivial actions shall be tried. Those who have been transported for life for stealing a few pounds from those who could well afford it, to quell their gnawing hunger, shall stand with those rich men who are looked on as worthy members of society; but if it be proved that they gained a halfpenny of their wealth by oppressing the poor or defenceless, I guess they'll get worse than transportation; and the poor convict will be walking off scot-free. What jolly fun that will be. I consider that day will pay us for all the bother we have had to get through this wretched life.

We returned to Tommy Roundhead's but found them in the same predicament as ourselves. They had been cheated considerably in their piecework and swore they would take out a summons for the recovery; but what with the doubts and the time they would be lost, they gave it up. That old saying about "possession being nine points" is as true as gold; if anything they ought to allow nine points and a half.

They had two little German boys with them before we came and one day after a shower came on, and having a newly-opened keg of gunpowder standing before the stores (they used a great deal for their work was all blasting) Tommy told the boy to go and cover it up. The next instant a tremendous explosion was heard and the boy was not to be seen. He had just lighted his newly-filled pipe and in stooping to cover the powder a piece of lighted tobacco fell into it, sending him a distance of two hundred yards over the other side of the cut, a shapeless mass of clay.[51] Now the expense of burial fell upon his mates and as his work was included in the rest, it being piece-work, of course Tom expected to be paid in full. But a thief is like a drowning man; he'll catch at a hair if there's a chance of getting anything by it, and Leslie deducted a fifth share for the whole of the time they had been at work, which even allowing he had a right to the boy's share, he had no right to a share for the other fortnight when the boy was dead.

Well, we all set off to Melbourne with the intention of making a fresh start for some diggings. We walked to Williamstown, that being the nearest but it was very dark when we neared the town and we had the satisfaction of getting bogged and wet through. We made up for it when we got there and enjoyed our hot glass and good bed. The fact is one would not know what it was to truly enjoy oneself if one did not have a few hardships. For instance, those who have never felt the pangs of starvation can't enjoy a good well-cooked meal as I can; it's like a sauce to one's meat, the thought of it is.

Old Ben got prodigiously drunk and it was easy seeing that his money would not last him long; it was because he was so foolish like that that his mates desired to get rid of him. I rather thought they were too hard on the old fellow, and so did Jack; because, although the company of a drunken man is anything but pleasant to a sober one, yet when an acquaintance gets drunk in your company it's a point of honour to see him through all dangers and difficulties, safe into that blessed harbour of refuge, blanket bay.

Now unfortunately Ben was worse in the morning, and Tommy and the others tried all they could to give him the slip. Anyone acquainted with Williamstown can be no stranger to the state of the roads through that delightful town, after a few days wet weather. The bogs of Erin are nothing to it. I remember Melbourne when those now fine roads were just like it. Helter-skelter through this bog we went to the steamer and I thought I should split with laughter to see old Ben, rolling from one side to the other, up to his knees in mud; then down he would go in the midst of it. He was in an awful mess, and although I could see that Tom wanted to get clear of him yet Ben thought they were only having a race. It was glorious fun! Having to wait for the steamer, all their running was of no use, and Ben came up panting and covered with mud which made them even more anxious to be rid of him.

We put up at the Western Dining Rooms and shortly after lost the run of him, for which none were sorry. If it was pleasing to himself to be in that state, why not? Though I had a melancholy presentiment that he would come to grief sooner or later.

I met Bill Taylor with Harrison in the Yarra Billiard Room, Harrison being marker; a young man of good education but being hard up had taken this billet. Bill had taken him into his books, as he usually did anyone in distress. Some people do the very opposite. Now he talked of getting monies from Turnbulls to take us all comfortably up to the diggings and set us at work. I have no doubt we should have done very well at that but it was ordained otherwise and I am not sorry for it. Which ever way one regards a thing, that which happens is better than that which might have happened – in after years I mean; and now it strikes me that I don't exactly know what I do mean. Oh, well! It does not matter much does it!

My foot broke out so badly that I could not move and was in much pain. To add to misfortunes, which some wiseacre has remarked never come singly, the money was done, and although Bill was in daily expectations, yet one can't exist on these things albeit they are very well as sauce to a good meal. So Jack, Tommy and little Bill had to go out to the quarries and look for a job, and I had to ask for tick at the Western which I got for a few nights. The bed was all I wanted. I did not take any meals, but occasionally got a crust from the bread basket on the sly. Well you can blame if you like, but don't do so until you have been in the same position, and then I'll give you leave. There is one thing at all events; it has taught me to be lenient to others for like offences.

At last Bill, tired of waiting, made a row with Turnbull and finished the business, thereby proving the hollowness of their friendship. He then went and asked the loan of some from another friend who instantly lent him thirty pounds, upbraiding him for not coming before. So now Jacques and he went up the road in search of the quarries where the others were, but after being out all day they returned unsuccessful.

Bill got my possum and coat out of pawn and we determined to try this new rush on the Sydney side. A great many people were setting off for there. It was called the Rocky River diggings. The passage money to Sydney was three pounds ten shillings each, so I purposed calling at my uncle's to get a fresh supply. We left a letter for Jack McGuiness telling him our reasons for going.

The foot was getting a little better, as I had been to the doctor's with it, but even yet I could not walk on it. We took our passage in the steamer *Yarra*, but it was so tremendously crowded and the fighting and swearing was wonderful.[52] I never saw such a badly-regulated boat before. It was quite the fault of the company, so greedy were they for gain. The cook and some others got their heads cut open in the struggle for provisions or berths, and none of us were sorry when her piston rod broke at the Heads and we had to turn back. It was quite dark when we got to Sandridge[53] where we slept.

VII

BEYOND THE BLUE MOUNTAINS

(The New South Wales goldfields via Sydney and Maitland. Paddle-steamer 'London', 687 tons registered. Commences August 12th 1856.)

A fine steamer called the *London* was now taken up by the S.N. Company and we were transferred into it.[1] This company monopolised most of the trade out of this port, they being so powerful that few can cope with them. They take passengers for a mere nominal rate, and I believe would take them for nothing rather than any other company should run with them. Many have tried but none have succeeded, at least out of this port. The Hunter River trade was solely theirs when I last came that way, but now a company of the residents of Maitland has clubbed together to put down their exorbitant prices. The others lowered their prices to no purpose and are now obliged to agree to be satisfied with half the trade. They are in possession of some very fine boats, but the accommodation ought to be much better for the money.

In the *London* we got on better for provisions but there were far too many passengers and more than half had to sleep how they could on deck. It was nice and fine. Two fights took place in consequence of a difference about giving money to the stewards, but not much damage was done on either side. Bill and Jacques were delighted with the scenery of Sydney Harbour, and indeed who is not? Bill was a true, pure lover of the beautiful in nature. Many of our fellow passengers set off for the Stoney Creek diggings[2] by the Bathurst Road, but we purposed going to Maitland to see how the Rocky River diggings were shaping.[3] It was with much difficulty I found a house to take us in. At last we succeeded in getting beds at J. Hutchinson's, the Willow Tree. He had, I believe, been in the fighting line but his charges were reasonable enough: one and sixpence for beds, and a shilling per meal at table d'hote. We were forced to stay here two days and then we got the boat.

My uncle received us very hospitably; would insist upon doctoring my foot which he smothered with bluestone and the pain was awful. He thought it was a bite from some venomous insect, but I believe it was only over-walking. We heard that the Rocky River diggings were quite done, and that the Louisa Creek were the best. They were about two hundred miles distant, a long walk with a sore foot. Fred was married and had settled down on his farm. Burgess said nothing about the farm he had promised me. Mrs. Burgess was very kind, but we only stayed there three days. He lent me ten pounds and Mrs. Burgess five pounds. We had a good supply of very nice corned beef with us, together with tea and sugar; altogether a good fit-out for the diggings.

The road is very intricate and winding, it has so many mountains and rivers to dodge. We frequently made short-cuts over these ranges and usually went some miles out of our way thereby. It was a great difficulty to get provisions on this road; few of the squatters would sell. They used to give at one time and glad of your company, but since the diggings they are much changed and they look with indignation upon the invaders of their sacred fortresses. To any but diggers they are still hospitable.

What beautiful places there are here up in the Blue Mountains! I can't describe them so it's no use trying. I could live and die here. What scope for an artist, for the geologist, for the naturalist, botanist and every other "-ist"; but still they seem to take little notice of the magnificent place. Whilst they are searching among barren fields of ice for things that when found will be of no use, this unsurpassed wild is thrown aside.

The reason is obvious – it is because it offers no impediment to the adventurer; its climate is the most salubrious, there are no wild beasts or any other pests but mosquitoes, or, what is better, there are few savage or warlike inhabitants. Yes, the reason why this country has been taken so little notice of by historians or others is because it has what no country since the foundation of the world has been able to boast of – it has no drawbacks. It unites the safety and security of an old and populous country with the freedom, wildness, natural beauty and non-taxation of the new. Africa with its pestilence, its wild beasts, its bloodthirsty aborigines, has attracted the pen of many adventurers and learned men; America, with its Red Indians who resisted slavery and invasion so long and successfully, its famines and other drawbacks, quickly rose from its original obscurity.

Australia now remains a vast field for the genius of man to display itself upon. Do you love Nature? Here you are! Here you will get it, unadorned, unsullied by the poisonous, bloodstained hand of man; no murders have been committed to gain possession of it, or comparatively few; none are required to keep it. In fact one has only to go there and one has everything that man could possibly wish for, without a struggle.

These ranges are in some parts sandstone, and in others a kind of conglomerate, in which one frequently perceives beautiful stones which may be valuable, for ought I know. In some parts they are composed of immense masses of granite rising thousands of feet into the clear blue sky, and not a soul, not a sound, to disturb the wild harmony of this grand scene. Bill and I would mount these tremendous mountains, the view we obtained at the top amply repaying us the fatigue. He was very fond of flowers and he was wont to be much excited at each novel specimen which came under his notice, and frequently exclaimed, "Oh, that my mother could see this or that one!" from which I am led to believe that she is fond of those beauties "which even Solomon was not arrayed like."[4]

Often when we had (after much and dangerous scrambling over almost perpendicular rocks which, had we missed our footing must have precipitated us to certain death in the valley beneath) arrived at the summit, we would stand entranced with the view thrown open to us on the opposite side. Miles of undulating forest land lay before us, studded with evergreens; clear pure rivers meandered over the sands of gold, the banks composed of the richest soil and shaded by magnificent trees which overhung the stream in various shapes; birds of every hue, of every shape fluttered around, flocks of white cockatoos flew screaming over our heads as if to enquire why we invaded their sacred bowers.

But what were all this? I have been told that some parts of England boast of as beautiful, but I don't believe it, for I've been nearly all over it. The most beautiful scene is naught without the glorious sun; it must be lighted up or it's dull and insipid. If one shivers in a damp, humid atmosphere one can look at nothing with zest. But here, how gloriously was it lighted and the atmosphere so clear, so pure, so heavenly; it's enough to bring a man on the point of death, to life and health.

Come here, ye poor consumptives, victims of foggy England; waive your extraordinary patriotism for once. You can take your luxuries, your black beaver hat, your broad cloth and your gloves; yes and even your roast beef. "I shall be bitten by mosquitoes and fleas," says you. "Well, that's no worse than to be bitten by frost. One thing you will lose; it is your taste for that black poison you call porter." Many will not own to losing that refined taste, but my belief is that one cannot stand it in a hot country. In London you will see bloated men drink their pot of Half and Half without taking their lips from the pot. I have seen the same kind of men in Maitland, coal-miners, calling for a nobbler of ale, or half a tumbler. Wouldn't the brave cockneys laugh at the "hide-AR"!

And although drunkenness is carried on to such a fearful extent in the towns of this country, yet I believe, from the progress teetotalism is making, that the country will eventually be as much noted for its sobriety as it now is for drunkenness. The greatest sinners always turn out the greatest saints, and these things if left to the people always sift down and find their level.

The world must advance, and the working classes are the ones to advance it. England, with all its talk about civilisation, is in about as dismal a state of ignorance and folly as any country in the world, and a little reflection would convince a person of the fact. Just con with an impartial eye the artificial state of society, the glaring humbug of caste, or the slavish worship of riches. Turn back the times a few years and see how curious and foolish those past chronicles appear; how it praised some person to the skies who was on the rise and predicted his future greatness; and how when he fell they knew all about it – had foreseen it; he was never fit for such an office; how one hears what the country demands is the right man in the right place, and goes on to tell you who the man is. What bosh it all seems now, but it read very well at the time didn't it?

Heigho, why everything is bosh! One reads a column eulogising some leader of a public charity fund, and how great and how good he was for putting his name down. I wonder it doesn't remind people of the text 6th of Matthew; you may depend upon it, you see *all* they give to the poor *in* the paper, and when it gets to its so called destination it would be well-sifted from passing through so many hands.

And when one reads of a glorious victory by Colonel So-and-So; how the gallant —th stormed the fort amid a shower of artillery which laid many a brave fellow low; and how the Colonel was the first to plant a standard on the wall; and how gallantly they bayoneted the besieged; and how the town is given up to be sacked by the soldiers; doesn't it seem strange that no-one remembers that God said, "Thou shall not kill or steal", and that our Saviour said that we were to "love our enemies", etc.

"Oh," says the war advocate, "if we were not to kill them, they would us – it's all fair fighting; and we ought to honour the brave defenders of our glorious constitution."

Does any rational being think for one instant that a man enters the army for the purpose of defending his country? Does he think that he cares one pin for his country? Of course, he doesn't! It's all twaddle. He enters the army to earn his livelihood, or, more frequently, dazzled by dress, drums and vanity; he wishes to carve himself a name; to gain honour and distinction; he cares not whom he kills; in fact it would make little difference if he did, for if he were told to cut down his father or brother he must do it. That has often been proved in riots when the military are called out to quell some disturbance caused by the starving millions who are kept down by this engine of tyranny and oppression. Do any of these advocates of war know the real practical misery of war? Do they think, as they sit in their luxurious rooms sipping their wine, what the real meaning of that paragraph is that they pass over so lightly and which sounds so well in the paper? Do they think of the thousands who are sent into the presence of their Maker unprepared, their blood-stained hands raised to heaven as witness against them, the poor widow and the fatherless little ones who are driven forth into wretchedness and crime? The English so seldom see the fruits of war in their own land that they grow callous of the misery they send out.

Perhaps they might think differently did they but see their country laid waste, their corn burnt up, their houses rifled, their wives violated, perhaps killed; for this is the true meaning of sacking a town. Men drunk with blood, wild, furious with brandy and passion, rush into your house, offer violence to those dearest to you, rob your houses. Such men as these in this infuriated state care not though they kill women and children; fancy your little ones treated brutally before your eyes, and you must not interfere or your life is not worth sixpence. Is this a thing for clergymen to uphold? To call a necessary evil? To say war has been from the beginning and we cannot help it? Even to raise their voices to the gentle, patient Saviour and ask Him to let victory shine on their murderous undertakings?

These are the wolves in sheep's clothing, preaching what they call the Gospel, which they pervert for their own lusts, from humility to tyranny and violence. They are just as much to blame, even though they do not uphold it, if they do not try to instill into the minds of their flock the "milk of human kindness."[5] It is because you are lukewarm, and neither cold nor hot, that I will "spew you out."[6]

And will you, O gentle Mothers of England, rear serpents, to go out in blue and scarlet, and spread desolation and death on the hearths of your foreign sisters? Beware, lest they turn and sting you! Think of your son, your strong beautiful boy, lying in agony on the damp sod, his fine form disabled and mutilated, with no gentle hand to smooth his pillow, or receive his dying breath, hurled into the presence of his Maker in the very act of taking the lives of his fellow creatures and rending the hearts of mothers and gentle sisters. And you do this for what? For an empty name, for shallow honours? Putting religion out of the question, what does it benefit him? He is heaping ashes on his own head; though he wade through a sea of blood and gets the honours, he gains but the yells of fools and perhaps a marble slab over his six feet of earth.

Would that I could do something in this great work. It seems so obvious to me that it is wrong, brutal and unnecessary that I can only wonder that among so many reforms this is scarcely touched on. All the great and learned men who write and speak so well cannot be blind to it; there must be many who are benevolent and good. A man with common sense cannot be off seeing the evils of the system; and yet on the most trivial slight, the smallest provocation, the nations rise and cry, "War, war, we will have blood, human blood!" You will hear Woman, tender loving woman, advocating it; learned and honest men rebuke it not; and boys from their earliest school-days are taught that it is noble and right to settle disputes by brute force; and the courage and cruelty of the bulldog are looked upon as the noblest attributes of Manhood. True moral courage they know nothing of; that there should be more remit in forgiving than in revenging; an insult is never allowed.

But I must return to my wandering with Bill and Jacques. Bill is at all events one of the peacemongers. I don't see what business I have with it here at all – we have it among the Blue Mountains. We lost our way several times; but got a good supply of grub from McDonnell's Station. The mistress, who is a widow, keeps it on. She is a kind woman, very fond of the baubees though. Bill quite won her heart with a few words of Gaelic, but I believe the rogue would sooner have won her daughter's, an exceedingly pretty dark girl, quite the artless Highland lassie of Sir Walter.

Mrs. McDonnell wished us much to see if we could find gold on the vicinity of her station. She was not averse to the diggers, spoke highly of the auriferous appearance of the place and said that she would find us in the necessaries; but on enquiry we found that she would like to be paid for them. A goldfield on her run would indeed be a fortune to her, as the squatter is allowed the privilege of monopolies in the trade in meat, viz. supplying all the butchers on that diggings, and some of them avail themselves of this to lay the prices on very heavy. She complained that her pigs were not domesticated, that many had left her and were now running wild, giving us permission to kill any we could catch. We saw a few in the bush and after several unsuccessful attempts found they were far too nimble for us.

From the Blue Mountains to Mudgee[7] the country presents a more flat appearance. We joined a party of sailors who were going up. When we came up to them they were hard up for grub and we therefore shared ours with them; which they returned on our arrival in Mudgee. The latter is rather a large town for so far inland, and, since the diggings, presents a very flourishing appearance.

Of course they all gave a very excellent account of Louisa Creek[8] which had formerly been worked by a company of quartz crushers, but was now thrown open to the public. Various accounts were given of the successes of this company. Some said their reason for leaving was that they had amassed so much wealth they wanted no more, whilst a few incredulous wretches (there are always such to be found, perhaps envious) said they were quite done brown. I confess I ranked among the latter, as I had seen no instance of the success of companies on the goldfields.

The place presented anything but a promising appearance, and yet they said it was a large rush. It was very different from a large rush the other side of the country, and was what they would have called fossicking in old ground, for it had all been turned up before. However there was no help for it and we bought a quantity of calico, stitched it together and made a fine large tent. With three flour bags, we made excellent stretchers, Jacques at the top, and Bill and I on each side and a nice bark table in the middle. Before the tent was finished it came on a heavy night's rain and we all got miserably wet. It did good however by filling the holes with water, thus enabling the diggers to wash their stuff without the expense of carting.

Being unacquainted with N.S.W. diggings I did wrong at the outset; for being unwilling to work in old ground which I considered fossicking, we went and sank in untried gullies, prospecting round the country. This kind of thing was always more in accordance with my taste, it is so much more exciting and romantic to try a place which has never been tried before. It raises up visions of countless wealth and the fame of being the first discoverer; but it is a poor game and requires a long purse which was not our forte, and continued failures drove us to resort to the old ground where we lost the few chances there had been by being too late. But bad was the best and we managed to get a little to keep life in, sometimes an ounce a week; poor work enough, but little contented us who had been lately on the brink of starvation.

Poor Jacques of the melancholy phiz – we used to chaff him sadly upon his little failing, which was too great a love for his little black moustache. Most likely it was envy caused us to laugh when he twirled it. Certain it was neither of us could boast of one like it. Bad luck always makes folks testy – one of my little failings was growling, and I used to growl, more than there was any occasion for, at Jacques who did what he could. No-one could do more; he was obliging and willing enough, poor fellow. He could join in the growl well enough too. And thus we passed a merry time in the evening, by growling, reading, smoking, singing, etc. We bought flour, it being cheaper than bread, but having no camp oven we made scones in the frying pan, like muffins, only that we rose them with carbonate of soda; a very bad thing indeed and I would not advise anyone else to try, for I already feel the bad effects on my digestive organs.

These diggings are famous for the heavy gold or nuggets found here, but they are very few and far between; although there have been instances of getting a three or four pound nugget at the bottom of a shaft, and then getting nothing more worth speaking of in the whole claim. The sinking is not deep, varying from the surface to fifteen feet. Another diggings was talked about, at the Iron Bark Ranges[9] about five miles from Stoney Creek, and this place was nearly deserted for it. We had bought a tub and cradle and were making a living here, and could not get our tools taken under two pounds. We might not do so well at the other place, but at all events we couldn't lose much for we hadn't much to lose, and so it was determined that we should go. A carter offered to take our tub and cradle for thirty shillings, together with tools and cooking utensils. We agreed and carried our blankets and tent ourselves.

It was but thirty miles, but an awful hilly road and with such a heavy swag we were obliged to make two days' journey of it. I like this travelling a good deal better than working for nothing; that is to say when the weather is dry and I haven't too much to carry. It's so jolly, as it were, not to be obliged to return, not to care how far you get or when you turn in, and to be all alone in the vast forest. Your only care, your only anxiety, is to get sufficient for the day. You are in the best of health and worship God at every step for all these glorious gifts.

On arriving at Iron Bark all our joyous anticipation of wealth vanished into thin air. It seemed even a more starve-gutted hole than Louisa Creek. However we pitched the tent and went to work, but for some time we could get nothing at all. Our tub and cradle arrived by the bullock dray very much damaged from the jolting over those tremendous hills. It seemed something wonderful for any dray to be able to make the passage at all. Our frying pan was gone and our billy smashed; a bad job we had made of it. Having no money to buy more, we managed with dampers and devils on the coals, and altogether were not nearly so comfortable here as at the Louisa. We got onto a hole paying about half an ounce to the load, which kept up the tucker, but it was coming down low for me who had left four ounces to the load on Maryborough, as not worth washing.

This ran out after a little, and the water being completely dried up from the continued washing caused us to shift our tent close to the Commissioner's who had reserved a water hole for the supply of the camp and prohibited washing therein.

We were now pretty close under the lion's paw, considering we never took out any licences. The troopers here are rather strict too, but we found more safety here than in the distance. They never thought any unlicensed diggers would be bold enough to come just under their noses. The licence here is ten shillings per month. In Victoria it was thirty shillings at one time; from that was reduced to twenty, and after many disturbances was abolished altogether. But I never paid any when I was getting no gold. What did I want with protection when I had nothing to protect?

There were a great many rushes about now which we followed up, but they were of very little good and we heartily wished ourselves back to Victoria, where although one starved a little while yet one had a chance of doing something good in the end. Now at this place almost anyone could make a bare livelihood and that was *all* anyone got. There is gold thinly scattered over the whole place and one can scarcely sink anywhere without getting the colour.

We fell upon another small vein of about three-quarters of an ounce to the load, and fossicked away at it for a good time, when there came a large rush at Stoney Creek about five miles off; and to this place I went and got some claims. The sinking was averaging twenty five feet, and very wet, but I believe the gold was much heavier and in large quantities.

Bill came out with me and we sank down to the drift, but the water rushed in so fast that it was impossible to keep it under until the surrounding parties, who were shepherding, went to work to try to keep the water under. But this the Sydney-ites could not be induced to do; they had never been accustomed to work in the water. So after cutting a channel into the creek, and much other work, we were compelled to leave it with a firm conviction that, if we could but get down, there was plenty of gold to repay our trouble, for some of the holes higher up where there was comparatively little water had got it very good. I saw ten ounces taken out of one bucket.

We tried several holes up above without success and were forced to return to our fossicking – "Dirty-stoned Gully", facetiously called so by Jacques from the peculiar stones found there resembling blue-bags and quite soft.

We managed to have a good dinner on Christmas Day, boiled a good pudding and sent a joint to the bakehouse, finishing off with a bottle of grog and going upon half rations the rest of the week; like true Britons who will go without all the week to have a good dinner on Sunday.

At last I got heartily tired of it, and seeing an advertisement in the *Sydney Herald* that the *La Hogue* – Captain Neatby who was a neighbour of Mr Hay's – would sail on the 10th, and thinking, from his having been kind enough to advertise for me the last time I was out, that he would give me a passage, I set off for Sydney. I thought that being idle and having my belly full was at all events better than working hard for nothing and seeing no chance of getting anything.

I said good-bye to Bill and H——. Only having fifteen shillings, ten of which I had raised on my coat, I had to be pretty sparing, having two hundred and twenty miles of mountains to go over. The only thing I cared about was the weather. If it kept fine it was all right and it was propitious at starting.

I never repent going on this journey, for I consider I've seen the finest, most magnificent scenery in the world. Mt. Victoria is about four thousand feet[10] above the level of the sea and the road which goes right over it is the most wonderful piece of work ever I saw. From here to Lapstone Hill is a fine road cut in some places out of the solid rock. Talk about old Hannibal crossing the Alps – it puts his pipe out entirely. By George, I'd sooner walk than ride over this bit – several conveyances have been smashed off Mt. Victoria. If you go a foot off the road there is a small chance for you – I guess you'd be off like a bomb-shell. Then there is Mt. Lambie about the same height but on a different principle – it's four miles from the bottom to the top, a gradual incline, and about the same distance down on the other side. And is it cold when one gets up? Don't mention it!

The varied scenery one meets with keeps up one's excitement the whole way across the mountains. Splendid waterfalls are to be seen on every side; or perhaps the better name would be torrents. Bounding from the mountains into the gullies and being filtered through sandstone, the water is as clear as crystal. Then there are the trees growing in all the most fantastic shapes; some horizontal, some obliquely, others being torn up by the roots. Then the prodigious masses of rock which have been hurled down, all jumbled together in that beautiful confusion which nature alone can arrive at. Then there are the birds, the goannas, opossums, flying squirrels, parrots of every hue, wallaby and sometimes kangaroo and emu.

And these magnificent ranges extend hundreds of miles to the northward past Morton Bay. They rise to such height about New England that the climate there, although in 30° Latitude, is quite as cold as Old England. The Rocky River diggings are up this way near Armidale. You can trace the ranges again to the southward right into Victoria. Although called by different names I should take them to be all the same range; and between these almost impassable mountains lie fertile flats and valleys which yield fine crops almost without any effort. How many thousands more still remain for the bold and the adventurous?

Nothing would please me better, if I had the means, than to follow these ranges from north to south. Some say it's impossible; pshaw! It was thought so to the cross the mountains at first, behind which are now fertile fields and populous cities; and well-grounded are they from all hostile attacks. Their standing army will require no pay and is the strongest they could have. It would take an enemy some time to get artillery over there if anyone had a mind to prevent them. Oh, how beautiful is Nature! How different from the works of man!

We had much rain on the journey – generally get it among the mountains. This did not suit my complaint at all. I fell in with four folks on the road and, although I care little for strange company, yet I thought that little could be lost in my present situation, and much gained – as it proved. One of them had travelled overland from the Ovens. He was one of the free and easy sort who do much more harm to themselves than to anyone else. He wished to stand nobblers at each public house. I had one with him, but refused to take any more, being unwilling to take from him knowing my inability to return it. The effect of the liquor soon began to tell upon him and he became noisy. It culminated about three o'clock when it came on to rain, and he, easily finding a friend willing to assist him in that not very difficult pursuit of spending money, soon got roaring drunk. The other chaps voted for leaving him and making for the next house.

I objected to leaving him, but proposed taking him with us. I managed to get him along at first, but we were soon left far behind. The road was very muddy and the rain began to fall. To crown it he got into a controversy with some campers and offered to show fight – proving his inability by falling headlong into the slush, and lay there rolling. A pretty fix I was in! Could I leave him there to be robbed, perhaps suffocated? I had seen such things done, but I could not do it, and my only alternative was to hoist him on my shoulders, to the great amusement of the campers who laughed at me for my pains. Out of obstinacy I got him clear of them and that was as much as I could do, for he was a big man and no small weight.

So all I could now do was to go on to the next public house and prevail on someone to come and help me with him. Luckily I found there those with whom I had been travelling, and with much pressing they came and helped to carry him along. After I had seen him a-bed I felt that my task was done. My blankets and self were wet through and, having no money to pay for a bed, I determined to sit in the tap [taproom] until I should be turned out. Luckily it appeared to be a house resorted to by bullock-drivers who were allowed to pass the night in this room, and the rain driving a pretty good many in, I was not noticed. There was a good fire and I passed the night on the floor pretty comfortably and partly dried my blankets.

The next morning was very lowering which, as Mt. Victoria lay before us in all its grandeur, was anything but pleasant. However it cleared up about ten o'clock and we all set off in a body. The two others would willingly have given the lushington the slip, and indeed so would I, but he stuck too closely on our heels; and as he had received a lesson yesterday he ventured not again so rashly.

We got no further than the bottom of Mt. Lambie when it came on a heavy rain and we took shelter in the public house, a large white building of a dull prison-like aspect, as unlike a public house as ever I saw anything. Not a soul was there but the publican's own household. The rooms were fitted up on the snug old English style, heavy, dark, mournful, not a sound to be heard save the rushing waters which now poured in angry cataracts down the sides of the mount. This had been guarded against by the prudent architect of this lone mansion. He had built on strong piles about four feet from the ground. One could fancy oneself in Venice or Amsterdam.

It would have been the greatest folly for me to have left this covering, and where could I go? For if I stepped off the platform I should be up to my waist; and I had not cheek enough to lie on the floor, so I was obliged to venture one and sixpence of my hoard for a bed.

The next morning the storm was over; everything was green and cheerful, the air so clear and transparent that one's spirits rose as if by magic. I have felt this feeling on a frosty morning in England sometimes, but there the cold marred the beauty of it. It is this which enables a man to bear such incredible hardships in Australia. In any other country I must have sunk under some of them, but here I was as jolly, wet as dry, without food as with it.

We had risen at daybreak so we pushed on four miles before breakfast. I then made a frugal repast with my own dry bread and their tea. Shortly after this my attention was attracted by what I at first supposed to be a snake in a rotten tree, but which proved to be an enormous goanna. We lighted a fire of wet leaves at the root and soon drove his nibs out, and, the nature of Man being bloody and cruel, we could not pass the harmless thing but must needs stone it to death, after having fought gallantly against a dog and four men, biting the dog's ear off and covering it with blood.

I would have willingly made a meal of him had I been alone, for I knew them to be good. I made the proposition and was laughed at; and being like the majority of my coward species, naturally afraid of ridicule, I allowed it to pass as a joke, thereby throwing away much excellent food which would have made any epicure's (Sayer included) heart rejoice. And all because we are too cowardly to fly against custom. This is the fruit of having company. Bad luck to it! He measured four feet and a few inches.

They were plentiful in this part, for we saw several more during the day. One was making for a bird's nest and we hid to watch his movements. He leisurely mounted the tree, about fifty birds fluttering and screeching round his head doing all in their power to arrest his progress; but in vain, his tough skin shielded him from their attacks of which he took not the slightest notice. He reached the nest which was on a slight high branch which bent with his weight. The birds grew outrageous at this point and attacked so furiously that I thought and hoped he would have been overthrown. But no, he snapped a young bird from the nest and threw him down. We now interfered and began to pelt the ravisher of feathered homes, and he, seeing himself surrounded, made a bold push by springing from the bough to the earth, at least twenty feet. So astonished were we that he was gone before we recovered ourselves sufficiently to give him chase. The bird was quite dead, but no marks of violence upon him but those caused by his fall. To these animals we may trace the cause of the scarcity of the feathered population. They are very numerous in this part of the country, but I never saw any in Victoria.

The next day nothing occurred of note. We passed several bullock drays and found several wild peach and cherry trees. The former fruit were not ripe, nor do I think they would ever get ripe in their wild state. The cherries were good but very small; the stones are on the outside, very much in an 8 shape. We also found a kind of fruit something like an olive in flavour which they called some name which I do not recollect.

The following day we crossed Lapstone Hill, the last one on our road. The scenery here was magnificent. The road, cut from the solid rock, wound round the side of the hill, the cliffs on one side rising perpendicular with trees and shrubs jutting out in a beautiful variety. On the other side was a deep ravine, the bottom of which could not be seen for the thick brushwood, but the sound of rushing waters (which was the only sound that disturbed the mighty silence) could be plainly heard. The water dashed down in small rivulets from the opposite mountain as clear as crystal. The road crossed this ravine by means of a rude bridge.

It was long 'ere I could tear myself from this "Arcadia", and when once we emerged from the hills a splendid view was suddenly opened to us. A mighty river, swelled by the late rains, rushed over an enormous plain. We were as if on a high wall in another country. This place is called the Emu Plains; long the theatre of oppression, crime and misery to those unfortunates we are indebted to for the fine road across these mountains which were once considered inaccessible. The labour on this road must have been enormous.

Much rain having fallen all this week, the Hawkesbury was swollen to such an extent as to endanger the bridge over which it foamed, and I feared would have prevented us from crossing. But I resolved at all risks to make the attempt and we succeeded, merely getting wet up to the waist. Our friend, the lushington, was not so fortunate. Some planks having been washed away, he managed to slip therein, although repeatedly warned of it by the folks ashore, who were watching our progress with interest. Luckily for him his blankets caught on a large nail and we quickly lugged him out with nothing worse than a fright and ducking. The latter is thought little of in this climate.

Much opposition was going on in the small town of conveyances to Parramatta, consequently it was very cheap. I put up at a public house from which the coach started next morning at five, and as I could not sleep out in a township I determined to venture three shillings for the public house, although that would run me out of the train from Parramatta to Sydney;[11] for I wished to keep enough if possible to take me over to Maitland.

It was a brilliant morning and after a good night's rest and the fine scenery I felt like another man, although I would prefer sleeping in the bush any night to a public house. Not so many mosquitoes and no fleas or bugs which are frequently to be found. Although I must say that the publics this side are invariably kept very neat and clean. We got into Parramatta early.

The others went by the train which was only a few shillings and would have saved me ten very long miles – no joke with a heavy swag on a hot day. But the country was beautiful and interspersed with fine seats and some very pretty gardens. It is mostly in a high state of cultivation; orange trees and roses are frequently seen and a very pretty effect they have too. But there is little water and I was precious thirsty. I asked a man for a drink whom I saw hauling up water from a well close to a public house. The water looked so delightfully cool, but he told me it was quite brackish. He invited me in and gave me some rum and water. How well one remembers such little kindnesses, when one is really in want. A penny given to a stranger without chance of reward is thought more of by the receiver than many pounds given by the rich to the rich.

I arrived in Sydney in the evening, and my ragged, worn appearance, and it being unusual to see diggers come down in this manner on this side, excited universal curiosity; and much did I curse their prying eyes as I walked to the Hunter River Boat, selecting the most unfrequented streets. Why should I, like a felon, fear the eyes of man? I feared not the solitude of the forest. Yet so it is. Pride increases with poverty. I had just enough money remaining to pay a steerage fare in the boat, and I was glad that I had been so sparing for I had expected to have seen Mason,[12] a fellow passenger per the *Red Jacket*, from whom I calculated to borrow a trifle. He originally had a horse bazaar; but I found he had given up business, so had I not had a reserve it would have proved disagreeable.

I arrived in Maitland the next morning. These Hunter River boats are fine ones. They leave Sydney at eleven o'clock at night, making Newcastle early in the morning. I walked to my uncle's with my blankets on my back. His home is about three miles from Morpeth, where the steamer stops. Rather surprised he was to see me; not very glad either I think!

I wrote to Captain Neatby requesting a steerage passage in his ship the *La Hogue.*[13] She was almost a new craft; he, being a general favourite in Sydney, from his careful seamanship and strict discipline and moreover a good man, got the command of all the new ships. He returned me an answer stating his willingness to give me a passage if I would send him an order on the Governor, Mr. Hay, for the twenty-five pounds, which I of course did.

It was on the 24th January, 1857, that I arrived at my uncle's after my pilgrimage. How sweet it is to look back after many roving years. He who does not learn by so doing has lived to little purpose. And to live in the past and future, to compare what one has done with what one might have done, is, after all that is said of its uselessness, a pleasure which I would be unwilling to forgo. How strange it is that one is obliged, as by an invisible power, to do that which he has no inclination for. Yet so it is. Yet folks say we are free agents. How can that be when circumstances over which we have no control exercise such a remarkable check upon all that we have purposed? Within the last few years, which appear to me like twenty at least, I have fully experienced the apparent fallacy of that saying which supposes us to be free agents. When I look back on what I intended to do and what I have done, how widely different they are – and if I were to commence again it would be with the same intentions.

How often have I experienced the truth of Bulwer's admirable maxim, that "Circumstances are fate."[14] Then why need a man add to the troubles which attend his life by thinking over them, and forcing his way against those troubles till they tear him? Rather let him float calmly and coolly down the stream of life, always acting in an honorable way and "doing to others as he would be done unto", yet at the same time not losing sight of the advantages which in the natural course of events will lie open to him on his way, and which he will be all the more likely to see if he takes things coolly.

But I did not look at things in that philosophical way a twelvemonth ago. But it's the best way after all. That's the content that poets rave about, the true religion which parsons call by another name, and the grand law that will always bring Mankind to its level no matter if their governments be called absolute aristocracy or democracy. Circumstance, that great leveller, will place them all on an equality and the philosophers can have a feast on their falls. When I get astray like this I feel very jolly just after the manner of the man who has got the first champagne bottle under his belt. Everything looks as through a coloured glass of a sweet roseate hue. But if I look at it the next day it's all dark and dreary, a kind of morning light upon an uncleared supper table. Oh, – horrid, insipid, lifeless and bosh, bosh, bosh!

The old man and I agreed not so well this time, although I believe that I managed as well as any of them. His was a very nasty temper. His sons had left him occasionally in consequence of his love of dominion. One day he had been to a regatta at Raymond Terrace and came home a little beery. He began knocking about his wife's son Jack who was simple-minded.[15]

I did not like that so much and foolishly interfered, thereby getting into the fire myself. He wished to know how I dared to leave his house whilst he was absent, that I had no respect for his property. To which, I, not yet having learned sense, or Christianity, which would have taught me that a soft answer turned away wrath, answered that being my own master I should go where I liked. He began about my dependency on him, that he had lent me money, that I was ungrateful and should not stay in his house another minute.

I replied in my usual foolish manner that I thought he was a mean man to throw his loan in to my face at such a time, that I would leave the house that instant and never cross the threshhold again. Mrs. Burgess acted as mediator – than which in any other role a woman never looks half so lovely – she was a good soul – quite the Southern disposition quick to love and also to anger. Her husband, when she was once roused, dared not overstep the mark. But in this case it was in vain; neither of us would give in, and although I knew that I ought to do so, to so much my elder, yet I also knew that if he was once bowed to there was no end to the servility he would demand as his right, and that now was the time to effect an equality.

I demanded my clothes and property, which he refused. The next morning I left the house, but it was only for a few hours. The wife sent for me and effected a reconciliation, and he, no doubt thinking that I would see his friends in England and he wished to get a good character, agreed, but I fancied that there was much dissimulation about his profession of love.

The ship had advertised to sail on 10th February [1857], but like all those London ships could not be depended upon, and continued to postpone her departure.

The last few days of my residence at my uncle's were passed as pleasantly as any of my life. The weather was beautiful and the fruit was very abundant; the peaches being plentiful enough to feed the pigs upon, and the grapes, oranges and apricots were magnificent. I went for several rides on one of the old man's horses along the shady banks of the Hunter which offers every gratification to one who loves Nature so well as I do. To add to all this, a very pretty little girl about seventeen stopped there from Sydney. Her name was Ellen – very unsophisticated indeed, but very delightful.[16] I was not long in making desperate love to her and was satisfied that my way was easy by being greeted with a warm kiss from her glowing lips the first day of our acquaintance – I was well-received. Oh, the joys of pure love in a genial clime! I could fill pages in relating the delights of our amorous meetings – how at first repulsed by the beauteous fair, whose pretended unwillingness but added to the enchantment of those rapturous moments; the pink hue of the light mosquito curtains on white damask; the excitement, rapture, warm bath and exhaustion; the round firm glowing orbs, the beautifully-rounded hips, the sweeping limbs, the melting dark eyes partly concealed by long half-closed eyelashes; the rich glowing lips, half-opened, displaying a dazzling set of teeth and a small piece of carnation tongue.

Such things bring the true lover of Nature to the seventh heaven – to press lip to lip in the lingering, ravishing kiss, to gaze into those deep caverns of the soul and to press that swelling bosom are, alas, bliss too pure to last – too like heaven for this mortal sphere. Let the cold virgins of the north who chide this kind of thing cease and leave their unloving clime; they will soon find the barrier of prudishness, which has too long kept them from such pure happiness, sink and crumble into dust before the glorious tropical sun. And let those who pride themselves on their virtue recollect that they have perhaps neither had nor are any temptation. I am sure there can be little wrong in using those pleasures sent us by the Great Architect to lighten the otherwise dreary path of life. Why were desires given to us if not to be satisfied, to be enjoyed?

Oh, Ellen! Long will those moments be remembered with melancholy delight. Long shall I linger over thy dear form and ponder over thy silky hair and sweet lips. If such things are sins, many must be laid to my charge, but not one for which I will more willingly suffer than for sinning with thee, dearest. Under the shade of a spreading gum tree did we sit, eating the sweet, cool grape and that glorious fruit for the thirsty, the watermelon, drinking at the same time the words of liquid love which fell from each other's lips. How beautifully she would sound them in her brogue, fresh from the land of the Shamrock, which to my ear is so sweet on the lips of a female, yet so low and coarse when pronounced by a male; refreshing ourselves occasionally with a kiss.

An old lady living next-door wished me to take some letters and packets to her brother, a Mr. Cole, supposed to reside at Islington, but from whom she had not heard for some time. I went to see several of the neighbours, friends living on the farms of the Hunter. They are very hospitable, and pretty remunerative places they have there too.

Drunkenness is the great drawback of this as well as many other Arcadias in this Island. My happiness was much modified by this great evil; the rows which it caused were disgusting and tedious.

The old gentleman's temper was failing and he was inclined to be pugnacious at times. I rose much in his estimation by coming to his rescue one day, for although his blows were tremendous at first, but he was soon blown. (No pun). I don't know how the row began. These two men, however, were half-drunk. The Governor put them out and, after many words, broke the jaw of one of them, but was quickly thrown by the other, and might have got the worst of it had I not turned the fellow off and pitched into him myself. Which albeit I am much against that kind of thing and would be unwilling to do for myself, I could not very well avoid it in this instance.

I borrowed three pounds from him when I left and that was all the money I had. I was unwilling to do that even, but could not manage without it. I left on 16th February, 1857 taking both their portraits with me, although Mrs. Burgess was not well pleased with hers and was inclined to keep it, for the same reason as my sister refused to let me have hers, viz. that it did not do her justice. What a pity they can't find some mode to make daguerreotypes more good-looking than the sitter really is! How they would take if it were so!

Ellen left a few days before me. She would not give me her address in Sydney, but would have gone home with me in the *La Hogue* willingly, and I daresay had I been differently situated I should have been tempted to make a consummate ass of myself as usual. When I arrived at Sydney I put up at the Willow Tree again; Joe Hutchinson, who had I think been a pugilist from Nottingham, kept the house, but it was a nice house and cheap. Bed, one and sixpence, meals a shilling.

I put my things on board the *La Hogue* and was politely greeted by Captain Neatby who had kept a berth in the steerage for me.[17] I felt half-inclined to ask after the health of Mrs. Neatby, but I afterwards found that it was as well I did not, for she being a Frenchwoman had left him in early life, he being far too sedate for her gay habits. They said that he allows her an annuity. If so, I should think he does not act wisely. He informed me that they purposed sailing on Thursday. These London ships are very irregular, it's a great nuisance.

Knowing no-one, I had rather a dull time of it. I passed the time principally in the Domain and along the harbour which was all in all to me. Strange to say I only met Nell in George Street on Friday and we were to sail that day most likely, so we had not much time together. She was with a female friend. From what I could learn they were milliners in Wooloomooloo, but I could not find where. My last shillings went in a bottle of sherry, and we then took a walk round by the Baths where there are some sweet secluded nooks for woodland play; but the day was too fine for much seclusion, and although we tried desperate love and were disturbed she promised to meet me in the evening opposite the Prince of Wales Theatre. But from some unforeseen occurrence she did not come, although I nearly lost my passage by waiting.

I slept on board that night, and very uncomfortable the first night on shipboard is, even though used to it as I was. So much noise, so stifling in the 'tween decks, and last not least, the maudlin drunkards' farewells. For most people think that they can't bid good-bye with sincerity without getting drunk, and many folks think it is a sure preventive to seasickness, although in fact it always makes them fifty times worse.

I remonstrated with some of them. Their answer was as usual made by an affectionate drunkard in that pure tone of brotherly love to all Mankind, "You'll 'cuse me, s-i-r-. This th' last nigh-ght. You'll 'cuse me asking you to d-d-drink with me, sir, and hope we have a g-g-good passage, and all be comfable." Here he grows affectionate – "I like you, sir. You're a m-m-m-an, and I'm a m-m-man. G-g-give me your hand, s-i-r-e!" This softened me but little, so I politely told him to go to the devil, and that if it was the last night we were to pass on earth together, I should want my sleep all the same.

Here a pugnacious drunkard – "Would p-punch anybody's head for twopence. He was a m-m-man too and didn't care a d-d-d——n for the biggest man that never was." A playful lushington trips him up for a lark and only nearly breaks his head. Here all talk a great deal, swear much, fight a little, make it up with many professions of eternal friendship, drink glasses round, have a song and finally, to the great satisfaction of the quiet inhabitants, fall under the table one by one, and slumber sweetly in a variety of picturesque attitudes.

Thus passed the first night at sea, or rather on board, interspersed by the bunk-boards falling out and having to put them pleasantly in without a light, or a nail tearing a lump of flesh out of one's rump. I had no mattress, only my glorious opossum rug which answered all purposes.

VIII

AN APPROACHING INHERITANCE

(Passage from Sydney to London in the ship 'La Hogue', Henry Neatby, Commander, 1331 tons registered. Commences February 21 1857.)

We got under weigh the following morning, Saturday, February 21st, 1857, and a steamer took us in tow. Another one full of the cabin passengers' friends was alongside, for the cabin [accommodation] was full of the most influential men of Sydney. Mort, the auctioneer, the great gun of the place, who a few years ago was a clerk and now is the richest man in Sydney, had the stern cabin for his wife and family, for which I heard he paid eight hundred pounds.[1] There were also a great many Jews – retailers, clothiers, publicans, horse dealers; the Colonial Secretary Riddle[2] and family together with a great many children. The fact is that I would prefer being where I was, to having a cabin passage.

Both steamers accompanied us outside the Heads and gave us three cheers on parting. The harbour looked beautiful. The weather was very fine but the wind light, which proved lucky for one of the steerage passengers who had taken one parting glass too many, and forgotten the time. The pilot boat put him on board for five pounds with the loss of some valuable clothes.

My berth was abreast of the main hatchway branching off from a narrow alley to the right. It contained two berths, mine being the top one which is better in cold weather, but not in hot, and if one happens to get a mate who has not been to sea before in the top berth it is not improbable that one may catch some of his stomach. There is more air in it though and that is something. Our place was very dark at first in consequence of a water cask being right over our skylight.

The deck was sadly in want of caulking but my mate had the worst of the leaks in the porthole at his side. His name was Rodd, from Essex. He had been to the diggings, talked largely of casinos and gambling, and took as much care to let folks think that he was a black-leg as a real one would have done to keep them from guessing it. Now I took this into my calculations and whilst others thought that he was a great rogue, I knew that there was little harm in him. There is little to be feared from one who talks much of himself, and much to be gained if one knows how to mark him.

Now there was in our mess, which consisted of four, myself and mate who were in the berth branching to the right, and Robinson and Andrews in the left branch. Robinson was a tall, quiet, gentlemanly middle-aged man who never contradicted anyone openly, very self-denying and generous in things of no use; he drank nothing in public, or little, but got quietly drunk in his berth and pretended sickness; he would willingly pay Andrews a full share for his extras, had no ready cash but many letters of advice on eminent merchants, was very loud in favour of strict principles in money matters and was never happy when he owed a shilling, until he paid it – but as for pounds he let them stand over. Very obliging was he to the females and very willing to give away the provisions of others to supply their wants. He thus gained much favour with the undiscerning, and although I don't pretend to be more so than the majority, yet strange to say my *friends* of shipboard usually turn out true friends in the *true* meaning of the word.

Andrews had brought a large stock of provisions with him such as cheese, bloaters, jam, etc., as also had Rodd and Robinson. I had none, or money either, nor did I want any for I preferred the ship's fare to their kind of humbug; but, as they seemed to think me singular, I promised, if they liked, to take a share and pay in London, which I did.

Andrews, a soft, old-fashioned chap, a rare study, had been a counter-jumper in Sholbred; a steady-going, very particular snob, he talked in what he thought a gentlemanly, but in reality in a very prosy, manner. He had been in the drapery line at Sydney and spoke much about the hardships he had undergone in ye same towne – "Will you believe it," he said to me, "that for weeks, yes on mature consideration, I may say weeks, we have actually been without a plum pudding" – drawling out the last word just as I was expecting nothing short of murder. "And moreover," he continued, "we had no – we had nothing better to drink than common Cape wine which they denominate sherry – and a common hair mattress to lie on. Sir, think of that!

"Persons who have been brought up in a certain way, with refinement like gentlemen, I may say perfect gentlemen, cannot put up with the hardships of the common herd, and I am assured that I should starve rather than submit to eat what I have not been accustomed to. You see me now in a very curious state," and he winked and whispered mysteriously, "We are on board ship now; but we shall not be here always. I have been accustomed to my little comforts, and my father has rather a comfortable little seat in Camden Town. I don't think! Oh, no, not at all," said he getting very ironical as he warmed on his subject.

I told him if he did not wish to be laughed at to keep all these things to himself, but he did not seem to take my observation kindly, and did not think me as gentlemanly a chap as that great friend of his, Robinson, of whom he spoke in the highest terms – who agreed with him in everything and then made a butt for the witty creature's funny remarks.

There was no-one that I cared much about. Glanhill and I were friends. He was an honorable chap and a well-educated one, but he knew little of men and manners and paid too little attention to his person. I learnt cribbage off him and we were continually playing together. And although the passengers were always at it, yet there was no playing for money. All our passengers were old Colonials, and very quiet they were. There are never half so many rows with old hands as with new ones; they get cooled down after a little colonial experience.

But how the spirit of gambling fructifies on board ship to be sure – cards, drafts, chess, bets, pitch and toss are all followed with avidity. And what a difference the tropical clime makes in folks! It takes all the stiffness out of them. Those who have been so very circumspect and so particular about the conventional forms generally go to quite an opposite extreme. Those gentlemen with the stiff leeboards, who call all those irreclaimable who do not bow to their forms and doctrine, are seen scattered about in every possible posture, and those who have the strength of mind to throw off their lethargy are, ten to one, gambling, flirting, swearing, drinking or some other equally culpable proceeding.

Now, there are the proper young ladies – you know what I mean! Lor, don't they draw in their horns! Oh, no! Not at all. Those who would frown down the slightest irregularity of speech or etiquette; who could not hear of being seen with a brother minus gloves, and who go into hysterics at a whistle or a cigar, who judge a man by his clothes, who never cared to avoid things positively sinful so that they did nothing unfashionable; these are the ones! What a change! Dancing with anybody, flirting with everybody, drinking frequently and gambling when laziness will allow.

Let no one boast of his virtue when it consists of a deficiency of temptation, and above all make allowances for everyone who commits a fault under circumstances or in situations which you have never been in; for the chances are ten to one that you would have done the same however much you might be confident of your own firmness.

By the bye, what strange attitudes one gets in on board a ship. All sorts of turns and twists to keep one's back from getting rusty, and in the bush the positions are no less peculiar. Suffice it to say that I can find little rest by sitting in an ordinary manner in a chair, like a Christian, as the saying is. Although there are so few specimens of that latter commodity that I have had no opportunity of judging how they do. From sitting under a tree at meals with my knees on a level with my chin, and in a variety of other ape-like postures my ideas of rest do not *rest* on chairs, unless one of those jolly, old-fashioned easy, or American rocking chairs, and getting one's feet on the mantlepiece.

We had no forms or tables in this steerage, and it was altogether as miserable a badly-accommodated hole as any ship ever I went in. There was much better accommodation in the *Red Jacket* for fourteen pounds than here for twenty-five, and the cabin was in proportion. Very little attention was paid to us steerage passengers. I only saw the Captain down on the main deck twice during the passage, and the doctor, like all the fraternity of ships at all events, was a humbug. Now Captain Milward[3] was round every day to enquire after health and comfort, and all complaints were sure to be attended to. But I think it more owing to the customs of the different towns that to any particular difference of the captains.

These London ships do not profess to pay much attention to the steerage or any other passengers, depending more on their freight, and a few select families who, having plenty of money, prefer safety to speed, the popular error being that these two very necessary articles cannot be united; but I feel assured that there is always more safety in a fast vessel, and that more vessels are lost by not carrying on enough sail, than by too much.

Now the Liverpool firms depend entirely upon their passengers especially the working class; a name is everything to them, and attention to the comforts and speed is indispensable. My firm belief is that no man ever went that long passage without growling at the ship, Captain, officers and all. The voyage is so long and tedious that if that small pleasure were to be taken away they could not exist. But I have been several times, have made it my study and I do not accuse a ship rashly. Our Captain was a good man and officer with that exception and that was merely custom, albeit a very bad custom that in respect to persons and the steerage, having so many less comforts requires all the more attention to their health.

Neatby was a remarkably careful man. He shortened sail every evening whether there were any appearances of a storm or not, and therefore we could not reasonably expect to make a very excellent run. He is like an old whaler. Mort spoke to him about it one night but Neatby sharply told him to mind his own business, that he was captain and would not submit to any dictation. I rather admired him for it, for, albeit it was rather galling to a man like Mort who might have had a large property at stake, yet no-one has the right to interfere with a captain or there is an end to all order and discipline.

The biscuits were not very good and were complained of. The Captain came into the steerage for the first time, and having listened, ate some, spat it out, looked at the cook and pointing to the words "Navy Bread" written there remarked that those words would never be written on bad bread – and with that he retired. A satisfactory explanation enough, but it did not improve the taste of the dog biscuits.

The beef also stank very badly and was anything but good. It was rectified a little but we should have been very poorly off but that we were very "old in the horn" as the saying is, and worked the oracle with the cooks, butcher and baker who were the best tradesmen ever I met with on board a ship. The former had been many years with this captain, the latter made the most exquisite pastry, and by giving them each a few pounds, half at the Cape Horn and the other half at London, we managed to get hot rolls for breakfast, soft bread every day together with fresh meat and pastry. Glorious work indeed for a sea voyage; so the owners gained little by sending bad things for our use.

London ships are said to be much better provisioned and more comfortable than those sailing out of Liverpool. I am sorry I cannot endorse it from experience. Certain it is that they are much dearer and it is the general opinion of the English that dear things must be good.

The Old Man was very attentive to sailing the ship; on deck almost always night and day except for meals. He trusts his officers little. He is a short man and from constant exposure to the wind his face has assumed the colour of boiled beetroot. Some folks might think he drank but I hear he abstained totally from all spirituous liquor. I applied to him for a few bottles of ale and porter. He was kind enough to allow me three bottles per week which, as of course I had to share with the others, came to a very small bite. However, occasionally coming the double on the steward, that is getting it from an under-steward today and some other tomorrow, we managed to do as well as could be expected. Several of the others asked him for a similar favour but he refused them, alleging that he only allowed Mr Smith because he knew his friends and he would not sell to steerage passengers. Which is by far the best plan, for when there is any allowed it always causes disturbances.

The weather was most infernally cold about a week after we left Sydney. I never felt so cold in my life; the sudden change from one hundred degrees Fahrenheit in the shade to below freezing point must be injurious one would think, but I felt no further ill effects.

March 17th [1857]. Rodd, who was continually up to some kind of lark, having got a tot, amused himself by pulling the clothes off the middy servant and, this little pleasantry causing the latter to show fight, much rowing was the consequence.

A man named Williamson was taken very bad with a succession of epileptic fits. He was in the next berth to ours making it very disagreeable. The ship's doctor paid very little attention to him, and although there could be no doubt that he was to die yet he might have been more prompt; at least such was the general opinion. No-one was appointed to watch him for the first ten days. He went on deck in a half-delirious state and, after walking about for a few hours, retired to the bed from which he never rose again. He died on the 4th April having recovered his senses a short time before he died and dictated a will to the doctor, leaving his effects to his wife.

Luckily for them that he did so, for on overhauling his trunk was a gutta-percha ball which was thrown on the deck; but someone hearing a chink examined it and finding it heavy opened it and found a hundred sovereigns inside. Had he omitted to make a will the chances are that on the things being sold by auction it would have been sold in the trunk. The person who bought might have had the honesty to give it to the widow. I say might – how are the chances there!

During his illness everything was very miserable. Foul winds, hatches battened down and the stink awful. Every ship ought to have an hospital on deck between the galley and main hatch. A very nice thing if he had been taken with small-pox or some other jolly infectious disease; besides not destroying the health of others, the sick man would have had a much better chance of recovery in a well-ventilated place. It would have been easy to have knocked up a bunk in an empty bullock stall, cleaned it out and made it comfortable. But no, what did the doctor care for the steerage? He played his cards for the ladies of the first – it was from them he expected to make his practice. One of the cabin passengers, a doctor, was more attentive.[4] However, he [Williamson] died and was sewn up in canvas, a bag of sand tied to his feet, the usual service read and he was consigned to his last home. It always seemed as though a great weight had been taken off the ship when a man is passed overboard and he is soon forgotten. Not so if a man falls overboard.

I never saw such an old beggar (as the Captain) to take in sail. There is little doubt about the sailing qualities of this ship being excellent; we passed all the ships we saw with the exception of the *Donald McKay* who hove to for a French ship but passed us shortly after keeping in sight for several days. I certainly thought she would have beaten us sooner and made a bet with Rodd that she would make the passage in a week less than us, and I only won it by two days. We walked past the ship *Carolina*, one of the White Star Line as well, but what we made in the day we would lose in the night by the Captain's infernal carefulness.

He was a part-owner of this ship and of several others belonging to Dunbar.[5] The most remarkable thing about him is that he has never been caught on deck by any chance, in any weather, without his black hat and kid gloves. He is a great swell and makes a great fuss escorting the ladies about the poop. I have heard that he orders the wine off the table a short while after dinner, much to the indignation of younger Riddle,[6] who has all the appearance of a Cornstalk, and likes his bottle. He would be very rackety if the Captain did not keep the reins pretty tight. His father appears a very jolly sort, too fond of the bottle to be very strict. And the Honorable Mrs. Riddle paid not the slightest attention to the children. The two girls were very great romps, very precocious and warm-blooded like most of the Sydney natives.[7] It is a remarkable fact that albeit many virgins cross the tropics, yet if they have the opportunity to act according to their inclination very few come out virgins – which leads to a common saying in Australia that "Maiden Cornstalks wear very small shoes".

Miss Hall, a very pretty girl of about fifteen years of age, the daughter of a wealthy Sydneyite, was caught in a berth with Bissott, the second mate, by Martyn, son of the horse-dealer, who reported the same to the father.[8] He had a private interview with Bissott, but what transpired there never came to light. Mr. Hall had had this daughter by his first wife, and had now married again to a very pretty Cornstalk by whom he had lately been presented with a daughter. She is not more than twenty. He is not a bad judge, an aged ram.

From the 15th April we had a foul wind for ten days and saw several ships. We crossed the Line on Sunday, 3rd May [1857] and luckily caught the north-east Trades and made a good run through the Tropic of Cancer. We had then calms and variables until 21st May, when we luckily got a strong west breeze which took us into the Channel where we lost it and got a dead muzzler from the eastward likely to remain so.

As I always take the first opportunity to get ashore, particularly to get clear of that cold dangerous Channel which is no doubt the most wretched part of the passage, I took Rodd's offer to lend me some tin and went ashore in a fishing smack for which they charged us ten shillings each. It fell quite calm shortly after and for about an hour we knocked about in a state of anxiety anything but pleasing; for had a breeze sprung up from the westward the *Hogue* would have been in London before us, allowing them the laugh of us.

We wished, very uncharitably, the foul wind to continue. The fishermen assured us that there had been light easterly winds for a considerable time past and that there was every appearance of a continuation. It was not long before a light breeze sprang up and caught us some time before it caught the other smack in which were several of the cabin gents, and to add to that ours proved far the faster boat. We went into the leeward of the breakwater and they to the west and altogether we got in nearly an hour before them.

The custom house officers boarded us and they demurred at allowing us to go ashore without a pass from the Captain or doctor certifying the ship to be free from sickness. However after many assurances that it was coming in the other boat they were at last satisfied. We were nearly torn to pieces by half-starved wretches who were desirous to carry our parcels. I was struck forcibly by the same thing when I last came home. One soon gets accustomed to it, however, and is able to look on the wretchedness of one's fellow men without horror. Rodd answered all the questions put him by a reporter readily, rather too readily; for he stated that we had beaten the *Donald McKay* and other things. The former was contradicted by Boing in the next paper.

We put up at a quiet hotel and Rodd would willingly have given Harry the slip, he being a rough Newcastle miner. We managed to do so for a time but he found us out afterwards. The town appeared to be overrun with girls and they were principally those who loved a little pleasure. Fine rosy-cheeked peaches, these Devonshire girls are, blonde, a complete red and white, forehead and breast like alabaster but cheeks plump and rosy, and lips oh-so-glorious! I certainly think they are preferable to any I have seen. We enjoyed ourselves much in their company.

The next morning we started for London by the eight o'clock train. The country looked very fine; everything was green; rather cold, yet methinks I could live in England if it was always summer. We arrived at nine o'clock, and very glad was I to get out. It was cramping work sitting in these close carriages all day. One would think that they were built for discomfort rather than comfort. The first class are well enough but there the price is so exorbitant and I thought more of a shilling now than I did of a sovereign then. Nothing like stern experience for teaching one of my calibre. We put up at Ann's, 24 Jervie Crescent, my mother's old servant, a good old soul and very kind she has been to me. I always like to stay with old friends if possible. Although I have little tact for making new friends, yet I like to keep to the old ones. Made a cast-down for Rodd on the sofa in the front room – he preferred it to a bed. I soon bundled the feather bed off, which lodging housekeepers always put on when they have new lodgers. Beastly, lousy things! I can never rest in them. And the sheets too, off with them, and let's have a plain mattress and blankets, then one can rise refreshed.

Rodd wanted a day or two in London, before he went to see his parents. The ship was not up yet and perhaps would not be for the next fortnight so there was plenty of time. I will join my log of Latitudes and Longitudes here. It's useful as a reference for any other voyage.

Days Out	*Date*	*Latitude*	*Longitude*	*Distance*	*Remarks*
	Feb.	*S.*	*E.*		
Sat. 1	*21*				*A steamboat towed us out of Sydney Heads – weather very warm with light winds and foul.*
2	*22*	*35° 53′*	*157° 25′*		
3	*23*	*36° 8′*	*152° 1′*		
4	*24*	*36° 29′*	*153° 12′*		
5	*25*	*37° 32′*	*152° 13′*		*Signalled a Chilean ship 'M—— Monte' for Valparaiso.*
6	*26*	*40° 25′+*	*152° 46′*	*175*	
7	*27*	*42° 49′*	*153° 46′*	*156*	
8	*28*	*45° 55′*	*156° 1′*	*206*	
9	*Mar.1*	*48° 44′*	*159° 9′*	*199*	
10	*2*	*51° 22′*	*163° 4′*	*222*	*Spoke the brig 'Arnon' from Launceston to London. 17 days out.*
11	*3*	*51° 30′*	*169° 4′*	*227*	
12	*4*	*52° 3′*	*174° 4′*	*194*	
13	*5*	*52° 30′*	*179° 25′E*	*200*	*One day gained.*
14	*6*	*52° 19′*	*175° 38′W*	*198*	
15	*7*	*53° 59′*	*170° 32′*	*200*	*Stronger breezes from North.*
16	*8*	*54° 56′*	*164° 13′*	*230*	
17	*9*	*55° 11′*	*157° 52′*	*220*	
18	*10*	*55° 31′*	*153° 17′*	*150*	
19	*11*	*55° 56′*	*147° 17′*	*203*	
20	*12*	*56° 10′*	*142° 59′*	*144*	
21	*13*	*55° 0′*	*135° 20′*	*270*	*Strong Westerly winds.*
22	*14*	*52° 47′*	*129° 50′*	*240*	

Days Out	*Date*	*Latitude*	*Longitude*	*Distance*	*Remarks*
23	15	53° 0′	123° 49′	220	
24	16	54° 38′	117° 51′	237	*Strong N-W winds.*
25	17	55° 56′	112° 2′	205	
26	18	56° 11′	106° 4′	211	
27	19	56° 45′	101° 3′	175	
28	20	57° 55′	99° 56′	77	
29	21	58° 29′	100° 6′	35	*Light breeze and calms.*
30	22	59° 4′	96° 56′	104	
31	23	59° 26′	90° 3′	216	*Weather miserably cold.*
32	24	59° 43′	84° 35′	169	
33	25	60° 50′	82° 50′	86	
34	26	61° 5′	80° 19′	75	
35	27	60° 28′	74° 16′	180	*Doubled the Horn.*
36	28	59° 13′	68° 13′	198	*Passed a full-rigged ship.*
37	29	58° 9′	63° 26′	160	*Spoke Barque 'Bentick' from Iquiqu to Cork. 59 days out.*
38	30	58° 12′	61° 27′	61	
39	31	57° 34′	58° 46′	95	
40	April 1	54° 58′	54° 14′	220	*Signalled ship S. S. 'Carolina' from Melbourne to Liverpool*
41	2	52° 4′	48° 46′	238	
42	3	49° 39′	45° 17′	231	*Signalled 'Donald McKay' hove to for French ship. J. Williamson died sewed him up and buried*
43	4	47° 58′	40° 35′	208	
44	5	46° 2′	36° 3′	215	
45	6	44° 23′	33° 18′	153	
46	7	44° 6′	31° 48′	66	
47	8	41° 11′	30° 18′	187	
48	9	37° 52′	28° 24′	217	
49	10	34° 45′	28° 21′	187	*Saw a strange sail.*
50	11	33° 32′	26° 41′	110	
51	12	31° 31′	24° 56′	150	
52	13	29° 32′	24° 24′	123	
53	14	26° 57′	25° 3′	159	
54	15	26° 27′	25° 30′	41	*Light and foul winds.*
55	16	25° 34′	23° 18′	130	
56	17	24° 16′	22° 14′	101	*Weather warm.*
57	18	23° 12′	20° 59′	104	
58	19	22° 43′	21° 20′	36	*A battle between Jimmy Ducks and Dick parted by the officers.*
59	20	21° 41′	20° 53′	65	
60	21	21° 5′	20° 40′	39	
61	22	19° 32′	18° 5′	20	*Signalled barque 'Alan' from Monte Video to London, 62 days out.*
62	23	18° 25′	17° 56′	109	
63	24	17° 25′	17° 5′	61	
64	25	16° 16′	19° 26′	102	

Days Out	*Date*	*Latitude*	*Longitude*	*Distance*	*Remarks*
65	*26*	*14° 19´*	*21° 4´*	*160*	
66	*27*	*12° 14´*	*23° 12´*	*177*	*Dancing on the poop. Scandal about B. and H.*
67	*28*	*9° 5´*	*24° 56´*	*182*	
68	*29*	*6° 55´*	*26° 31´*	*196*	
69	*30*	*4° 35´*	*28° 9´*	*171*	*Spoke ship 'Epaminondas'.*
70	*May 1*	*2° 46´*	*29° 20´*	*130*	
71	*2*	*1° 54´*	*29° 30´*	*52*	*Crossed the Line.*
72	*3*	*1° 31´*	*29° 34´*	*28*	*Weather very hot with calms and light breezes.*
73	*4*	*48´W*	*30° 48´*	*139*	
74	*5*	*3° 12´*	*32° 16´*	*182*	*Strong wind sprang up. N.E.*
75	*6*	*6° 6´*			
76	*7*	*8° 57´*	*37° 52´*	*232*	
77	*8*	*12° 14´*	*40° 33´*	*254*	*The first Gulf weed seen.*
78	*9*	*15° 18´*	*42° 38´*	*223*	*A pig killed for steerage.*
79	*10*	*18° 38´*	*44° 42´*	*233*	*Saw a bird called Bosun – lives on fish – a marline spike head.*
80	*11*	*21° 36´*	*46° 42´*	*211*	
81	*12*	*23° 57´*	*48° 15´*	*165*	*Lost NE Trade winds.*
82	*13*	*25° 42´*	*48° 33´*	*107*	*Fight between Dangar and Crawford.*
83	*14*	*27° 29´*	*47° 24´*	*127*	*Wind light and foul – saw several dolphins & school of black fish.*
84	*15*	*29° 33´*	*45° 56´*	*146*	
85	*16*	*31° 38´*	*43° 46´*	*166*	
86	*17*	*32° 6´*	*42° 8´*	*87*	*Sighted Western Islands.*
87	*18*	*32° 38´*	*42° 26´*	*57*	*Sent a boat on board the 'Epaminondas' from Shields to New York – got some English papers.*
88	*19*	*33° 53´*	*40° 27´*	*86*	
89	*20*	*35° 9´*	*39° 30´*	*96*	
90	*21*	*35° 59´*	*38° 55´*	*61*	*Calms and variables – 17th the 'Henry Frances' whaler sent a boat on board with letters – Spoke the 'Europe' French ship from Martinique to Havre de Gra 18 days out.*
91	*22*	*38° 44´*	*36° 1´*	*213*	
92	*23*	*41° 30´*	*33° 3´*	*220*	
93	*24*	*43° 54´*	*29° 3´*	*223*	
94	*25*	*45° 20´*	*25° 1´*	*195*	
95	*26*	*46° 5´*	*19° 16´*	*248*	*Strong westerly winds.*
95	*26*	*47° 8´*	*14° 12´*	*217*	*There was a day gained on the 5th March. I have allowed for it here instead.*
96	*27*	*48° 51´*	*10° 30´*	*195*	*Passed a great many small boats – dead calm – spoke French fishing boat – steady rain.*
97	*28*	*49° 3´*	*7° 11´*	*127*	

Wind east – hailed two fishing boats on the afternoon of the 29th [May, 1857]; sent the mail on shore in one with some cabin passengers, went ashore myself in another. The ship arrived at East India Docks Tuesday night, June 2, 1857. Total 102 days.

Now about the first thing for me to do was to get made a man of by the tailor. Accordingly I went to Nicol, (a friend of Mr. Richmond's) and got measured for a suit of clothes. I had a long yarn with him about the aforesaid and to unravel a mystery which until the last two years had remained shrouded by the curtain of silence, and which, although I care little about it, shall still remain so.[9] As I shall have to wait some time for these clothes I rigged myself out as well as possible and went down to the Governor to see how they were and fish for some ready money. He was anything but pleased at the sight – would as soon have seen the devil. However I managed to screw out ten pounds, but it was like drawing teeth and he swore that the account was overdrawn, which I very much doubted. Mrs. Hay was much better but was still an invalid.

June 1st 1857. I paid Rodd the money he had lent me, and which pleased him much. His brother and sister called to see him. She is a nice little girl, some affection about her, very black hair and dark round the eyes, the peculiarity of the Essex girls. This one was the youngest. He was continuing at war with his eldest; but I think it a fact worthy of remark that younger sisters are always more affectionate to elder brothers than vice versa. I called upon Fanny the same day, losing no time – thinking she might be anxious to see me, but might have saved myself the trouble. She was out at Miss Brown's, an invalid with a few thousands per annum; couldn't find a soul at home, although I'll swear I heard someone run upstairs. I went away in high dudgeon. There was nothing to be got out of me now, and what did anyone care for me! A bitter feeling arose within me. I had no home, not a soul to care for me.

Rodd set off for Essex to see his mother who had just heard of his arrival and had written off instantly such an affectionate letter that it made my gall rise more to think that I never had or knew what a home was. As for a rich man's London home I would not give a d——n for it; but a pure country one, no matter how humble, so that it had love therein .... As far as I can judge there is nothing blunts the feelings and paralyses the affections more than trade, and nothing makes us more selfish than money-making. It has its advantages; one of the greatest is that it wipes off many narrow prejudices.

I called on Fanny again in a couple of days. She kept me waiting an hour and then made her appearance, greeting me in an everyday style. I was just about to be off when she came in, and of course not in the best humour. She talked in an affected half-fashionable slang, looked much stouter and gayer, and, although much improved in appearance, had not in manner or temper. The fact is she is getting too old; she ought to have been married three years ago.

That's the way with a great many of these London girls; they are always on the lookout to begin where their parents left off, and the latter are also on the lookout for what they call good, (meaning 'money') matches. The consequence is that they never go off at all, and become bad-tempered old maids. It's all very well when girls have got a tidy fortune hanging to them; then they can command a good match, but, hang it all, is a sensible man going to marry a woman fit for nothing but small talk and nonsense, and no money either? Oh no! must have either – home, money or be a useful housewife not wanting a couple of servants to wait on them. Helpmates indeed! Pretty helpmates those helpless town hot-room dolls would make.

This kind of idleness which is thought so necessary to make young ladies is one of the worst customs ever introduced into any country. It undermines their health, temper and morals. They always have, or fancy they have, something the matter with them; hence the diabolical custom of family physicians. In ancient times, particularly among the Jewish nation, the women were skilled in the healing art. The culinary of course must have preceded it, for without it the former were thrown away. Those folks who write about women's rights should consider this, and thus point out the road by which they can right themselves by teaching them to be women and not things.

As to temper and morals, what can be worse for the former than idleness? The slightest thing chafes an idle person, They become great talkers from having nought else to do and great talkers invariably say things which they are afterwards sorry for, besides wounding the feelings of others by their careless thrusts. Scandal becomes into favour, novels are the rage, everything appears through a coloured glass; they long for change, their passions become inflamed, their talk wanders much on love affairs, but the strict ways of society keep them within bounds and they gratify their desires by those improper means which are the only ones thrown open to them, which destroy their health and if they ever marry deform their offspring, thus inflicting a cruel wound on society; but one that it well deserves.

Look on this picture and then say with pride – this is the way we train Englishwomen. The system must be quite new for it could not last long without inflicting a serious wound on the nation. Many of the sores we see around us in our everyday walks are its results, but folks close their eyes and will not trace them to their true source.

Now I had little or no experience of the female sex when I came to England last in 1855 but I learnt much during that few months. Then I would have married any woman at a moment's notice who would have been foolish enough to give me encouragement, but now I was much changed and so were they in my eyes. From nineteen to twenty-one are two very dangerous years; if one escapes these he is more likely to go single until he really marries, or thinks he does, for love. At all events he'll be more reasonable in his choice.

I heard Eliza had cut Sweetman and was going to be married to Slark, her old flame – in the words of the poet, "Woman thy vows are traced on sand". I was not sorry for this as I had been made a fool of at his instigation, and one likes to be rid of those who have seen them in their foolish moments. She is a nice good-tempered girl but ought to have been spliced three years ago.[10]

I called and saw James Burgess and family; all quite well. They appeared better pleased to see me than any of my other friends, having nothing to give and everything to receive. All self in this world. I promised to bring William's portrait next time, about whom they wished to pump every possible thing and were surprised to find me silent. The fact is I never can mouth it when I'm pelted with questions – 'spect it's bashfulness. I found that Mary Ann Burgess had sailed for Sydney with the intention of going to their uncle's in the ship, so she must have passed me and will arrive in Sydney about the time I got home. I guessed how it would be on enquiring into her character and finding that they would not suit each other long, or else my name's not Smith. They may go on well enough at first but it would not last; so at least thought I, but did not tell them so.

June 5th 1857. Dined with the Governor and despairing of getting more tin borrowed two pounds off Charles. Mrs. Hay looked much better.

June 6th 1857. Andrews called, having on a remarkably flash suit, a blue tie, red shawl, pattern vest and green tartan trousers. "There," he remarked in a tone of triumph, "I told you all that it would not last for ever; it's over!" (In a theatrical tone.) "My foot's on my native heath, etc., but" (sadness) "Robinson has excapitulated and has not returned my money. I saw him when the ship arrived, attired in a gorgeous cloak; he waved his hand to me to be seated, said that he'd pay me tomorrow, and altogether appeared such a gentleman that I couldn't doubt his word; but he has gone – left last night for Bristol!"

I laughed until I nearly choked myself at the poor wretch. I had an idea before that London counter-jumpers were pretty smart fellows, but he's the worst snob ever I met. He went on with a yarn about the respectability of his friends and his father's house on Tavistock Hill. These kinds of folks always try that game, just as if anyone cared if they deduced their birth from fifty kings. So I paid him and this got rid of him quickly.

Walking along Oxford Street the same day I met Mr. and Mrs. Hall. Miss Hall looks very wild and stares about her as if lost. The last I saw of them they were dragging the unsuspecting husband into a milliner's shop – poor, poor fellow! I had had a kind of flirtation with their nursery girl. She was an Irish lass and had been some time in service in New South Wales. I naturally supposed it all right, thought she liked to enjoy herself and made love to her, to which she seemed to take very kindly; so I left her my address and asked her to drop a line to meet me in London, but as yet I had not heard from her.

Miss Hall appeared very stout ... some badly disposed folks might have imputed to improper causes, but I thought only that the sea voyage had suited her, of course.

In the evening I met a girl yclept Jane with whom I had a quick conversation at the corner of Kingsgate Street. She, confiding creature, proved a regular screw (got up outrageously, but in fact a bundle of old rags). This is a bad neighbourhood.

7th June 1857. Had a cut in with J. Burgess. He's very kind, but not quite pushing enough, poor fellow, and has had no luck. Poverty's the greatest crime a man can be guilty of in this world, and is punished more severely than any other. He has some nice daughters; the youngest will be very pretty in time but it's such a wretched neighbourhood that they can't grow healthy. I promised to drop a line to Mary Ann, which I did. Called on Fanny, 22 Queen's Square[11], going home. Frank Hay and sister and Fred D. were there – talked humbug. I sat still and moralised on the two sides of the picture, thought of getting up a panorama of the inside of the houses of a single street of London, the rich and the poor, side by side, at the same minute. How amusing it would be and remarkable too; only they would preach a yarn about invading the sanctity of their homes. The girls thought I was asleep. Aha!

9th June 1857. Saw Fred at his offices today, Austin Friars. Went in smoking. A man leaving him made some remark on it I did not catch, don't think he liked it either. Spat out of the window as well and thereby endangered folks beneath – cursed the country and wished I was out of it.

10th June 1857. Dined at Burge's. Lizzie had been out paying bills. Girls like even that, anything in the spending line. Mary Ann[12] had some of her charity school children home and gave them a feed. It's getting quite fashionable "to teach the young" idea now, and a very good thing it is too; although it's only the name of teaching with most of them, but still it's better than nothing. Fanny went out at half past ten to a party at Mrs. Novelli's, grandly togged out for the occasion with an absurdly monstrous skirt yclept "crinoline".[13] It must be a very large room to hold twenty like her. Mrs. Novelli was one of her chums at Queen's College.[14]

11th June 1857. Went to the Opera and saw *Don Giovanni*; the first time that season; the house was crowded and a tremendous crush at the door. Saw Piccolomini, the popular songstress; funny little woman, always nodding her head. The secret of her success is that she is natural. Guilini had just come out. He had indeed a sweet voice. I managed to get a seat down the centre walk. This is about the finest ventilated house in London, but one can't hear very plainly up here.

I met a young lady, yclept Kate, going out, a very pretty girl. We went up James Street together and afterwards had a first-rate supper at Quin's; lobsters, port and brandy. Both got well-screwed, got facetious and attempted to curl the waiter's hair with the tongs, which little pleasantry occasioned a squall which ended in foul breath.

I presented a five pound note in payment of the supper which, after scrutinising very severely, he refused to cash. I quietly pocketed the note, took Kate's arm and de-camped armed with an empty bottle with which I walked into the street, threatening anyone with a slight contusion who offered to stop my way. I then threw the bottle among the lobsters in the window and walked slowly away taking up Coventry Street. As soon as I was out of sight of the shop, however, I took along faster, being unwilling to have a barney with any policeman, for I had seen one of the waiters after one. Turning down Princes Street I said goodbye to Kate, at the same time making an appointment to meet her opposite Morley's in Trafalgar Square on Saturday. I then jumped into a hansom and off home.

Called the next day and paid Quin who was very obsequious and apologised for not cashing it, stating as a reason a case which occurred to him a short time ago by which he became the loser of ten pounds. I was too late to meet Kate on Saturday for which I was sorry, not knowing her address and having promised to make her a present. I looked through the Haymarket occasionally but did not find her till the latter end of the week. We went to the Adelphi together and from there to Jessop's, finishing up at the Hotel de Paris.

I made an appointment to go to Richmond with her in a few days, for I did not know how to pass the time at all; and living by myself having no company but those I paid for, it was a miserable life after all. But still I preferred it to starvation, and I had come to look at things in a more philosophical light than the last time. I divided my days better; read, wrote and drew a little, had a chop for breakfast. (By the bye I used to have eggs but I find that my digestive organs have been destroyed by eating so much carbonate of soda in my bread on the Sydney diggings, so I was obliged to give them up.) I dined at some of the houses in Cheapside.

I think I tried half the dining rooms in London, having a peculiar aversion to being asked, as is the custom in this country, "Waiter, sir, please, sir?" It is a most infernal imposition and costs one half as much as would keep one. Why don't the masters give their waiters a salary? It's a beastly begging system and one can't even get common civility in London without putting one's hand in one's pocket. It comes very hard upon poor clerks who receive such wretched salaries. And if those who have plenty give, the fellows treat those who can't afford it with contumely. Therefore I made a practice on principle of never entering the rooms again if they asked me for "waiter", and also refusing to give anything. What infernal rogues they are to be sure.

I occasionally indulge in a pint of claret this hot weather, so I dropped into the Queen's Inn at the corner of Skinner Street; had some cold mutton and a pint of St. Julien for which they had the cheek to charge eight shillings – six shillings for the claret and two shillings for the meat – and even asked, "Waiter, sir, please sir?" as coolly and demurely as if nothing had happened. Now I could have gone round the corner to Ball's and got a fine hot plate of *à la mode* or boiled beef for sixpence, potatoes one penny, bread one penny and a pint of porter twopence; or sent out for my pint of claret and never paid more than two shillings for it. It takes a man a long time to find out the cheap places in London. Now there's the Guildhall Dining Rooms very good, Lake's middling cheap ones in Gracechurch Street, and one or two in the Strand. When I had no invitation on Sundays I generally tried the Albany in Piccadilly.

I did not go so much to Burge's as I formerly did. The old lady who was my great favourite being occasionally laid up with severe fits, the management of the house fell on some of the young ladies, and they had been brought up in a different and more frivolous school than the mother. The consequence was that the house assumed a very different aspect.

It is perhaps a strange taste, but I'd sooner talk to an old lady any day than to a young one of the present day. The latter are either so senseless that they can take no part in commonsense conversation – nothing else but frivolous small talk seems to go down – or else they are so pert and self-willed that they think it clever to make jokes at others' expense, and will not bear with anyone who is unfortunate enough to express a difference of opinion. One who cracks jokes at others with a view to show one's own smartness, not thinking or caring for their feelings, is in either sex despicable, but especially so when they proceed from lips which cannot with decency be answered as they deserve.

I dined with the Hays occasionally and was working quickly into the good graces of the Governor and was hoping to be able to get my money on the 28th August, which was my birthday and the day which I, of right, attained the age of twenty-one and when according to the will the property was to be delivered to me. The Governor demurred about giving it up to me on the plea that the certificate of baptism was dated 4th December and the time of birth was not named. But I argued the point with him and had hopes of convincing him how much it would be to my benefit to give it up and let me get out again; and although he was very obstinate yet I had hopes.

I dined with the Burges now and then, but I did not altogether like it for I thought I perceived a coldness and distance which was not so before, and although I was invited frequently to Sunday dinner yet it appeared as though it was only done as a return for Fanny's being so often away from home, and her occasional treats to some of the girls. I'm such a proud upstart that the slightest sign of coldness, although frequently unintentional, fires me up, and that has been the cause of a great many of my misfortunes.

I have lately found it advisable for my health and well-being to keep from all unnecessary excitement, never to get into an argument about politics or to contradict folks unnecessarily. I can agree with few folks about here in the former and an argument worries me. But as Shakespeare says, "It is easier, etc." and this kind of idle life was playing Old Nick with my morals and money. All I thought of was making all kinds of love, and quiet sprees.

Rodd came up the other day and enticed me to Cremorne where we went the usual round of what is called fun, such as dancing, drinking, shooting at inanimate rabbits which are made to revolve in the most natural way in the world, the bowling alley in which the ladies show off their agility and a thousand other ingenious little ways which don't cost one anything – oh no, not at all!

A young lady of course accompanies one and feels very dry about every five minutes. One would think that a hot wind was blowing inside some of these girls. The waiters bring one execrable brandy and worse wine and they don't charge anything extra – certainly not! If you go to the bar the waiter hands you what you want from the barman – they are so polite – and then salutes you quietly with, "Waiter, sir, please sir"; and if one gives him less than sixpence he looks so pleased, of course he does, why not! The fireworks are really worth seeing. I never saw anything to beat them, and the lady who walks over the bridge looks in a rather perilous position; and after that there's some more dancing, a great deal of drinking, love-making and a little fighting.

Rodd had been dancing with a young lady from the ballet at the Princess, a very nice little girl, but she did not take to him at all; for although he was the last person, from his talk, one would have imagined to be bashful in the presence of these sort, yet he had nothing to say at all, and she showed decided preference to me and asked me to dance with her. But as he began to show symptoms of great jealousy and I had no money to fool away in this game I made quietly off home like a good boy.

The next night Rodd slept at my place. He talked of going out (to Australia) again soon and taking his younger brother with him. He also wanted me to go down and see his mother and stay for a few days, which I promised to do by and bye. The money was running short and the Governor had refused to forward any more, so although I could have borrowed from Frank or Charley I would rather go to a money-lender and pay an enormous percentage. Ann recommended me to a friend of hers, Alfred Smith residing in Whitecross Street, and from him I obtained nine pounds on accepting a bill for ten pounds payable in five months. Pretty good interest too.

I had received a letter from Anne Hogan, Hall's nursery maid and had taken a walk with her in the park. But it happened in a remarkable manner that the girl was one of those peculiarly unsophisticated ones who can't see above two inches before their noses, and she, it appears, thought that I was going to marry, although I'll declare that I never gave the slightest intimation of such a thing. And indeed, had I thought that she was anything of a maid I should never have spoken to her, for I have a peculiar horror ....

EPILOGUE

How tantalising to have the fourth notebook of 'memorandums' finish in mid-sentence. James indicates that he would have avoided the flirtation and love-making with Anne Hogan if he had known 'she was anything of a maid.' He did give her his address so that they could meet in London, but was in full retreat when marriage was mentioned.

If the fifth notebook had survived it would no doubt have recorded the final six months in London and yet another voyage to Australia. We presume James collected his inheritance on or close to his twenty-first birthday and was, at last, completely independent. He chose to return to Australia in a fast wooden clipper called the *Scottish Chief*, described as a handsome ship, 'built especially for the passenger trade'. It was advertised to depart from Liverpool on 5 February 1858, but records show that it left three days later. It was a vessel of 1,052 tons built at St John, New Brunswick, in 1856 and was under the command of Captain Peter Buchan. 'James M. Smith, age 22, gentleman' did not take a first-class cabin, appearing in the list of 'intermediate' passengers. They reached Melbourne on 8 May, back in the land he had grown to love. One family story has him going into business as an accountant. His uncle, William Burgess, died on 28 July 1861 and left him 50 acres (20.25 hectares) on the Hunter River at Nulla Nulla, Hinton, near Morpeth in New South Wales.

Despite his earlier rejection of an offer to gain experience on a farm in England, James took up the land and became intensely interested in agriculture. The farm included an area of river flats with rich alluvial soil and was not far from the junction of the Hunter and Paterson rivers. As well as the flats there were gently sloping hillsides with a southeasterly aspect offering a panoramic view over the Swan Reach towards Raymond Terrace and Newcastle.

It seems likely that the only dwelling on the farm in James's early years was a slab hut, which later became the kitchen. Three rooms were added to the south: two bedrooms and a sitting room, with a wide verandah along the front taking advantage of the view. Later still, at right angles to the kitchen, a large room known as the dining room or ballroom was added which had access to the earlier rooms by a wooden walkway. At the far end of this room was another bedroom known as the boys' room and again a verandah ran along the whole length.

The farm, like others in the area, was most likely producing wheat, maize and vegetables when James took it over. By October 1864 he was confident enough to write to the Maitland *Mercury* on rust in wheat, the importance of drainage and the problems of mineral deficiency in soils. Prior to writing to the *Mercury*, he had published an essay on these topics and the importance of science in agriculture. This was presented to the 'landed proprietors' in the area with additional copies to be distributed amongst their tenants or customers.

In 1863 grapes were planted on 8 acres (3 hectares) with more acreage planted during the following two decades. A surviving page from the catalogue of the Calcutta Exhibition of 1883-84 details four of the wines entered by James Montagu Smith of Nulla Nulla Vineyard at Hinton. The first was a liqueur wine of a 'sweet, tawny red colour', vintage 1880; the second 'a sweet white shiraz', vintage 1882: the third 'a dry red made from Black Hermitage grapes' planted in 1868 and the fourth 'a dry white made from Shepherd's Riesling grapes' planted in 1863. The vines were trained to stakes and wire trellises and mostly grew on sandy alluvial soil with a white gravelly subsoil.

In March 1871, James had decided to let or sell all but 15 acres (7 hectares) of his land. The newspaper advertisement describes it as 'Nulla Nulla Vineyard of 10 acres, out of flood reach, and 25 acres of river bank land.' No sale or lease eventuated and we know from the 1883-84 catalogue that the total area of vineyard was by this time 13 acres (5 hectares). It also tells us that some of the vines were on 'a steep hillside' which would be the slope below the high ground on which the house was situated. The vines on the lower levels proved not to be out of flood reach during the 1893 floods. It is said that so much damage was caused that the vineyard was abandoned and the farm converted to dairying. Government records of 1885 show that J. M. Smith of Nulla Nulla, Hinton, held 50 acres and possessed seven horses, ten cattle and two pigs.[1] The 50 acres had been part of 200 acres (81 hectares) conveyed to William Burgess by the original grantee Francis Eagar in 1845.

James married Marion Harmon at Morpeth on Thursday 6 December 1866. Marion was the daughter of Michael and Agnes Harmon and was around eighteen when wedded. Her place and date of birth are not known. There were ten children of the marriage: Viola 1867, Harold 1868, Frank Hay 1870, Fanny 1872, Montagu 1874, Charles Stuart 1877, Lancelot Hinton 1879, May 1883 (died at birth), Reginald 1884 and George Stansell Septimus 1886. They attended the Hinton State School in an era when it was a small but busy town with a flourmill, three churches, two stores, a school of arts and the school. On the 3 June 1869, James became secretary of the Hinton School of Arts, just one facet of his interest in community affairs. He was remembered as a keen debater and a frequent contributor of letters to local newspapers.

Life at home centred around the rambling weatherboard house with its flower garden and kitchen garden. These were protected by a fence and just outside of this grew Moreton Bay figs. They were a haven for flying foxes and Viola later recalled seeing 'native bears' (koalas) in the trees on the farm during her childhood. 'Nulla Nulla' shared a wharf with the neighbouring farm, although use of the river for transport declined after railways came to the area.

Pride of place in the house was given to the well-stocked bookcase. It contained a forty-eight-volume set of Sir Walter Scott's *Waverley* novels, *Robinson's History of Europe*, twelve books of plays in the series, *London Theatre*, most of the popular poetry books and a book of guided walks around Sydney, dated 1856. Viola, now remembered as Auntie Vyla, never married and lived in the old home with her brother Reginald until her death in 1940. She looked after 'Father's books' including the four surviving notebooks. She chose for her own reading 'modern' romance novels and is said to have had one or two gentleman admirers.

Reginald, Viola's second youngest brother, was injured in a riding accident at age ten, and was partially deaf, being able to speak only in a whisper. Taunted at school, he retreated to a life on the farm and ended his days in a one-roomed cottage built for him after the old house was demolished. The eldest son, Harold, a bachelor, remained at home and helped his mother with the running of the farm. He died in 1918 and George, the youngest member of the family, took over the farm having returned from World War I with an injury which resulted in the amputation of one leg. He had a small cottage built lower down the hill from the main house and brought home his bride to help him carry on the farm. He raised a family and led a very active life.

Other members of the family made their lives elsewhere and exhibited varying degrees of attachment to the old family place. Montagu and Charles spent some time in Tasmania at the Queenstown copper mines before returning to New South Wales. Monty eventually settled on a farm at Kincumber near Gosford, while Charlie farmed in the Maitland area. Lancelot, after trying his luck near Tamworth, bought a farm from Walter Scott at Wallalong. Frank went to Sydney and worked for the railways. Fanny fell in love with a marine engineer, Herbert Fuller, who worked on the dredges in the river and they married in 1894. George had gone to the canefields before World War I and bought a farm on the Johnson River in North Queensland. When war came he enlisted in Townsville in 1917, and never returned to the north.

James Montagu Smith and his wife Marion had more than twenty-one years together, although Marion's widowhood lasted for over thirty years. James died on 15 May 1888 and was buried as he requested under the tuckeroo tree overlooking his beloved 'Nulla Nulla'. Marion died on 22 December 1920 and is also buried on the farm.

James was diagnosed as having heart disease and was offered no hope of recovery. Characteristically, when he made his will he asked that his heart be examined after death, 'so that if possible the medical fraternity should have an opportunity to gain any information thereby, and thus render any benefit that could be obtained from such a course to suffering humanity'. Notes written on a small piece of paper in March and April 1888 tell us of the sad days leading to his untimely end. This is the kind of record-keeping that James must have done throughout his life; with those from the 1850s being the basis for the 'memorandums'. He records on Sunday night 18 March 1888: 'Have been better since attack of last Thursday night – had shivering fit tonight and breath shorter and pain in jugular.'

On Wednesday 4 April, he called on Dr Russell who found him better, said there was no aneurism and gave him a sleeping draught and iron tonic. "To April 12 inclusive – general health better but cough more frequent, ostridulous [*sic*] sound in breathing, also pain in the chest and neck on coughing and signs of a lump there although not visible.'

Just over a month later, on Tuesday 15 May, James Montagu Smith died at the comparatively young age of 51, leaving a wife and nine surviving children between two and twenty years of age.

At least he had those years as a family man. Two of his good friends on the Victorian goldfields, Jimmy Barr and 'Dan' Mather, had died tragically in their thirties. James Jackson Barr, the 'Wee Hairy Man', died of starvation in the bush near Rushworth, Victoria, in 1861, aged 35, while Andrew Mather was buried in a mine collapse at New Bendigo (St Arnaud) in 1868 aged 36. His sister Fanny Smith was a spinster, aged 44, when she married 37-year-old bachelor Arthur George Dallas at Paddington, Middlesex, on 2 December 1880. Sadly, she died on 1 July 1884, and was buried at London's Kensal Green Cemetery.[2]

James might well have drowned at sea in 1851, but survived and went on to have many more remarkable experiences. He found both loyalty and love and, with his wife Marion, created the kind of enfolding family he so much longed for as a young man.

His newspaper obituary begins with the following: 'The remains of Mr Montagu Smith, of Nulla Nulla, Hinton, were carried to their last resting-place on May 17th. By his request, he was interred within his own grounds, and was followed to the grave by nearly all of the male population of Hinton.' At the conclusion we read, 'Hinton has lost a good citizen, Mrs Smith a kind and loving husband, and his family an indulgent and loving father.'

NOTES

INTRODUCTION

1 James quotes the poet John Langhorne (1735-1779) in vol. 2 of his 'Memorandums' (see page viii).

2 Charles Smith is described as a merchant in his widow's death certificate of 1846. A Charles Smith of Herne Bay was an engineering contractor in 1844 and was bankrupt by early 1845.

3 Church rate books for Herne Bay have this property marked 'empty' in 1845. The Herne Bay Historical Records Society.

4 Charles Hay married Ann Walker on 7th October 1815 at St Mary Magdalen, Bermondsey. The family were Ann (1816), Eleanor (1819), Francis (Frank) Theodore (1822), Richard Walker (1824), Maria (1826) and Charles (1828).

5 James writes in April 1855 that the Pier Hotel was built at great expense but was now let for nothing.

6 These were Thomas Telford's St Katharine Docks in London, begun in 1827, and Isambard Kingdom Brunel's Box Tunnel on the London to Bristol railway, which took from 1836 to 1841 to complete. In its time it was the longest tunnel in the world, employing more than 1000 men in its construction.

7 At the end of vol. 1 James notes that he has not yet had sons. The first was born in 1868.

Chapter I – ON THE BLUE BRINY

1 The original gives the year as 1850, which seemed to leave large gaps in time. On investigation it was confirmed that the *Lancastrian* arrived in Melbourne on 1 May 1851, indicating that James had made the fairly common slip of writing the previous year on the first day of the year.

2 On census night 30 March 1851, Elizabeth Willans, widow, aged 40, was at 75 Paradise Street, Rotherhithe, with her daughters Elizabeth (22), Mary (17) and Martha (12) and son John (15). Her late husband, John Alnutt Willans, was killed in the accident in 1838. British Census 1851; General Register Office Index of Deaths.

3 Records show that the *Lancastrian* was built in Liverpool in 1848.

R.T. Langley was captain in 1851 and the vessel was owned by his father. It was 503 tons registered, not 567 tons as James states. Lloyds Register of British and Foreign Shipping, 1851.

4 This was Albert Read (1811-1902) born at Steyning, Sussex, the son of Benjamin Read and Jane Fitzwalter. He was admitted as an attorney, solicitor and proctor for the Port Phillip District, Supreme Court of New South Wales on 4 June 1851. Supreme Court Roll.

5 Agnes Jane Read, daughter of Albert and Mercy Read, was baptised at Steyning, Sussex, 15 July 1838, so James is correct in estimating that she was 12. She married John Box at Brighton, Victoria, in 1856 and had five children. She died in 1924 aged 85. British Vital Records; Registry of Births, Deaths and Marriages, Victoria.

6 Albert Read often defended the 'underdog'. On 18 January 1879 he appeared for some of the Kelly sympathisers at Beechworth Court. He is also believed to have defended Ned Kelly on a horse-stealing charge. His grandson was Judge Albert Leonard Read (1893-1970). A great-grandson, John L. Read, was a judge of the County Court, and Richard M. Read, also a great-grandson, has been appointed a Crown Prosecutor in Victoria.

7 Chips is the traditional nickname for a carpenter. In this case it was the ship's carpenter.

8 At first called 'The Beach' or 'Liardet's Beach', Sandridge became Port Melbourne in January 1884. N. U'Ren & N. Turnbull, *A History of Port Melbourne*, OUP, Melbourne, 1983, pp. 147-8.

9 The steam sloop *Reynard* and the brigantine *Arab* had sailed from Hong Kong on 2 June 1851, for Pratte's Shoal, in the hope of rescuing a British crew which had been stranded there. On 6 June the *Reynard* was caught on the same shoal and subsequently broke up. The *Arab* was able to rescue all of its crew as well as the crew of the vessel they were seeking. *Daily Alta,* California, 5 August 1851, The Maritime Heritage Project 1999, http://www.maritimeheritage.org/ships/wrecks.html.

10 *Brookes' Gazetteer* of 1861, gives the following: 'Whampoa, a town of China, province of Quantung, on an island in the Canton River. Merchant vessels stop at this town and communicate with Canton by means of boats. It is 45 miles North of Macao, and 10 south of Canton'.

11 Anjer Point lighthouse was an important reference for vessels passing through the Sunda Strait.

12 Jacko was a mongoose, an Indian animal of the civet family and a noted slayer of snakes and rats.

[13] English composer and performer Henry Russell (1812-1900) wrote the melody for 'A Life on the Ocean Wave' in 1838. The words James comments on were in fact written by the American poet, Epes Sargent (1813-1880). Oscar Fay Adams, *A Dictionary of American Authors*, Houghton Mifflin, Boston, 1901, p. 327.

[14] Baptised at St Mary, Rotherhithe, on 1 February 1822, Francis Theodore Hay was the eldest son of Charles Hay, guardian of James and Fanny Smith. In 1836, Frank was apprenticed to his father, a lighterman on the Thames. Records of The Company of Watermen and Lightermen of the River Thames, 1759-1897.

[15] This comment reflects the anti-Semitic attitudes of the age in which James is writing. In contrast to this stereotype, Benjamin Disraeli, grandson of a Jewish merchant of Italian descent, entered the British Parliament in 1837 and twice became prime minister.

Chapter II – SAILORS AND CONVICTS

[1] Richard Smith Stuart, Commander of the *Sir Robert Seppings*, was born at Portsmouth, Hampshire, c. 1815. His wife Charlotte gave birth to their son, William Thomas Stuart, in Hawthorn, Victoria, in 1854. In the 1881 British Census they are living at Deptford, Kent, with Richard as a master mariner age 66 and William as a mariner age 26. British Census, 1881; Victorian Pioneers Index, 1837-1888.

[2] First mate Thomas James Clark (Chief Officer).

[3] Charles Dibdin (1745-1814) was an English songwriter who wrote just under 100 sea songs along with almost 70 dramatic pieces. *Chambers Biographical Dictionary*, Edinburgh, 1990, p. 416.

[4] The convict transport *Sir Robert Seppings* departed Woolwich on 18 March 1852 with 220 female convicts and a number of children. Mary Petty had her three-month-old daughter Sarah in her arms when she came on board at Woolwich. (See also p. 313) The baby survived the voyage, but died a year later. Archives Office of Tasmania; General Register Office (London) Index of Births; Tasmanian Pioneer Index, 1803-1899.

[5] The ship's log reads: 'Thursday 8 am June 17th 1852, Latt 42° 00´ S. Long 84° 110´ E. James M. Smith Ordinary Seaman, when checked by the Chief Mate for negligence became very abusive and saying "You b...y b...r now I'll pitch into you," on the Second Mate going to him to bring him aft, he struck him in the Face giving him a Black Eye, the same seaman having, ever since joining the ship, given much Trouble and abusive Language to the officers at Different Times – Put him in Irons and Solitary Confinement for Twenty Four Hours – [Signed] R.S. Stuart Master, T.J. Clark Mate, L.T. Cunningham M.D.' Public Record Office, London. XC 155101 BT 98/3046.

6 Surgeon Superintendent Lennox Thompson Cunningham was married to Jane Forster in Edinburgh, Scotland, on 22 December 1832. International Geneological Index.

7 The Brickfields hiring depot was situated in North Hobart, off Argyle Street. The North Hobart Football Oval now occupies the site. James's statement that convict women were soon hired is not supported by other evidence. It is said that the supply of convict labour greatly exceeded demand in the mid-1850s. P. Howard, *To Hell or to Hobart*, Kangaroo Press, Kenthurst, NSW, 1993, p. 147.

8 "The Cascades" refers to the Female Factory established at the Cascades, South Hobart, in the late 1820s.

9 Bridget Lyons (age 42) died on 14 June 1842. Five children died, not three as James states. All were between six and eighteen months. Daily Sick Book, Convict Ship *Sir Robert Seppings* 1852, PRO London, Adm.101/68.

10 This is Samuel Wilson, ordinary seaman.

11 James lost his notes of the voyage on the *Sir Robert Seppings*, so while details are accurate, the dates can be out. The events leading up to his two months in prison took place six days after their arrival. The Official Log reports as follows: 'Thursday 5/30pm July 15th 1852. Hobart Town. James Smith Ordinary Seaman when the boatswain ordered him aft to keep the necessary look out refused to go, the Mates went forward when he again positively refused to obey their orders, they then took hold of him to bring him aft. When he made every resistance as likewise made use of much abusive language in the presence of myself and the Surgeon I was under the necessity of putting him in handcuffs (his conduct was so violent) until 8 pm when I put him in the Prisoners box for the remainder of the night, the next morning he refused to go to his duty, the same seaman on Wednesday evening refused to keep his lookout, his conduct throughout this voyage has been of the worst description..' [Signed] R. S. Stuart, Master, T. J. Clark, Mate. Public Record Office, London. XC 155101 BT 98/3046.

12 Official Log, *Sir Robert Seppings,* Saturday 10 am, July 17 1852, Hobart Town: 'James Smith and Joshua Nunn Seaman, taken before the Police Magistrate and Sentenced to Two Months imprisonment with hard Labour in the House of Correction.' [Signed] R. S. Stuart, Master. Public Record Office, London, XC 155101 BT/3046.

13 The Hobart Town Prisoners' Barracks or Penitentiary, known as the 'Tench' by the convict population, was first occupied in 1821. While the barracks were demolished in the 1960s, the church, built 1830-33 over solitary confinement cells, has survived and is opened to the public by the National Trust.

14 Drawings of the treadmill at the Hobart Town Prisoners' Barracks have survived.

15 The convict transport *Sir Robert Seppings* left Hobart Town for Norfolk Island on 19 or 20 August 1852. It departed Norfolk Island on Monday 13 September 1852. Ship's log; Report of the Select Committee.

16 James Dalton and Andrew Kelly were in a party of six or seven convicts who escaped on 28 December 1852. In an attempt to swim past the dogs and guards at Eaglehawk Neck, Dalton and Kelly were the only ones who did not drown. They were in fact hanged in Hobart on 26 April 1853, not in Melbourne as James states. Their conviction was for shooting a police constable in Tasmania. Allan M. Nixon, *Stand & Deliver: 100 Australian Bushrangers 1789-1901*, Lothian, Melbourne, 1991, pp. 46-7.

17 The Cascades was a landing place on Norfolk Island, not to be confused with the Cascades Women's Prison south of Hobart.

18 Captain Stuart, giving evidence before the Select Committee on the conduct of the convicts during the voyage, presents his version of events: 'About 9 o'clock that morning, when fore-hatches were taken off for the purpose of getting up the supply of water for the day, one of the sailors, going into the hold, discovered one of the prisoners trying to conceal himself away in the hold among the water-casks, which he instantly reported to the Captain of the guard, and the officers of the ship and four of the guard jumped down below, each armed with a cutlass and pistol: they first of all found that the coal-hole scuttle-hatch, which had been secured by two iron bars, had been broken open – a sentry was placed immediately under that to prevent any more men from coming down – then they searched through the hold, and found 6 prisoners concealed away amongst the casks. These men were immediately passed on deck, placed in irons, and kept on deck for the remainder of the voyage.' *Convicts by the Sir R. Seppings*, Van Diemen's Land, 1852, Archives Office of Tasmania.

19 The Report of the Select Committee, 19 October, gives the number as six or eight men wounded and these were brought up on deck one by one and had their wounds dressed. *Convicts by the Sir R. Seppings*, Van Diemen's Land, 1852, Archives Office of Tasmania.

20 The official log of the *Sir Robert Seppings* reads: 'October 13th 1852, 2 AM, Hobart Town. Deserted from the ship taking away one of the Quarter Boats, Charles William Blake Carpenter, Joshua Nunn Seaman, William Cosgrove Seaman, David Morgan Seaman, James Smith Seaman, George Yeldham Seaman, Thomas Howse Apprentice.' [Signed] R. S. Stuart, Master, T. J. Clark Mate. Public Record Office, London, XC 155101 BT 98/3046.

21 Peppermint Bay is now called Woodbridge.

[22] Port Cygnet Hill would seem to be a reference to Mount Cygnet. It is east of Gardners Bay and south-east of Cygnet.

[23] The records show that James was recaptured by 25 October, and as they escaped on the 13th, it was really only 12 days at large.

[24] Brown's River is now called Kingston Beach and being only 13 km from Hobart has become an 'outer suburb'. In 1852 the inland Proctors Road was the main link.

[25] Superintendent James Boyd went on to be Commandant at Port Arthur from 1853 to 1871.

[26] Governor Denison was [Sir] William Thomas Denison (1804-1871). He was appointed Lieutenant Governor of Van Diemen's Land in April 1846, a post he held until his appointment in 1854 as Governor of New South Wales and Governor-General of the Australian Colonies. *Australian Dictionary of Biography*, MUP, Melbourne, vol. 4, pp. 46-53.

[27] Eight solitary confinement cells were built in the vaulted foundations of the chapel at the Hobart Town Prisoners' Barracks, also known as the Penitentiary or 'Tench'. Some of these are still in place, giving visitors an insight into the conditions experienced by refractory prisoners.

[28] William Shakespeare (1564-1616), *As You Like It*. Act II, Scene 1.

[29] The *Harriet Nathan* was a three-masted barque of 126 tons, built in 1844 by William Williamson of Hobart Town. It had one deck and a square stern, being 81.7 feet (25 metres) long. It was built as a whale ship and was named for the wife of a member of the firm Nathan, Moses & Co. The launch took place with a public ceremony on Monday 19 November 1844.

[30] The *Alert* was a two-masted schooner of 91 tons, built in 1846 on the Bellinger River by George Brown. It left Launceston on 24 March 1853 and sailed to the Leven River for a cargo of palings. At that time the town of Ulverstone was not yet established. The official register closes with the words: 'Lost August 1854'. R. Parsons (comp.) *Ships of Australia and New Zealand before 1850,* part 1, Magill, South Australia, 1983, p. 6.

[31] A lushington is someone who drinks to excess, a drunkard. More familiar in modern times as a 'lush'.

[32] The *Sword Fish* was a wooden two-masted brigantine of 168 tons, built in Hobart Town in 1850 by John Watson. It had one deck, a square stern and was 86.9 feet (26 metres) long. Captain John Clinch was its owner and was well known in the coastal trade. James was probably on the voyage that left Hobart Town on 26 May 1853 and arrived in Melbourne on 7 June with passengers and sundries. The master was William Lyon.

[33] 'St George's Rocks' probably refers to Georges Rocks north of Eddystone Point on Tasmania's north-east coast. A vessel sailing through Banks Strait could pass close to these rocks.

[34] A 'catspaw' is a light breeze which ruffles the water surface over a small area. In this case it was enough to carry the vessel away from the rocks.

Chapter III – IN PURSUIT OF GOLD

[1] Called the 'Black Forest' because bushfire had blackened the tree trunks. At that time the most recent were the terrible 'Black Thursday' fires on 6 February 1851.

[2] William Daniel Collyer held Spring Plains station at the time James and his mates camped overnight. Brothers John and William Collyer had acquired Spring Plains (20,000 acres or 8,100 ha) in March 1851 and Wild Duck Creek Station (30,000 acres or 12,150 ha) in 1852. They were in the area east of Kyneton and Redesdale. J.O. Randell, *Pastoral Settlement in Northern Victoria*, vol. II, Chandos, Burwood, Victoria, 1982, pp. 156-7.

[3] The Bush Inn at Gisborne had been a notable stopping place since the 1840s.

[4] The Black Forest Inn was between Gisborne and Woodend (Five Mile Creek) at a place called Middle Gully, later known as Lower Macedon. Mr Hunter, the landlord, had a reputation for harbouring bushrangers. Isaac Batey, *Gisborne Gazette*, 27 September 1912.

[5] The deaf-adder is not found in Australia although there is a death adder in the northern regions. In Central Victoria, this could be a reference to a tiger snake or a brown snake, both of which are venomous.

[6] Forest Creek was at that time the name for the gold diggings along the creek from Expedition Pass and Golden Point through the localities that became Chewton, Wesley Hill and Castlemaine.

[7] The Old Post Office site, to the south-east of the centre of present-day Chewton, remained a landmark when a new post office was opened near the Government Camp in Castlemaine.

[8] The mia-mia is a traditional Aboriginal shelter, usually built in the manner described, but without the bed ticking, which was a cotton cloth used to cover mattresses.

[9] Lushington Hill is south of the Castlemaine-Newstead road, west of Campbells Creek and close to Winters Flat.

[10] A glass of Geneva Gin. JDKZ was a favourite brand on the goldfields with its heart-shaped label on a tapered, square bottle.

[11] In an 'Erratum', James adds that in a large rush to Jones's Creek (later called Waanyarra) his mate Dick lost a 15-pound nugget (5600 g or 5.66 kg).

[12] Variations on this story can be found in other recollections. In 1904, Richard Thimbleby related how in early 1853 he was told that such a tragic event had recently taken place near the Five Flags Hotel at Campbells Creek. *Records of the Castlemaine Pioneers*, Rigby, Melbourne, 1972, pp. 195-6.

[13] As yet the location of Growlers Hill has not been fixed with certainty. It was most likely the southern end of the hill immediately behind the Government Camp at Castlemaine.

[14] Edward Hammond Hargraves (1816-1891) basked in the notoriety of being the 'official' discoverer, although John Lister and William and James Tom were later found to deserve the credit for finding 'payable gold'. James rightly points out that gold had frequently been found before, 'but no notice was taken of it'. Hargraves had been a sailor, settler, publican, storekeeper and gold digger, but was not a geologist as James states. *ADB*, vol. 4, pp. 346-7.

[15] Ophir was not on the Turon River as James states. It was at the confluence of Lewis Ponds Creek and Summer Hill Creek, a tributary of the Macquarie River.

[16] The large waterhole or 'Great Water Hole' was described in May 1854 as being near the 'Old House at Home' on Campbells Creek Road (*Mount Alexander Mail,* 27 May 1854, p. 3.) James writes that it was under Growlers Hill. Henry Leversha recalled in September 1880: 'In December, 1851, water was very scarce, and nearly all the wash dirt had to be taken to a big waterhole somewhere below where Johnston's bakery is now.' This places it close to present day Johnstone Street, downstream from Sheriff's Bridge. *Records of the Castlemaine Pioneers*, p. 13.

[17] Diamond Gully is 2 km south-west of the Castlemaine Post Office, close to Lushington Hill and Winter's Flat. Early maps show a Diamond Hill, Old Diamond Hill and Diamond Flat.

[18] This deluge is possibly the one described by Richard Thimbleby in recollections presented to the Castlemaine Association of Pioneers and Old Residents in October 1904. Thimbleby dates it to August 1853. *Records of the Castlemaine Pioneers*, p. 196.

[19] An egg-laying monotreme, the platypus (*Ornithorhynchus anatinus*) has long been a protected species and still inhabits the creeks in the Mt Alexander region.

[20] Tom Berman may have legally married the 'Ministering Angel'; there is no official record. Registration of births, deaths and marriages began in Victoria

on 1 July 1853 and took time to be fully implemented, especially on the goldfields, with their transient populations.

21 Charles Joseph La Trobe (1801-1875) was Superintendent of the Port Phillip District from 1839 up to the formation of the Colony of Victoria in 1851, when he became Lieutenant-Governor. He was replaced by Sir Charles Hotham in May 1854. Alan Gross, *Charles Joseph La Trobe*, MUP, Melbourne, 1956.

22 William R. Jackson was a Baptist preacher and possibly a storekeeper.

23 'Itchcock' was the auctioneer and businessman William Hitchcock (1810-1867). In about 1854 he erected the Hall of Castlemaine in Hargraves Street, a large structure of wood and canvas used as an auction room and later as a theatre. In July 1855 it was advertised as the Theatre Royal at the Hall of Castlemaine. Raymond A. Bradfield, *Lola Montez and Castlemaine: Some Early Theatre History*, undated, p. 50.

24 The new miners' licence was introduced in September 1853. A licence for one month cost one pound and for three, six and twelve months, two, four and eight pounds, respectively.

25 The first hotel licences on the Mt Alexander Goldfield were issued from 21 September 1853. The first in Castlemaine was for the Victoria Hotel, owned by Jennings Coliver. Frank McKillop, 'Early Castlemaine', *Mount Alexander Mail*, 3 November 1908.

26 In colonial times, Victorians were called Cabbage-patchers. South Australians were called Crow-eaters and keep up their 'Crows' identity in their Adelaide football team.

27 The rush to Tarrengower took place in November-December 1853. The name Maldon soon supplanted Tarrengower for the town that developed as a result of this influx of diggers.

28 'Jimmy' Barr was surely James Jackson Barr, born in Glasgow's Gorbals area in 1826, the son of Peter Barr and Susan Jackson. In mid-1853 he signed the Bendigo petition for goldfields reforms. He was a friend of Andrew McIntyre, one of the three people charged in relation to the fire at Bentley's Eureka Hotel in Ballarat in 1854. He died of starvation near Rushworth, Victoria.

29 The 'Hawick man' was Andrew 'Dan' Mather, the son of James and Janet Mather (née Lillico), born Damside, Hawick, Roxburghshire, Scotland, on 21 September 1831. In the 1851 Census he is a 19-year-old merchant (woollen draper) living with his widowed mother at Wilton, Roxburghshire. He and his younger brother Robert were soon off to the Victorian goldfields. Tragically, Andrew was killed in a mine collapse at New Bendigo (St Arnaud) on 24 November 1865. *St Arnaud Mercury*, 2 December 1865.

[30] Porcupine Flat diggings was an area to the north-east of Mt Tarrengower and reached a peak of activity in the first half of 1854. The Tarrengower correspondent in the *Mount Alexander Mail* of 27 May 1854 wrote: 'The attraction of Porcupine Flat still continues to cause a great rush to that spot.'

[31] The statement of being west of the Loddon River, and also references to 'a vast plain on the banks of the Loddon' suggests north of Carisbrook and as far north as Kingower.

[32] Known as Loddon River or Catto's Run, this 64,000-acre (25,920-ha) holding was taken up by John Catto in 1841. The main homestead was in a bend of the river about four miles (6 km) south of Bridgewater.

[33] At this time Tom Bryce and Donald Kesson Campbell were partners in business. In January 1856 Donald married Tom's sister, thus linking two Glasgow families. The parents on both sides were married in the Gorbals in the 1820s so it is likely they were neighbours. Moving 'D. K. Campbell's' stores in response to rapid population shifts must have required both effort and good judgement.

[34] Avoca goldfield in north-western Victoria began early in 1853. By June 1854, the Main Lead had attracted 14,000 diggers. J. Flett, *The History of Gold Discovery in Victoria*, Hawthorn Press, Melbourne, 1970, p. 454.

[35] The White Hills, in this instance, was a location that became the town of Maryborough.

[36] William Shakespeare, 'There is nothing either good or bad but thinking makes it so.'

[37] 'Penny Gaffs' were the upper floors of shops used for cheap performances of dancing and singing.

[38] American passenger wagons were usually given a simple suspension of leather thoroughbraces. They were square-lined and much plainer than the stylish Concord 'jack' coach or the English coach with its metal springs.

[39] Catherine Hayes (1818-1861) was an Irish-born opera and concert singer. She was the first great name in European opera to visit Australia.

[40] James uses the alternative spelling for Ballarat, the more common form. Both spellings were in use in the 1850s.

[41] Andrew McIntyre was one of three men arrested and tried for the burning of Bentley's Hotel. He was taken into custody at Geelong and was not present when the battle took place at the stockade. Born in Glasgow, he married Margaret Kerr on 19 May 1850 in the Gorbals. A daughter, Margaret Eureka McIntyre, was born at Ballarat on 25 February 1855. The family had returned to Glasgow

by September 1859. Reg. BDMs, Victoria; IGI.

42 The battle of the Eureka Stockade took place in the early hours of Sunday 3 December 1854. An attack by military and police forces took the miners by surprise, and only 150 were in the stockade. They were greatly outnumbered and the fighting lasted a mere 10 to 15 minutes. Five soldiers were killed, including Captain Wise, and 12 were wounded: 25 miners were killed and a number died later of wounds. Subsequent reforms made the defeat into a victory long celebrated as a landmark for democracy in Australia.

43 Cunningham McFarlane (c.1818-1897), a watchmaker and jeweller from Edinburgh, was at 165 Elizabeth Street. *The Melbourne Commercial Directory* for 1855, compiled by James Butterfield.

Chapter IV – CAPE HORN AND HOME

1 The *Chicora* was built in Maine in 1847 and was registered in Boston, the owners being Bassett & Co. After April 1855 it was registered in Anvers, Belgium. Bureau Veritas, Registre de Renseignements sur Navires 1854-5.

2 John Myers had a wife and young son living at Cowes on the Isle of Wight (see p. 122-3).

3 Captain Garrett was almost certainly Samuel Beattie Garrett. A warrant had been issued by the Adelaide Bench for his apprehension for 'Larceny and Embezzlement'. On 22 November 1854, Constable Alfred Burt was at Tankards Hotel, Lonsdale Street, Melbourne, holding a warrant for his arrest. *Victorian Police Gazette*, 24 November 1854, p. 560.

4 A kind of storm petrel, a sea bird.

5 William Hockin's Commercial Hotel was on the corner of Elizabeth and Lonsdale streets, Melbourne. *Sands & Kenny Melbourne Directory*, 1857.

6 The grampus is a member of the dolphin family.

7 Rio Sao Francisco is a river in Brazil which flows into the sea between Aracaju and Maceio.

8 Maceio is a seaport of Brazil, situated on a small peninsula between the sea and the Lagoa do Norte.

9 A 'Universal Code of Signals' for the merchant service was introduced in 1817 by Captain Frederick Marryat (1792-1848). Captain Marryat later became well known as the author of sea stories based on his experiences in the Royal Navy. *Chambers Biographical Dictionary*, p. 976.

10 Fernando de Noronha is an island in the South Atlantic belonging to Brazil. The convict settlement was called Remedios. *World Pictorial Gazetteer*.

[11] Nicholas I (1796-1855) was Emperor of Russia from 1825. He died on 18 February 1855.

[12] The Crimean War (1853-1856) saw Britain, France, Sardinia and Turkey fighting against Russian expansion in the Black Sea region.

[13] Edward Bulwer Lytton (1803-1873) English novelist, playwright, essayist, poet and politician.

[14] Lord John Russell, (1792-1878) was an English statesman and notable reformer. He was Prime Minister from 1846-1852.

[15] Robert Burns (1759-1796) Scottish poet of humble origins, much loved by Scots both at home and abroad. 'A Man's a Man for A' That' is a song for equality and the brotherhood of man, written some 18 months before the death of Burns in July 1796.

[16] Lansdowne Place adjoined Brunswick Square in the parish of St Pancras. It was opposite the Foundling Hospital and is now called Lansdowne Terrace, while the hospital site is now Coram's Fields Playground.

[17] Myers appears in the 1867 *Isle of Wight Directory* as: 'John Myers, Lodging House, Rose Mount, Bath Road, West Cowes'.

[18] Captain George Allanack is recorded as being master of a number of vessels on the Australian run, including *Enchanter* and *Chicora*.

[19] William Patterson appears in the 1881 Census as a British subject born in Paris. He is an architect and surveyor living with his wife Emily and their three children at 123 Camden Street, St Pancras, London.

[20] Queens Hotel.

[21] John Stokes Esq., physician, had married Hetty Betty Dean in Limerick, Ireland, on 3 March 1838. Mrs Dean was Mrs Stokes's mother and at around 75 would have seemed like a grandmother. Her late husband, William Dean, had been paymaster of the 25th Regiment (King's Own Borderers). Herne Bay Historical Records Society.

[22] 'Lind' almost certainly refers to Jenny Lind (1820-1887) the famed Swedish soprano. She was a supporter of charities, so could well have been involved in a benefit for the those affected by the Crimean War.

[23] In 1851, George Burge, in partnership with I. C. Johnson, set up a cement works at Frindsbury on the Medway and at a young age his son, George William Burge, succeeded to his interests in the business. Harold Gough, Herne Bay.

[24] The Crown Inn was in High Street, Rochester, publican George Willson. *Post Office Directory for Kent*, 1851.

[25] Harriott Chancellor Willson, daughter of George and Harriott Willson, would turn 20 on 1 July 1855.

[26] This was probably Frederick Dinely.

[27] Richard Winch conducted a school at 1 The Terrace, Herne Bay, Kent, from c. 1839 to the mid-1840s. The establishment was started in 1834 by William Butt. Herne Bay Historical Records Society.

[28] This was Thomas Frederick Robson (1822-1864). He worked with playwright J. R. Planché who was adapting French fairy romances to the English stage. First performed in London in 1854, *The Yellow Dwarf (Le Nain Jaune)* was given the full title of *The Yellow Dwarf and the King of the Gold Mines*. Sydney Lee (ed.) *Dictionary of National Biography*, Smith, Elder & Co., London, 1900, p. 63.

[29] George Burge (1795-1874) was an engineering contractor who carried out the designs of great 19th-century engineers such as Thomas Telford and Isambard Kingdom Brunel. In 1841 he constructed the foundations for the Széchenyi Chain-bridge at Budapest. Harold Gough, Herne Bay.

[30] Charles Louis Napoleon Bonaparte (1808-1873) became Emperor of France after the constitution was dissolved in December 1851. He married a Spanish countess, Eugénie de Montijo, on 29 January 1853. *Chambers Biographical Dictionary*, p. 1066.

[31] Edward Richard Wright (1813-1859) played his last performance at the old Adelphi in June 1858. *Dictionary of National Biography*, pp. 102-3.

[32] This is Rose Anne Fesenmeyer, born in London in 1808. She was a witness to the will of Mary Ann Smith in 1846, and was living with her at St Johns Wood.

[33] Strand Theatre, Westminster, London.

[34] *The Cricket on the Hearth*, by Charles Dickens (1812-1870), was first published in 1845.

[35] William Shakespeare, *Troilus and Cressida*, Act III, Scene 3.

[36] Frederic Burge, son of George and Emma Burge, was born on 24 August 1844.

[37] Clift and Fisher were solicitors for the Herne Bay Pier Company.

[38] Charles Cornelius Gardiner (c. 1800-1866) was appointed Pier Master at Herne Bay in 1844. He was a great character, known to some locals as 'The Bloody Bulldog' One of his inventions was a double-barrelled cannon which fired two projectiles linked by a chain that stretched apart to mow down a line of troops. Harold Gough, Herne Bay.

39 Mary Anne Keeley (1806-1899) was married to actor Robert Keeley and their daughter, Louise Annie Keeley (b. 1834), was also on the stage. Jack Sheppard (1702-1724) was a famous highwayman.

40 The Adelphi Theatre was at 411 The Strand, London. John Timbs, *Curiosities of London*, 1855, p. 713.

41 The remarkable Crystal Palace, built for the Great Exhibition in Hyde Park, London, in 1851, was moved to Sydenham in 1852.

42 Janet Mather (née Lillico) was the mother of gold diggers Andrew 'Dan' Mather and Robert Lillico Mather.

43 Charles John Kean (1811-1868).

44 'Yclept' is an archaic word meaning 'named'.

45 Captain Henry Neatby had placed the following advertisement in the *Argus* (Melbourne), 14 November 1854: 'Should this meet the eye of James Montague [*sic*] Smith Supposed to be at Mount Alexander he is requested to communicate with Henry Nealby [*sic*], Ship *Vimiera*, Sydney, New South Wales.'

46 Cyrus Legg was associated with Charles Hay. He was born at Bermondsey in 1813 and married there in 1836. The Legg family were wool-staplers. IGI, British Census, 1881.

47 Hassocks Gate was the name given to a station on the London to Brighton line opened in 1841. Now known as Hassocks, it is situated in West Sussex.

48 'L'homme propose et Dieu dispose' is from the treatise, *De Imitatione Christi* (*On the Following of Christ*), by Thomas à Kempis (1379-1471) a German religious writer. *Chambers Biographical Dictionary,* p. 818.

49 'That undicover'd country, from whose bourn /No traveller returns...' William Shakespeare, *Hamlet*, Act III, Scene 1.

50 'sailing the cars up and down' refers to the tramway used to transport people to the end of the pier and back. Three cars ran on rails and were propelled by a sail on one of them. If the wind was not favourable, the luggage porters would push it along. Captain Gardiner the Pier Master was usually in charge of 'Old Neptune's Car'. Harold Gough, Herne Bay.

Chapter V – GREATER EXPECTATIONS

1 Willam Burgess (c.1804-1861) born Lambeth, Surrey, was a brother to James's mother. Tried at Croydon, Surrey, on 4 August 1831, he was convicted of receiving stolen goods. He arrived in Sydney on the convict transport *John* (3), on 8 June 1832. Convict Indent 32/1282156, State Records of NSW.

[2] The *Red Jacket* was a record-breaking extreme clipper ship launched at Rockland, Maine, 2 November 1853. On her maiden voyage from New York to Liverpool she logged 413 sea miles in 24 hours, becoming one of the seven fastest ships in sailing history. Basil Lubbock, *The Colonial Clippers*, Brown, Son & Ferguson, Glasgow, 1955, p. 52.

[3] Myers must have left his wife to operate the lodging house at 3 Pelham Place, West Cowes, Isle of Wight. The 1867 directory has the entry: 'John Myers, Lodging House, Bath Road, West Cowes.'

[4] Barnard Beckham died at Barham, Victoria, in 1881 aged 51. The inquest states that he had heart disease. Victoria Pioneers Index 1837-1888.

[5] Ebenezer Seater and his wife Janet were from Westray and Papa Westray in the Orkney Islands. IGI.

[6] This is Matthias Hector O'Halloran who rose to the position of captain of the *Red Jacket* on the return journey, due to the death of Captain Milward (see p. 160).

[7] Joshua Walker had married Ruth Anna Hirst. Her sister was Sarah Jane Hirst and they were the daughters of James Hirst and Lucy Wood, who were married at Halifax, Yorkshire, 29 February 1824. Sarah Jane married Samuel Haigh in Melbourne in 1858 and was around 36 when the first of their four children arrived. She was 90 years of age when she died in 1914 at Hawthorn, Victoria. Reg. BDMs, Victoria; IGI.

[8] A Charles Bullock is listed as a miner at Long Gully (Bendigo) in the 1856/57 Electoral Roll for the Victorian Legislative Assembly.

[9] Ellen Conroy from Tipperary was 24 and is surely the person who married Michael Phelan in 1857. Ellen Phelan, the daughter of Thomas Conroy and Mary Corcoran, died in 1875, age 45. Passenger list of the *Red Jacket*, 1855, Public Record Office of Victoria; Victorian Pioneers Index 1837-1888.

[10] Martin Massey Milward was master of a number of ships on the Australian run. He married Eliza Addison at St Luke Old Street, Finsbury, London, on 7 September 1830.

[11] A calumet is an Indian peace pipe – a long tobacco pipe used by native Americans on ceremonial occasions. *Macquarie Dictionary*.

[12] Sebastopol was under seige for 11 months until successfully stormed by the French in September 1855. The *Red Jacket* sailed on 20 September with the news that the Malakoff Tower had fallen and that the whole southern side of Sebastopol was in the hands of the allied force. The news had been anticipated by a vessel from Calcutta which carried a brief telegraphic dispatch received

via Agra, telling of the success of the allied arms. *Mount Alexander Mail,* 7 December 1855.

13 Matthias Hector O'Halloran was master of the *Red Jacket* on voyages to Australia in 1856, '57 and '58. Unassisted Immigration, 1852-1889, PROV.

14 The Melbourne and Hobson's Bay Railway was officially opened on 12 September 1854. Australia's first steam railway provided a vital link between Sandridge (Port Melbourne) and rapidly growing Melbourne. From November 1854, a ferry service ran from Sandridge railway pier to Williamstown.

15 Eugene McLaughlan built the Yarra Family Hotel in 1853-54. Situated on the corner of William and Flinders streets, it was of three storeys in stone and brick and had 26 rooms and a large cellar. Michael Cannon, *Melbourne after the Gold Rush*, Loch Haven Books, Main Ridge, Victoria, 1993, p. 323.

16 John Wilson was a widower from Newcastle upon Tyne. His eldest daughter Elizabeth (b.1828) was on the *Red Jacket* with her husband James Jopling. Also on the voyage were daughters Mary (b.1832) and Eleanor (b.1835), and son John, age 17. Passenger list of *Red Jacket*; PRO, Victoria.

17 Eleanor Dorothy Wilson went on to marry Scottish-born James Herschell in 1856 and they had 11 children. After some ten years in Bendigo they moved to South Melbourne. Sadly Eleanor died in 1883 at the comparatively young age of 47.

18 Laurence Sterne (1713-1768), *A Sentimental Journey through France and Italy*, 1768.

19 The *Telegraph* was built by J. & G. Thompson of Glasgow in 1854 and registered in Sydney by the Australasian Steam Navigation Company. It was a 352-ton iron paddlesteamer, 193.9 feet (59 m) long, with a two-cylinder 220-horsepower engine. Ronald Parsons, *Australian Coastal Passenger Ships*, Magill, SA, 1981, p. 173.

20 Maria Burgess was born in New South Wales in 1811, the daughter of John Graham and Charlotte Mann. She married Frederick Wilson at St Matthew's, Windsor, in 1827 and they had sons Frederick (b. 1829), John (b. 1832) and William (b. 1834). Maria was widowed in 1836 and in 1837, convict William Burgess obtained permission to marry her. In August 1837, Maria petitioned to have her husband assigned to her to work in her butcher shop at Windsor. With a Ticket of Leave granted to William in 1840, the couple went on to become successful in various business interests in the Morpeth–East Maitland area. Maria died at Nulla Nulla, Hinton, on 4 August 1869.

21 A rush to California from Sydney and other Australian ports began in 1849.

22 The George and Dragon Inn at East Maitland is still standing and operates as a restaurant and accommodation house in fine colonial style.

Chapter VI – HARD TIMES IN TOWN AND COUNTRY

1 The *City of Sydney* was a steamship built in Scotland in 1851 and registered in Sydney by the Australasian Steam Navigation Company. R.H. Parsons, *Australasian Coastal Passenger Ships*, Magill, South Australia, 1981, p. 192.

2 The legendary firm of Cobb & Co. was founded in 1853 by Americans Freeman Cobb, John Murray Peck, John B. Lamber and James Swanton. The vehicle would have been a Downing & Sons coach, built in Concord, New Hampshire. Leather 'thoroughbrace' suspension was ideal for the road conditions. E.D. Potts & A. Potts, *Young America and Australian Gold*, UQP, 1974, p. 90.

3 Catherine Hayes (1818-1861), the Irish-born opera and concert singer, appeared at the 'Princess's Theatre', Criterion Hotel, Bendigo, on 31 December 1855. A further two concerts were held on Thursday 3 January and a special 'reduced price' evening for the busy diggers on the following Saturday. *Bendigo Advertiser*, 29 December 1855, 3 January 1856.

4 This would have been the first Shamrock Hotel, not as grand as the later buildings on the site.

5 J. N. Williams's Victoria Hotel was established in Pall Mall, Bendigo, in 1854.

6 John Wilson from Newcastle upon Tyne (see previous chapter) must have refused to lend James money.

7 The Bible, Matthew 7:1 'Judge not, that ye not be judged.'

8 Mary and Eleanor Wilson were on the *Red Jacket* with James and he had advised their father to send them to Bendigo by coach rather than have them travel on top of a wagon (see previous chapter).

9 An advertisement in the *Argus* (Melbourne) 8 December 1855 reads: 'If this should meet the eye of John Burge, late of Herne Bay, his friends are anxious to hear from him, and if he would write to his old friend James Smith, George and Dragon, East Maitland, he will give him particulars from home.'

10 This is a reference to the historic Porcupine Inn, established in 1847 and commonly known in the early days as Hawkins' Inn. For some years it was the closest inn to the Bendigo diggings with a licence to sell liquor. By the late 1860s it was in a ruinous state. The site is north of Harcourt, adjacent to the present Porcupine Overpass. Frank Cusack, *Bendigo, A History*, Heinemann, Melbourne, 1973, pp. 20, 34-5.

[11] Sawpit Gully was later named Elphinstone. Prior to the general licensing of hotels on the goldfields in 1854, it was a place where spirits could be sold in bulk and was notorious for sly grog shanties, thieves and prostitutes. Cusack, p. 34.

[12] The 'diamond snake' is not found in Victoria. By the description it could have been a small tiger snake (*Notechis scutatus*).

[13] The Tam-O'-Shanter Hotel, Lothian Street, North Melbourne, proprietor George Murray, is in the 1860 *Sands & Kenny Melbourne Directory*. Perhaps it was an unlisted boarding house before this time.

[14] Whitlaw is difficult to identify. James notes later in 1855 that he was going to Anderson's Creek with a friend to start a store. In 1859, Whitlaw and Gibson have a store at Brown's Diggings (Scarsdale). *Victorian Police Gazette*, 4 August 1859, p. 305.

[15] Now called the Maribynong River, it was formerly the Salt Water River.

[16] Fulton & Smith, ironfounders and millers, were at 131 Flinders Street East in 1856. *Melbourne Commercial, Professional and Legal Directory for 1856*, John Needham.

[17] Liardet's Beach became part of Sandridge, later renamed Port Melbourne.

[18] The *Sir Colin Campbell* sailed out of Hobson's Bay on 16 September 1856, bound for Callao, Peru. *Argus* Shipping Movement Index 1856-1860, Marion Button (comp.), Gisborne, Victoria, 1993.

[19] Construction of the Geelong to Melbourne railway began in September 1853 and it was officially opened on 25 June 1857. Leo J. Harrigan, *Victorian Railways to '62*, Victorian Railways, Melbourne, 1962, pp. 33-4.

[20] Laurence Sterne (1713-1768), *A Sentimental Journey through France and Italy*, 1768.

[21] At this time De Pass Brothers & Co., merchants, were at 107 William Street. The brothers were John, Mitchell and Michael De Pass. *Needham's Melbourne Commercial Directory*, 1856.

[22] Omeo was a remote goldfield in the Victorian Alps. Prospecting began in the early 1850s and there was a rush in 1856 to Livingstone Creek. Flett, p. 170.

[23] In the 1859 *Melbourne Directory* (Tanner's) we find John McMillan, Drayman, 29 Courtney Street, North Melbourne.

[24] This would be the Royal Hotel at 33 Victoria Street East, North Melbourne. *Sands & Kenny Directory*, 1859.

25 Daisy Hill diggings were between Maryborough and Amherst. The first rush (Cowley's) was in December 1852. B. Osborn and T. Du Bourg, *Maryborough, A Social History 1854-1904*, Maryborough City Council, Maryborough, Victoria, 1985, p. 19.

26 Simsons Ranges and Simsons Diggings were names given to the locality which was rushed from the middle of 1854 and became the Maryborough goldfield. The Simson brothers settled in the area from 1840.

27 The Alma Lead is north-west of Maryborough in the Timor Creek Valley. The Adelaide Lead is south of the Alma, being intersected by the Maryborough to Avoca road.

28 'There is a tide in the affairs of men...' William Shakespeare, *Julius Caesar,* Act IV, Scene 3.

29 Jimmy Barr or the 'Wee Hairy Man', was surely James Jackson Barr (1826-1861).

30 Avoca was attracting diggers at least as early as February 1853. A large-scale rush began later in that year. Flett, pp. 254, 454.

31 Ebenezer Seater (1822-1899) and his wife Janet Seater, née Read (1831-1890), remained in the Avoca area for the rest of their lives, a long way from their birthplace in the Orkneys, the very northern extreme of Scotland. IGI; Reg. BDMs, Victoria.

32 D. K. Campbell's store was one of the first buildings in what became the town of Maryborough. In 1904 another storekeeper, Thomas Morrow, wrote that he and D. K. Campbell were the first to erect stores on what became the main street of Maryborough. *Maryborough and Dunolly Advertiser*, 28 June 1904.

33 Jane Bryce and Donald Kesson Campbell were married at the Church of England minister's house in Carisbrook, Victoria, on 4 January 1856. Janet was the daughter of John Bryce and Grace McAdam and gives her age as 24. Donald was the son of Hugh Campbell and Janet Kesson and gives his age as 28. His parents were married in 1824, so even if 29 or 30, he was not, as James states, 'old enough to be her father'. Donald was notable in public affairs in the growing town of Maryborough. He was president of the hospital in 1858, in 1860 laid the foundation stone of the Presbyterian Church and in 1861 was elected as chairman and councillor of the municipality. By June 1861 he was off to New Zealand, chasing yet another gold-rush and died at Dunstan's in 1863. A son, Hugh Campbell, was born in Melbourne in 1862. Reg. BDMs, Victoria; IGI; Osborn & DuBourg, pp. 142, 149, 170.

34 Buninyong as a town dates back to the early 1840s and was well established by 1851 when Thomas Hiscock discovered gold in the district. Peter Griffith,

Three Times Blest, A History of Buninyong and District: 1837-1901. Buninyong and District History Society, Buninyong (Vic.), 1988, p. 17.

[35] Gold was discovered at Chalk Hill near Buninyong early in 1856. Flett, p. 370.

[36] New Bendigo diggings were the beginnings of the town of St Arnaud.

[37] Thomas Campbell (1777-1844), *Pleasures of Hope*, first published 1799.

[38] Chalk Hill is 2.4 km south of Buninyong. Flett, p. 370.

[39] Green Hills is 1.6 km south of Buninyong. Gold was discovered there in early March 1856. Flett, pp. 370-1.

[40] Under the *Goldfields Act* of June 1855, the position of Commissioner was abolished. Wardens and local courts were now administering each mining district by early 1856, when James was in the Buninyong area. We presume James means the Mining Warden. Cusack, p. 13.

[41] There were two Brunel tunnels noted as great engineering feats. Sir Marc Brunel (1769-1849) was responsible for the Thames Tunnel from Rotherhithe to Wapping (1825-1843). His son, Isambard Kingdom Brunel (1806-1859), designed the Box Tunnel on the Great Western Railway (1836-1841). *Chambers Biographical Dictionary*, pp. 219-20.

[42] Frontage claims were described in the Regulations at Ballarat in 1856 as applying to all recognised leads or gutters and were to be of an indefinite width until such leads or gutters were found. These claims were a specific measurement in front, with eight men to each claim. *Ballarat Times*, 24 May 1856, p. 2.

[43] The town of Beaufort grew out of the Fiery Creek Diggings.

[44] William Reid, draper, 212 Bourke Street, appears in the *Melbourne Commercial Directory* for 1855.

[45] R.C. McTaggart was the legendary 'Johnny Allsorts' who claimed that he sold everything in his store except snowballs and fresh pilchards. Henry Leversha, *Records of the Castlemaine Pioneers*, p. 11.

[46] The Separation Inn was on the east side of the Ballarat-Geelong Road at Gheringhap. It was opened by Michael O'Meara in 1851, but by 1853 he had moved on. In 1854 a township subdivision was laid out around the inn although no town developed. Geelong Historical Society; *Investigator*, September 1978, p. 98.

[47] This is Batesford, 48 miles (77 km) south-west of Melbourne on the Moorabool River. *Bailliere's Victorian Gazetteer*, 1865, p. 30.

[48] Captain Franicis Cadell had been granted a thousand pounds to clear the Murray River of snags. That figure, at one pound per mile, was considered entirely inadequate. *Bendigo Advertiser*, 5 July 1856, p. 2.

[49] By October 1856 the railway being built from the Geelong end had extended 10 miles (16 km) and was beyond Duck Ponds (Lara). Leo J. Harrigan, p. 34.

[50] Duck Ponds was a station on the Melbourne to Geelong Railway on the Duck Ponds Creek. It was later renamed Lara.

[51] This incident was related to James after the event, so while his outline of the story is correct, he incorrectly states that the victim was a 'little German boy'. In fact James Anguin was from the West of England and was 20 years of age. The inquest found that he died on the 'Werribee Railway' on 23 May 1856, due to an explosion of gunpowder. Inquest, PROV: VPRS: 24/P Unit 33, file no. 338/1856.

[52] The paddlesteamer *Yarra* was 337 tons (registered) and had a two-cylinder 200-horsepower engine. It was built in Scotland in 1851 and was registered in Sydney by the Australasian Steam Navigation Company. R. H. Parsons, *Australasian Coastal Passenger Ships*, p. 192.

[53] Sandridge was the early name for Port Melbourne.

Chapter VII – BEYOND THE BLUE MOUNTAINS

[1] The *London* was built at Port Glasgow in 1837. It was a two-masted paddle-steamer with a 380-horsepower engine. Bought by the Australasian Steam Navigation Co. in July 1856, it was sent to Hong Kong to be sold in 1861. Parsons, p. 122.

[2] Stoney Creek diggings were on a narrow strip of tableland running parallel with the Macquarie River, south-east of Wellington, NSW. A rush to this area took place in mid-1856.

[3] Rocky River is 22 km south-west of Armidale, NSW.

[4] 'Consider the lilies of the field...' St Matthew 6:28 'And yet I say unto you, That even Solomon in all his glory was not arrayed like one of these.' St Matthew 6:29.

[5] William Shakespeare, *Macbeth,* Act I, Scene 3.

[6] The Bible. Revelation 3:16. 'So then because thou art lukewarm, and neither cold nor hot, I will spue thee out of my mouth.'

[7] The 'Village of Mudgee' was gazetted in 1838. Well-situated in an upland valley of the Gudgegong River, it benefited from the various gold strikes in the region, but grazing remained its real wealth.

8 Louisa Creek was rushed at the beginning of July 1856 as a result of the Great Nugget Vein Company's claims being opened to the public. Gold Fields report, Senior Assistant Commissioner Johnson, 28 July 1856. Votes / Proceedings of the Legislative Assembly, NSW, 1856/7, vol. 2.

9 'Iron Bark' was one of the rich surfacing spots in the vicinity of Stoney Creek. In early October 1856 it was said to be 'lately discovered'. By 1866 it was called Ironbarks and described a postal and mining township, 40 km west of Wellington. *Bailliere's New South Wales Gazetteer and Road Guide*, 1866.

10 Mt Victoria is 1044 metres or 3424 feet, not quite as high as James states.

11 The first official train from Sydney to Parramatta was on 26 September 1855.

12 Francis Mason had travelled to Sydney to marry a brewer's daughter.

13 The *La Hogue* was a 1331-ton vessel built in Sunderland, Durham, in 1855 for Duncan Dunbar.

14 Edward Bulwer Lytton (1803-1873).

15 John 'Jack' Wilson was included in his stepfather's will to receive: 'board, washing, maintenance, support and necessary and proper comforts...' for his natural life. William Burgess, No 5145, 1861, Probate Division, Supreme Court of NSW.

16 Ellen or 'Nellie' has not otherwise been identified. She may have been a friend of the Burgess family.

17 James notes that Henry Neatby had a share in the *La Hogue*. The principle owner was Duncan Dunbar. It was a popular vessel on the Australian run and, at 1,331 tons, one of the largest frigate-built ships ever launched. B. Lubbock, *The Colonial Clippers*, Glasgow, 1955, p. 148.

Chapter VIII – AN APPROACHING INHERITANCE

1 Thomas Sutcliffe Mort (1816-1878) was born at Bolton, Lancashire, and arrived in Sydney in February 1838. He began as a clerk at Aspinall, Browne & Co. and with the experience gained in local overseas commerce, he went on to become a very successful businessman. His visit to England in 1857-59 saw a worsening of the hypochondria he had suffered since a riding accident in 1855. *Australian Dictionary of Biography*, vol. 5, pp. 299-301. The *Sydney Morning Herald* of Friday 20 February 1857 announced in the ship advertisements: 'THE VICTORIA STEAM-PACKET having been placed at the disposal of Mr. Mort, will leave the Circular Quay, TO-MORROW, Saturday, morning, at 7 o'clock, for the purpose of accompanying the ship La Hogue to sea. The friends of any passengers by this ship are invited, should they feel disposed to make the trip.'

2 Campbell Drummond Riddell (1796-1858) had been appointed temporarily as Colonial Secretary in January 1854, but was now a Member of the Legislative Council, having been nominated in May 1856. He had also been Colonial Treasurer. Riddell is also notable for having built 'Lindesay' at Darling Point on Sydney Harbour in1834, said to be Australia's first domestic example of Gothic Revival. *Australian Dictionary of Biography*, vol. 2, pp. 377-9.

3 Martin Massey Milward was master of the *Red Jacket* on James's 1855 voyage.

4 This would be Dr McKellar who was travelling to England with his wife. List of cabin passengers, *Sydney Morning Herald*, 20 February 1857.

5 Duncan Dunbar was a notable ship-owner. After his death in 1862, his interest in *La Hogue* was purchased by Messrs. Devitt & Moore. Lubbock, p. 148.

6 Rodney Stuart Riddell, son of Campbell Drummond Riddell, was born 7 November 1838, making him 19. New South Wales Pioneer Index 1788-1888.

7 Louisa Riddell was born in 1841, so was 15 or 16 at this time. Her sister, Caroline Mary Riddell would have been 13 or 14. Some ten years later Caroline would marry Louis William Knowles on 29 September 1867 at St Pancras Old Church, London. Also on the *La Hogue* were Frances, b. 1852 and baby Herbert, b.1854. ADB, vol. 2; British Census1881; IGI.

8 The Hall family had Anne Hogan as their nursery maid to help the young Mrs Hall with the baby. The young man who told Mr Hall of his daughter's assignation would be Henry D. Martyn, son of Charles and Elizabeth, born in Sydney in 1839. List of cabin passengers, *Sydney Morning Herald*, 20 February 1857; New South Wales Pioneer Index 1788-1888.

9 The mystery might have been the disappearance of Charles Smith in 1844, or perhaps it was related to the transportation of his uncle, William Burgess.

10 Eliza Burge married William Slark on 28 July 1858 at St Pancras Old Church, London. Eliza is given as the daughter of George Burge, 'Railway Contractor', and William Slark as the son of William Slark, 'Gentleman'. William junior was a miller and his father, Captain William Slark, a JP and Deputy Lieutenant of the County of Kent. Eliza and William lived at Parndon, Essex, in the 1860s, but by 1871 were at 9 St George's Terrace, Herne Bay. Number 7 was the childhood home of James Montagu Smith. Herne Bay Historical Records Society.

11 Number 22 Queen Square was in the parish of St George the Martyr, Holborn, London. It was close to the Burge residence at 1 Lansdowne Place. Fanny also lived in adjoining Devonshire Street in 1852/53.

[12] Mary Ann Burge, daughter of George and Emma Burge, was baptised 27 May 1833 at St Matthew, Brixton. She apparently did not marry and in the 1881 Census is living with her mother and sister Caroline at 32 Hawley Square, Margate, Kent. All three are living on 'income derived from houses'.

[13] The crinoline dominated the fashion scene in Europe from 1856. They reached their greatest width in the 1860s, having become a subject for much humour and complaints in the press.

[14] Sarah Helena James had married Augustus Henry Novelli on 7 September 1853 at St Andrew, Marylebone.

EPILOGUE

[1] Parliamentary Return of Landholders (NSW) 1885. Index, comp. Liz Vincent.

[2] GRO London, and memorial card in family collection.

GLOSSARY

albacore A medium-sized tuna of warm seas.

baubee Scottish term for halfpenny.

bend To fasten ropes of sails.

belay To secure (a rope) by winding around a pin or rod in a holder.

bight Loop or bent part of a rope.

binnacle Stand of non-magnetic material in ship's hull for housing the compass.

bog-trotter A rural Irishman.

bolt rope Sewn on edge of sail to strengthen it.

bonito Type of tuna.

bower anchor An anchor carried at the bow of a ship.

bowie knife Heavy sheath knife with long single-edged blade.

bowsprit A large boom or spar running out from the stem of a sailing ship to carry its sails forward.

bulwark Ship's protective side at outer edge of deck.

bumper Cup filled to the brim, especially for toast.

calumet Long ornamental tobacco pipe used by North American Indians.

carbine Short rifle for cavalry use.

chain locker Box-like steel structure below the forecastle where anchor is stowed.

chip (chippie) A carpenter.

choler Biliousness.

claim A portion of public land to which a claim is made for mining.

cleat Piece of wood or iron consisting of a bar with arms to which ropes are belayed.

clew Ball of thread. Lower corner of a sail to which a sheet is attached.

cognomen Nickname.

cornstalk Person born in Australia, esp. in NSW.

cuddy Small cabin on ship (under the poop).

dace Small carp-like fish.

deal Fir or pine wood.

diggings A mining area.

double To sail around, e.g. a cape

duff A flour pudding boiled in a bag.

forecastle Seamen's quarters in forward part of a merchant vessel.

fluking Gaining or passing (of a ship).

fly Light single-horse public carriage.

flying jib A triangular sail set forward of the jib.

gantline Rope temporarily made fast through a block for hoisting.

gasket One of several bands used to bind a furled sail to a yard.

goanna Large Australian lizard (genus *Varanus*).

gutta-percha Tough rubbery substance.

half-fourpenny Intoxication.

handspike Bar used as a lever.

halliard (halyard) Rope used to hoist or lower sails.

hawse Part of ship's bow with holes for cable to pass through.

hawser Small cable used in mooring, towing.

hooker Fishing boat with hook and lines instead of nets.

hocus To drug (someone).

jack Seaman or sailor

jib Triangular sail in front of foreward mast.

jib boom Spar forming continuation of bowsprit.

jury mast Temporary mast replacing broken one.

lead An auriferous deposit in an old riverbed.

lee The side away from the wind.

lighter Flat-bottomed boat for transferring goods from a ship to a wharf.

lushington A drunkard.

marline spike Pointed metal or bone implement used to separate strands of rope.

martingale Short spar under the bowsprit for staying the jib boom.

mast headed Sent to the top of the highest mast as punishment.

mizzen Lowest sail on mizzenmast.

mizzenmast Aftermost mast on a three-masted vessel or the third on a vessel with more.

moosedeer (mousedeer) Very small deer-like ruminant.

nobbler Small glass of spirits or wine.

pee (of anchor) The point of anchor.

poop Enclosed space in aftermost part of ship, above the main deck.

pooper To take seas over the stern.

painter Rope for fastening a boat.

puddling Working together water and earth rich in clay to separate out any gold.

puddling machine Usually operated by horse, steam or other power to puddle earth containing ores.

pump well A compartment around ship's pumps to protect them from damage.

quarter deck Upper deck between the main mast and the poop or stern.

reef Strips across a sail for taking it in or rolling it up in a high wind.

roadstead A place near shore where ships may ride at anchor.

royal mast Next above topgallant mast.

scouse A baked food served to sailors.

scud To run before a gale with little sail set.

scuttle A small opening in deck with a moveable lid.

shellback Experienced sailor, esp. an old one.

shepherding Retaining a claim without working it.

shicer A duffer or unproductive gold-mine.

skilly Thin soup or gruel once used in prisons or workhouses.

spoke Communicated with passing ship by voice or signal.

staysail A sail hoisted on a stay, e.g. a triangular sail between two masts.

stripes Strokes with whip or rod as punishment.

spun yarn Cord made from rope yarns loosely twisted together.

tackles Gear and rigging used in handling ship.

ticket of leave Document entitling a convict to freedom of occupation and lodging within a given district until the original sentence has expired.

topgallant Mast, sail, yard, or rigging immediately above the topmast and topsail.

unbend Unfasten ropes or sales.

vingt-et-un A card game in which the object is to score twenty-one.

whim A large capstan turned by horsepower for raising material from a mine.

windlass Device for raising weights on a cable.

yard A long cylindrical spar with a taper towards each end and slung crosswise to a mast and suspending a square sail.

yclept Archaic word for 'called' or 'named'.

CONVERSION TABLES

The following table is to help readers understand measurements used in the main text. Money values given below represent theoretical rates only. They do not allow for inflatory factors.

One halfpenny = ½ cent
One penny = 1 cent (approx.)
One shilling = 10 cents
One pound = $2

One inch = 2.45 cm
One foot = 30.5 cm
One yard = 0.914 m
One mile = 1.61 km
One acre = 0.405 ha

One ounce = 28.3 g
One pound = 454 g
One ton = 1.02 tonnes

One pint = 568 ml
One gallon = 4.55 litres

BIBLIOGRAPHY

ADCOCK, W. E. *The Gold Rushes of the Fifties*. Poppet Head Press, Melbourne, 1977 (first published by E. W. Cole, Melbourne, 1912).

ANNEAR, ROBYN. *Nothing But Gold*. The Text Publishing Company, Melbourne, 1999.

BATESON, CHARLES. *The Convict Ships, 1787-1868*. Brown, Son & Ferguson, Glasgow, 1959

BILLIS, R .V. & KENYON, A. S. *Pastoral Pioneers of Port Phillip*. Stockland Press. Melbourne, 1974.

BRADFIELD, RAYMOND A. *Lola Montez and Castlemaine: Some Early Theatre History*. Published Castlemaine, (Vic.) undated.

——— Castlemaine, *A Golden Harvest*. Lowden Publishing Co., Kilmore (Vic.), 1972.

BRAND, IAN. *The Convict Probation System: Van Diemen's Land 1839-1854*. Blubber Head Press, Hobart, 1990.

CANNON, MICHAEL. *Melbourne after the Gold Rush*. Loch Haven Books, Main Ridge (Vic.), 1991.

Castlemaine Association of Pioneers and Old Residents. *Records of the Castlemaine Pioneers*. Rigby, Adelaide, 1972.

Convicts by the Sir R. Seppings. Report of the Select Committee, Legislative Council, Van Diemen's Land (Tas.) 1852.

'Early Castlemaine: A Glance at the Stirring Fifties', McKillop, Frank. Series of articles in the *Mount Alexander Mail*, November 1908 – April 1909.

EVANS, WILSON P. *Through the Rip, Ships and Seamen of Old Port Phillip*. Rigby, Melbourne, 1978.

FLETT, JAMES. *Old Pubs: Inns, Taverns and Grog Houses on the Victorian Gold Diggings*. Poppet Head Press, Melbourne, 1979.

——— *The History of Gold Discovery in Victoria*. The Hawthorn Press, Melbourne, 1970.

GOUGH, HAROLD. *George Burge, Herne Bay's Founding Father,* parts 1 & 2. Bygone Kent, 2001.

GRIFFITH, PETER. *Three Times Blest, A History of Buninyong and District 1837-1901.* Buninyong and District History Society, Buninyong, (Vic.), 1988.

HARRIGAN, LEO J. *Victorian Railways to '62,* Victorian Railways. Melbourne, 1962.

HARRIS, HELEN DOXFORD. *Digging for Gold: A guide to researching family & local history in Victoria's Central Goldfields.* Self-published, Melbourne (Vic.).

HOCKING GEOFFREY. *To The Diggings! A Celebration of the 150th Anniversary of the Discovery of Gold in Australia.* Lothian Books, Melbourne, 2000.

HOLLETT, DAVID. *Fast Passage to Australia.* Fairplay Publications, London, 1986.

HOWARD, PATRICK. *To Hell or to Hobart.* Kangaroo Press, Kenthurst, (NSW), 1993.

HOWITT, WILLIAM. *Land, Labour and Gold: or Two Years in Victoria: With Visits to Sydney and Van Diemen's Land,* 2 vols. Longman, Brown, Green & Longmans, London, 1855.

JOHNSON, WILLIAM. *Gold Fields (Western Districts),* vol 2. Government of New South Wales, Sydney, 1856/7.

LAWSON, WILL & Shiplovers' Society of Tasmania, *Blue Gum Clippers and Whale Ships of Tasmania.* Georgian House, Melbourne, 1949.

LEE, SIDNEY (ed.). *Dictionary of National Biography.* Smith Elder & Co., London, 1900.

LEWIS, MILES. *The Essential Maldon,* Greenhouse Publications, Melbourne, 1983.

LUBBOCK, BASIL. *The Colonial Clippers.* Brown, Son & Ferguson, Glasgow, 1948.

MACFARLANE, IAN, (comp. & ed.). *Eureka from the Official Records.* Public Records Office of Victoria, Melbourne, 1995.

MERCER, PETER & ELIZABETH (eds.). *The Penitentiary Chapel & Criminal Courts, Hobart.* National Trust of Australia (Tas.), undated.

MOORE, BRUCE (ed.). *Gold! Gold! Gold! The Language of the Nineteenth-Century Australian Gold Rushes.* Oxford University Press, Melbourne, 2000.

MYERS, PAULINE, *The Great Majority: Obituaries of the Forest Creek Pioneers from the Mount Alexander Mail*, part 1: 1855-1885. Self-published, Castlemaine (Vic.), 1990.

NICHOLSON, IAN (comp.). *Log of Logs: A Catalogue of Logs, Journals, Shipboard Diaries, Letters and All Forms of Voyage Narratives 1788 to 1988,* vol. 1, 1990: vol. 2, 1993; vol. 3, 1999. Self-published, Yaroomba (Qld), 1990.

NIXON, ALLAN. *Stand & Deliver! 100 Australian Bushrangers 1789-1901.* Lothian, Melbourne, 1991.

NUNN, HAROLD. *Maryborough (Vic.) 1854-1954.* Self-published, Maryborough (Vic.), 1959.

PARSONS, RONALD. *Australian Coastal Passenger Ships* Self-published, Magill, (SA), 1981.

——— *Australian Shipowners and their Fleets (Vessels enrolled at Launceston 1830-1859).* Self-published, Magill, (SA), 1992.

——— *Australian Shipowners and their Fleets*, book 12 (Hobart to 1859 A-L. Self-published, Magill, (SA), 1989.

——— *Ships of Australia and New Zealand Before 1850*, parts 1 & 2. Self-published, Magill (SA), 1983.

POTTS, E. DANIEL & POTTS, ANNETTE. *Young America and Australian Gold: Americans and the Gold Rush of the 1850s.* University of Queensland Press, St.Lucia (Qld), 1974.

RANDALL, J.O. *The Campaspe District,* vol. II, *Pastoral Settlement in Northern Victoria*, Chandos Publishing Company, Melbourne, 1982.

RIEUSSET, BRIAN. *Penitentiary Chapel.* National Trust of Australia (Tas.), Hobart, 1986.

ROSS, BRYCE. *Diggings' Directory*, Melbourne, 1852.

Royal National and Commercial Directory and Topography. London, 1839, facsimile edn. 1993.

SANDS, MOLLIE. *Robson of the Olympic.* Society for Theatre Research, London, 1979.

SALTER HAROLD. Bass Strait Ketches. St David's Park Publishing, Hobart, 1991.

SERLE, GEOFFREY. *The Golden Age: A History of the Colony of Victoria 1851-1861.* Melbourne University Press, Melbourne, 1963.

SHERER, JOHN. *The Gold-Finder of Australia.* Clarke, Beeton & Co., London, 1853.

SPREADBOROUGH, ROBERT & ANDERSON, HUGH (comps.). *Victorian Squatters.* Red Rooster Press, Melbourne, 1983.

SYME, MARTEN. A. *Shipping Arrivals and Departures Victorian Ports*, vol. 2, 1846-1855, Roebuck, Melbourne, 1987.

TIMBS, JOHN. *Curiosities of London.* David Bogue, London, 1855.

WALSH, BASIL. *Catherine Hayes: The Hiberian Prima Donna.* The Irish Academic Press, Dublin, 2000.

WELLS, WILLIAM HENRY. *A Geographical Dictionary or Gazetteer of the Australian Colonies*, 1848, facsimile edn., The Council of the Library of New South Wales, Sydney, 1970.

WHITWORTH, ROBERT (comp.) *Bailliere's New South Wales Gazetteer and Road Guide*, Sydney 1866.

WITHERS, WILLIAM BRAMWELL. *History of Ballarat.* Published by the *Ballarat Star* newspaper, 1870.

ACKNOWLEDGEMENTS

We owe a great debt to Jean Truebridge (née Smith) for preserving and transcribing her grandfather's journals. She is the pivotal figure in a continuing story, and has been vitally involved in the preparation of this book. My wife Barbara was the catalyst for developments that led to the publication of these important memoirs. Her great-great-grandmother, Mary Petty, was a convict on the *Sir Robert Seppings* in 1852. Barbara read in the *Log of Logs* that one James Montagu Smith had written of that fateful journey, so she wrote to Jean Truebridge who kindly sent back the relevant pages from her typed transcription. These graphically described the voyage from London to Hobart Town, with an emerging sympathy for the women and children who suffered under such terrible conditions. We had already read the report of the ship's surgeon, and knew that Mary Petty came on board with a three-month-old baby in her arms.

Now here was the story from the point of view of a young sailor. Barbara wrote back to Jean thanking her and asking if we could read more of these fascinating 'memorandums'. And so the full text eventually arrived. The entire work was so enthralling that Barbara read it all on the Saturday after it arrived. On 8th July 1996 she wrote, 'I am very much of the opinion it would make a wonderful published work.' From the initial correspondence a friendship developed, with hopes of publication becoming a shared dream.

Due to the nature of the original typed transcription it was necessary to re-type this text into a word-processing format. Barbara's daughter, Jane Ashton, began the process and completed chapter one. The balance of the work was typed by L'rainne Siostrom and proofread by her husband Bob. They are long-time friends who joined a growing circle of James Montagu Smith admirers. Zoë Murphy designed the book with a real enthusiasm for the story.

My own research was assisted by author/historian Harold Gough of Herne Bay, Kent. Harold also lent three engravings from his own collection. Other research was undertaken by Carolynn Boucher of St Albans, Hertfordshire; Fay Johnson of Melbourne; Ann Prendergast of Sydney; Elisabeth Wilson of Hobart and Harry Boyle of Maitland. My daughter Sarah Cuffley helped with checking the transcriptions against the original journals.

Thanks are also due to the following individuals and institutions:
Mary Akers; Archives Office of Tasmania; Australian Institute of Geneological Studies; Bendigo Library, Victoria; Rebecca Beswick of Bradford District Archives (West Yorkshire Archives Service), UK; Castlemaine Art Gallery and Historical Museum, Victoria; Castlemaine Historical Society, Victoria; Brian Cuffley; David Cufley, Kent, UK; John Dance; Helen Darling, Scottish Borders Archive and Local History Centre, Selkirk, Scotland; Bill Davies; Albert Dean, UK; Pat Evans; Geelong Historical Records Centre; Carol Greenwood of Central Library, Bradford, UK; Janet Hawkins; Herne Bay Historical Records Society, Kent, UK; Alleyne Hockley; Rita Hull; Institution of Civil Engineers, London; Valma Kent; Maryborough Library, Victoria; Midlands Historial Society, UK; George Milford; Diana Mitchell-Dorrity; Sue Mooney; Laurie Moore; Jane Nagy, Surrey, UK; National Library of Australia, Canberra, ACT; Betty and Bruce Osborn; Port Stephens Family History Society; Public Records Office, London; Public Record Office of Victoria; Queen's College, London; Raymond Terrace Historical Society, NSW; Registry of Births, Deaths and Marriages, Victoria; Joseph Fitzwalter Read, UK; Richard M. Read; Joan Reese; Brian Rhule; Sally Routledge; Gillian Simpson of the Australian National Maritime Museum; Sue Spliet; State Library of Tasmania; State Library of Victoria; State Records of New South Wales; James Taylor; Janice Taylor of Wirral Archives Service, Birkenhead, UK; Geoff Walker; Syd Welsh; Dot Wickham; Ken Williamson, Kent, UK; Clive Willman; Woodend and District Heritage Society, Victoria; and Stephen T. J. Wright, London Research Service.

INDEX